IELTS

IELTS 雅思口语宗师力作

舌尖上的雅思

钱多多 编著

中国人民大学出版社
· 北京 ·

口语，多多益善

语言学习的首要目的之一就是沟通。

通过沟通，我们可以注意到我们曾经关心或者忽略的信息，可以从不同的角度思考问题，也可以感受到不一样的生活和学习经历。于是，我们更容易体会到生活的乐趣。

一口漂亮的英语能够使沟通更加顺畅。

通过不同词语的使用，通过不同语音的调整，通过不同句法的叠加，你会觉得“弦外之音”奥妙无穷。是的，这就是语言的艺术。

沟通能力也是雅思口语的主要测试目的之一。

雅思口语分为三部分，Part 1和Part 2都是对话形式，Part 3是独白形式。

不管是哪一种形式，重要的是内容，因为准确回答问题是沟通的基础。

沟通的前提是真实的个性化。

准确回答问题不是评判观点，而是要体现个人对问题的真实理解，这才是进一步讨论的基础。如果是“背诵答案”，一定会在无形中失去沟通的乐趣，当然也不会得高分。

“人本论”和“人存论”是很好的突出个性化的方法。

人本论和人存论都是以题目和个体特征为基础，找到答题切入口，并快速组织答案的方法。如果你能真实地表达自己，那么对方也愿意耐心地讨论更多内容。

口语要求准确表达，这也是有效沟通的重要前提。

口语测试强调词汇、语法、句型的准确、灵活使用。所有的表现形式都是为内容服务，从而达到有效沟通的目的。

如果希望自己说得精彩，编码口语学可以起到很大作用。

如果希望自己的话引人入胜，那么正确的语音、合理的内容分布、有逻辑性的展开、自然的衔接都非常重要。这样对方也会在你的精彩回答中，发现你的沟通诚意和出色的沟通能力。“编码口语学”在这方面有非常突出的贡献。

人本论、人存论和编码口语学的实质是借助题目要求，激活潜在的语言能力，并激发沟通热情，达到有效沟通的目的和效果。

人本论、人存论和编码口语学是钱多多老师对雅思口语以及整个口语培训的杰出贡献。这三种方式都强调个性化，跟语言学中的variety相契合，能充分促进语言交流，不仅符合雅思的测试目的，更符合口语学习的目的。

当然，除了以理论为基础，这本书的信息量也足够大，不管是对备考信息的总结还是对整个真题题库的描述，都体现了钱多多老师丰富的经验和扎实的语言基础，此处不再一一赘述，大家可以从答案及其点评中感受到。

祝各位考生考分多多益善！

吕蕾公众微信号：lvlei1973

吕蕾微博：http://weibo.com/lvlei1973

吕蕾博客：http://blog.sina.com.cn/wonderfullei

吕蕾

真明师

很荣幸应邀为本书写一篇序。

随着互联网教育大潮的来临，中国英语培训行业的现状变得“名”师泛滥，“明”师稀少。

我见过各种各样的“名”师。或以预测押题炒作，或常雇用水军造势，或以娱乐励志扬名，更有低价盗买真题而后高价卖出者，考生却趋之若鹜，称其为“名师”。

这名利得来快，一时火，有争议，不长久。

另一类名师，他们不仅精研学术，明白考试的来龙去脉，强调学以致用，累积而至教学创新，而且还善于调节学生情绪和心理状态，懂得科学的进步过程，能够传播东西方文化和无价的人生智慧。这一类老师有长久的大名气。为了区别于前者，我称之为“明师”。

在当今中国的雅思培训行业中，这样的真明师不超过十位，钱多多老师是其中的佼佼者。

雅思口语考试测试语言的本质功能：人与人之间的口头交流能力。所有的考题设计均来自于留学生、移民在国外的真实生活交际场景。遗憾的是，很多考生怀着一种纯粹的应试心态，仅把雅思口语当作一种考试来备考，把重心放在了模板和预测押题上，最后浪费了时间，没有学到真功夫，成绩也不理想。

要想真正学好英语口语，考生应该以备战雅思为契机，认真了解雅思口语的官方评分标准，学习有科学性地拓展思路，有逻辑性地组织语言，系统地提升口语表达技能，这样才能真正提高口语水平，同时轻松拿到雅思口语考试高分，一箭双雕。此乃智者所为。

这本《舌尖上的雅思》是钱多多老师的心血力作。它强调交流以人为本，为雅思口语教学正本清源。《舌尖上的雅思》不只是一本优秀的雅思教材。希望有幸看到这本书的读者能体会到它的真正价值。

劉洪波

前 言

12年磨一剑，著书以分享。在和雅思考生多年的不断接触中，我发现口语是大部分考生出国留学路上的一大拦路虎，如下绝望的感叹不绝于耳：

多叔，我都考了4次雅思了，每次口语都是5.5分，怎么办？

多叔，我总分是7，可是口语只有可怜的5分，怎么办？

多叔，我听力都考到8分了，可是口语最高只有5.5分，拿着那份“沉重”的OFFER，它却要求我单科不低于6分，我都考了5次了，再考真的要疯掉了。

面对着这群追梦的年轻人一个个迫切的追问和一次次失望的泪水，我除了被他们屡败屡战、再启征程的精神所打动，更明白了作为一名口语老师的责任。

从2003年教授第一拨雅思考生，迄今已有10多个年头了。我也苦恼过，彷徨过，以前也像现在的绝大多数雅思教师一样，要么带着学生狂练，要么让学生去记忆素材，但我发觉这些方法都是自欺欺人，收效甚微！于是，在2009年，我邀请数位国内及英国权威英语教育专家成立中国首个雅思听说研究中心——多叔雅思，其中包括本书的部分资料搜集者：前任雅思考官Dr. Robert Burton，感谢他为本书提供雅思官方相关资料。我们针对学生做了大量的口语测试实验，系统、精准地分析了雅思口语的评分标准，有了惊人发现：如果考生能激活对特定考题的思维细胞，产生清晰自然的思维渠道，同时满足考试评分点要求，就不难提高雅思口语成绩。为了实现这一目标，我们教研团队将心理学和统计学融入口语思维体系，创立“四大黄金法则”“人本论”“编码口语学”等神奇方法，快速激发考生的语言组织能力，使其最大限度地做到流畅表达！

我们后来通过数年的教学实践，不断完善方法体系，力求尽善尽美。同学们的一个又一个喜报让我们的付出得到了回报，有同学从6分到8分，有同学从4.5分到7分，这些在传统雅思口语教学中“不可能完成的任务”，在我们面前变得不再那么难以完成。我不敢说每个同学都能提高这么多，但是口语能力实质改善和成绩有力提升在短期内是可以实现的。有考生说我是“雅思口语思维派”的鼻祖，我淡然地笑了，仅希望口语不再成为考生心中的痛。

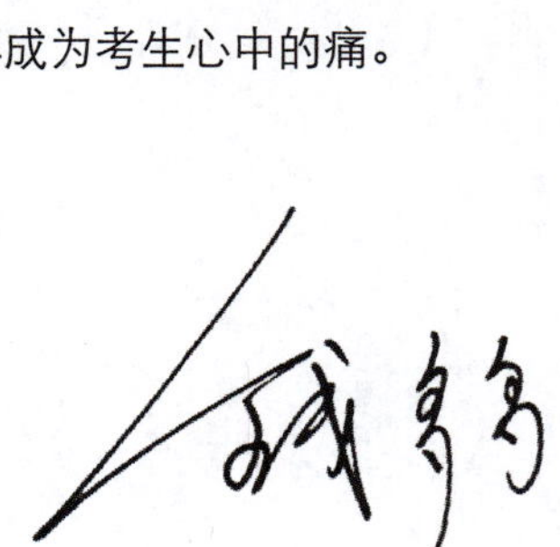

目　录

第1章

雅思考生不可不知的

8大“口语术语”

一、蹲点

这个“蹲点”不是指游戏中蹲点来狙击对手，雅思考试的“蹲点”是指提前到你所在的考点等候考完出来的同学，问刚考过的题目。这些考题会在后面甚至第二天出现，概率非常大。提醒当天下午考试的同学最好收集同一考场的题目，第二天考试的需要收集当天全部题目。

二、换题

在雅思考试的12个月中，雅思“换题”已经成为了公开的“不能说的秘密”，1、5、9三个月题库会进行一次刷新，因此同学们在这三个月的月初尽量不要参加考试，以免成为小白鼠。

三、预测

由于了解换题的基本规律，雅思老师会对1、5、9三个月的考试题目进行归类，分别对2、3、4、6、7、8、10、11和12月中的考题进行预测，因此除1、5、9三个月外的口语话题还是趋于稳定的。值得一提的是，每个换题季，都会约有1/3老题从上季题库中剔除，由新题补充，最终形成新季题库。从新季的第一个月首次考试到月底最后一场考试，新题基本上会陆续出炉。

四、考试流程

参加口语考试要记得带身份证，以备查验。提前30分钟到考场进行拍照、验证身份。接着到考场门口等考官来接你，切记不要敲门，因为考官已经很累了，他休息一会儿自然会来找你的。考官出来见你，会问你：“Did you take your cell phone?”有时候会拿着名单先用拼音核实性地说出你的中文名，你点头即可，你要老实地回答有没有带手机，如果没带就说“NO”，带了就说“YES”，然后他会让你关机。

进入考场，雅思口语考试正式开始。

(1) 大概流程

整个雅思口语考试分为三个部分，大体过程如下：

介绍部分（=验明身份，不属于以下三个部分）通常有四个基础问题（25～30秒，实际考试会有变动）。

Part 1 生活交流

4～5分钟，考官通常会问4组话题，每组话题一般有4个小问题，实际考试会有变动。

Part 2 个人独自

重点在于述说个人经历(3～4分钟)

1分钟思考时间（允许做笔记，要记关键词）

1～2分钟个人独白（原则上，考官不允许打断，实际情况中，考官有时会打断）

1～2 个后续问题（实际情况有所变动，有时不问）

Part 3 深入讨论

4～5 分钟，通常是两组话题，一般由考官根据Part 2考生作答随机提问，实际考试有所变动。

(2) 具体流程

考官打开录音笔后，考试正式开始：

介绍部分（身份检查）

Item 1. 尽管介绍部分不是考试主体，但仍然是考试的一部分。考官的录音笔会记录你所说的，同时考官也会注意你的语言表达质量及所犯的错误。

Item 2. 该部分的目的是检查考生是否能够使用“合适的答案”回答一些核实身份的问题，“合适的答案”指的是简单干脆，不需要回答得长或者在回答完问题后附加多余的信息。

Item 3. 介绍部分通常以基本的打招呼开始，如“Good morning/afternoon, can I see your identification please?”之类的表达。

Part 1

在介绍部分完成后，考官会引出第一组话题，然后问你一些相关的小问题。第一组问题通常会是：你的家（家乡在哪里、现在住哪儿等问题）或者你的工作/学习（工作还是学习、喜欢与否等问题），或者名字（含义、起名习俗等问题），实际情况有所变动。

紧随其后，考官会问其他两组问题，通常是和日常生活息息相关的。每季最新Part（以下简称P）1题库，可参考www.ieltslearn.com（雅思学习网）。

如果考生不太明白题目中的个别单词，考官会给予一些帮助，但是这会暴露出你的词汇缺陷，考官也会因此初步判断你的口语水平在5或者以下，因为考官认为这些问题对考生来说是最基本的。

当考官告诉你他将会给你一个topic，这表明第一部分正式结束。

Part 2

第二部分开始的时候，考官通常会这么说：

I'm now going to give you a topic and I'd like you to talk about that topic for one to two minutes. Before you start to talk, you'll have one minute to think about what you're going to say. You can make notes if you wish on this paper. Do you understand?

随后，考官会给你一张A4纸大小的卡片（官方规定是卡片），即话题卡，但是实际上很多考点有不同方式，甚至有考官直接指着“话题书”里的一个话题给你看。

当考官给你卡片的时候，官方规定他必须说“I'd like you to describe...”，然后读出话题。在卡片上通常会有4～5个小要求（这些小要求考官是不会读的），你的个人独白必须满足所有要求。卡片上的“you should say”意味着：

You should include these points but you can also say more than just these points.

在1分钟准备时间里，我们该做些什么呢？

Item 1. 读话题卡（记住：这个时候就可以开始思考该说些什么了）。

Item 2. 读完后，你要快速决定要说什么，很多考生在犹豫中度过了1分钟。

Item 3. 根据每个小要求，思考下自己该说什么，并同时快速记下关键词（记住：把精力主要集中在思考观点和词汇上，不要过多思考句子该怎么组织，本书后面将会介绍神器“编码口语学”，瞬间激活同学们的组织思维）。

1分钟结束后，考官会提醒你将会有1～2分钟时间去展示个人独白，通常会这么说：“Can you start speaking now, please?”（= Please start speaking now.）

当你在说的时候，你可以保留卡片，但不要一直盯着卡片或自己记录的要点，适当的眼神交流也很重要。比如你可以看一下自己记下的关键词，然后看着考官说，再重复以上动作。

考官被要求在你进行个人独白的时候，不允许打断，即便他没有听清或听懂，但事实上有不少考官在1分半钟的时候将你打断。

当到2分钟或者你停止个人独白的时候，考官将有可能会说：“Thank you.”

通常情况下，考官会提出1～2个后续问题，这些问题和P2中你所展现的信息高度相关，目的在于体现考官对你的个人独白感兴趣，你只需要做简短回答。同时，这些问题有时候也在暗示在P3考官可能会问哪方面问题，使你提前进入P3的讨论节奏。

P2话题分为四大类：

Item 1. People

Item 2. Objects

Item 3. Places

Item 4. Events

不论是哪类，话题都和你的生活和经历直接相关，也就是说你必须讲出个人情况，而不是客观或粗略描述。很多考生喜欢买市面上的素材来背答案，这些答案往往是在客观描述一件事物，如近期考题Describe a movie that you dislike，素材中大篇幅在说这部电影多么糟糕，但似乎和你没什么关系。考官对此表示非常厌恶。

考生在P2的个人独白时间最好是1分30秒～2分钟，不要太短，尽管超过1分钟已经符合题目要求，但是尽可能地展示更多信息可以更充分展示你的语言能力。实际考试中，如果考官觉得你说得非常不错，但时间仅在1分钟左右，这时候考官会提示你可以继续说下去。考官被要求严格将作答时间限制在2分钟以内，超过即可打断。需要注意的是，考生在时间未到却已经结束或无法继续下去的时候，请告知考官，如Well, that’s all I have to say.没有任何表示则会被扣流利度分数。

考生没有权利要求更换话题，即便你非常不喜欢话题卡上的话题或对该话题没有相关信息可说。因为剑桥官方认为这些话题都是一些日常生活中会接触到的。中国考生时常认为无话可说，是因为大部分中国考生在找观点的时候遵循“假大空”思维方式。关于如何快速有效寻找合适观点，本书在后面第3章有专题讲解。

考生在个人独白时要时刻记得不要将P2变成正式的演讲，你的个人独白要像日常对话中的自然描述。

P2 话题示范（雅思高频考题）

Describe a famous person who is important to your country.

You should say

who this person is

how you know about the person

what sort of life they had before they became famous

how this person became famous

and explain why this person is important to your country.

Part 3

考官在开始P3的时候，通常会这么说：“We've been talking about the topic of part 2 and now I'd like to ask you a few more general questions related to this topic.”

P3在形式上和P1一样，都是你问我答，但是在P3，考官一般会根据问题书或自己设计问题来提问考生，这些问题通常情况下是根据你在P2的作答提出的。在很大程度上，P3就是讨论甚至辩论，实际考试中，考官有可能会对你就某个问题回答的某个点感兴趣，从而刨根问底。考官也有可能另起炉灶，问一些和P2毫不相干的问题。

官方要求考官在P3最好问两组话题，一般每组话题有5个小问题。根据时间情况，实际考试中问题个数有所变动。

考生在P3中用词要比P1、P2稍微难，尽量使用学术表达词汇，因为第三部分的问题更加复杂和抽象，是一些“general questions about people and life in China”。

既然P3是讨论，就不能像P1一样只是简单回答问题，而需要尽可能地展开话题，甚至展现新的论点，这样考官可以和你深度讨论下去，从而获得更高的分数。关于这一方面，书中第4章会详细介绍。

五、眼神交流

在雅思口语考试中，眼神交流是非常重要的，尽管这不是评分点，但是会对你的口语成绩产生隐性影响。眼神交流不仅仅是看着考官眼睛那么简单。合理地进行眼神交流的考生会被考官认为是个成熟的口语表达者。雅思口语考试是面对面的交流，眼神的沟通有时候会产生意想不到的效果。

(1) 多少眼神交流合适

眼神交流要适度，通常要像你和朋友说话时的眼神交流状态。考生要学会暗示自己把考官当成自己的朋友，千万不要觉得考官是你的命运大神。如果实在太紧张，偶尔看考官的脸部也可视作眼神交流。考生可以在和朋友练习口语时注意眼神交流的训练。

(2) 眼神交流的好处

首先，眼神交流能够提高自信心，考生进考场后一般都非常紧张，有些考生就干脆一直躲避考官的目光，你问什么我就答什么，其实呢，如果你一开始努力和考官进行眼神沟通，你会发觉过不了多长时间你就完全适应了，甚至能够激发你的表达欲望，同时给考官留下非常好的印象。

其次，眼神交流对流利度有不可小觑的帮助，有同学认为流利度指的就是不能停顿，这个认知是错误的，有效的停顿是流利度的一个必要因素。当我们说完一个观点或句子后，我们可以看着考官停顿一下，然后移开目光继续说，考官会认为这样很自然。当我们对所说的话不太自信的时候，看一下考官可以帮助我们了解考官是否能听懂，同时可以稍微停顿下，这样做的话，如果感觉考官比较疑惑，可以赶紧说“what I mean is...”“so my main point is...”来救场。

六、成绩复议

考生在口语成绩出来之后，如果发现成绩和自己的预期相差太大，可以通过雅思官方网站申请复议。在雅思四项考试中，只有口语考试有主观评分成分存在，其复议成功率在四项中是最高的。复议时最好加份复议信，说明考试情况，以提高成功率。

七、评分方式

口语考试考查语音语调、词汇、流利度、语法，四个评分点满分都是9分，考官分别给出整数分数，然后取平均数，口试最终成绩为整数或半分。考官不会给3个Part分别打分，考官在Part 1已给四个方面打分，再在Part 2和Part 3进行调整。如平均下来不是整数或半分，考官会往下找下一个最近的整数或半分（如5.75 = 5.5，7.25 = 7.0）。

八、评分标准

雅思口语官方评分标准

A Detailed Description of the Band Scores

In this table, the candidate is called “she”, instead of “he or she”.

Item	9分
Fluency and Coherence (& Cohesion)	Fluency • This candidate speaks as fluently as native English speakers. That is, she speaks at the natural speed and continuity of native speakers. • She occasionally shows hesitation or occasional pauses when speaking about the most complex or abstract concepts or when recalling examples, just as a native speaker sometimes does.
	Coherence • When this candidate speaks at length, such as in Part 2, the listener (the examiner) feels that the long answer has a sense of “wholeness” and completeness. • Similarly, when she speaks about several aspects of a complex topic, the examiner can effortlessly follow the flow of ideas because the relationships between ideas are clearly spoken. To achieve this, she makes full use of “cohesive devices”, such as the introductory words of sentences. • When topics are introduced by the examiner in the form of questions in Part 1 and Part 3 or the task card in Part 2, she fully develops these topics by speaking “expansively” to a degree that is suitable. That is, she never gives very short answers to questions.

Vocabulary	Vocabulary Range • The candidate shows all the vocabulary attributes of a reasonably well-educated native English speaker (but not necessarily equal to a highly educated native speaker). • The candidate has a wide enough vocabulary to fully converse about all topics in depth. Flexibility and Precision of Meaning • The candidate shows an accurate knowledge of small differences in meaning and usage between similar or related words, including the more advanced vocabulary. Idiomatic Usage • The candidate uses idiomatic language quite often, naturally and without errors. This includes a few examples of less common or more advanced idiomatic language.
Grammatical Range and Accuracy	• A Band 9 candidate shows the strong grammar of a reasonably well-educated native speaker. The only mistakes are the kind of minor mistakes that even some reasonably well-educated native speakers may occasionally make.
Pronunciation	• The candidate sounds like a native English speaker, or like someone who speaks "international English" (such as American English influenced by British English or British English influenced by American English). • Possibly she has a slight hint of her native accent. • In general, the candidate shows all the pronunciation features of a native English speaker with the only errors being the kind of errors that even reasonably well educated native English speakers might occasionally make.

Item	8分
Fluency and Coherence (& Cohesion)	Fluency • The candidate speaks almost as fluently as the Band 9 candidate but there might be a few times when she hesitates slightly to find the correct word or grammatical structure to use. However, these occasional hesitations are usually when she is trying to express the most abstract or complex ideas, as in Part 3 and her hesitations are usually to search for ideas. Coherence • Most of this candidate's language is fully cohesive, as for the Band 9 candidate. • However, the examiner might occasionally feel that the candidate could have used a more natural choice of cohesive device (i.e., A choice that native speakers would chose). • As for the Band 9 candidate, she shows the ability to fully develop her answers, using examples and a suitable amount of relevant extra information.

Vocabulary	Range ● The candidate has a wide enough vocabulary to discuss all topics in depth. Flexibility and Precision of Meaning ● She accurately shows knowledge of small differences in meaning and usage between similar or related words. That is, she shows strong flexibility in her usage of vocabulary. Idiomatic Usage ● She shows good knowledge of common idiomatic expressions. ● She uses a few examples of less common idiomatic vocabulary in a natural way but occasionally might have some minor inaccuracies in their usage. Paraphrase ● If needed, she shows the ability to accurately communicate meaning using other words when she does not know the precise, more advanced word that an educated native speaker would use. ● She is very skilful in rephrasing sentences or phrases when she wants to add clarity to or amplify her meaning. Style ● She shows a very accurate understanding of the appropriate level of formality to use in her choice of words. This includes the possible, occasional use of quite informal language, if it is suitable for the conversation. Collocation ● She shows strong knowledge of collocation (= the most natural and common combinations of different words), although she may occasionally show minor inaccuracy with less commonly used words.
Grammatical Range and Accuracy	Errors ● This candidate is similar to Band 7 except for the fact that she makes fewer grammatical mistakes than a Band 7 candidate. ● Perhaps she makes 1 to 5 minor mistakes in the whole test. These mistakes are usually made when producing the most advanced structures. Grammatical Range ● This candidate shows the ability to use the most advanced grammar, effortlessly and usually accurately. Complex Sentences ● She speaks using complex sentences most of the time and shows a wide range of connectives to form these sentences.

Pronunciation	Accent ● The examiner might be able to recognize the candidate's native accent but it is (usually but not always) slight and does not interfere with the English pronunciation in any way. Understandability ● The pronunciation is very clear and accurate. The examiner rarely or never needs to ask the candidate to repeat anything (except in the case of the examiner having poor hearing or the candidate speaking too softly). Basic Sound Accuracy ● All the vowels, consonants and diphthongs are pronounced very accurately, the way a native speaker pronounces them. Sentence Stress ● Almost all the time, the candidate places the sentence stress on the correct word, although there might be one or two times when the examiner feels the wrong word was stressed. ● To a greater degree than a Band 7 candidate, this candidate makes use of sentence stress to express meaning or for emphasis. Intonation ● The candidate frequently shows the ability to vary her intonation to express meaning. Speed of Delivery and Chunking ● The candidate shows the ability to consistently vary her speed by speaking in "chunks" of word groups. Word Stress ● The candidate might make a rare error in placing the stress in a multi-syllable word on the wrong syllable but these errors would be in less common words and they would be the type of error that some native English speakers might make.

Item	7分
Fluency and Coherence (& Cohesion)	Fluency ● This candidate is able to speak continuously most of the time with no apparent effort. However, she hesitates occasionally when searching for a word or the correct way to express herself. ● Possibly she self-corrects her language more than once or twice, when speaking more complex language.

<table>
<tr><td>Fluency and Coherence (& Cohesion)</td><td>Coherence
• The flow of her ideas is easy for the examiner to follow. To some extent, she (wisely) chooses to avoid speaking about the most abstract or complex ideas and this helps her to speak coherently. That is, she tries to speak in somewhat simpler terms than the Band 8 candidate. (In contrast, the Band 8 candidate attempts to express herself almost at the same level and the same degree of complexity as when speaking her own language while the Band 7 controls this impulse to some extent.)
• This candidate shows frequent usage of a good range of connective phrases and expressions.
• However, the examiner notices that the range of this knowledge, and the understanding of the usage of these “connective devices” may still be a little restricted. That is, the examiner can sometimes think of better ways to connect ideas than what the candidate spoke (i.e., the candidate occasionally uses a connective device a little inappropriately) or the candidate sometimes doesn’t use a connective phrase when one should be used.
• She shows a good ability to develop her answers (e.g., adding an appropriate amount of suitable extra information or extending a discussion topic).
• Although her ability to extend discussion questions in Part 3 is much better than the “rudimentary” level of a Band 6, her ability in this area is still below that of the Band 8 candidate who is able to “fully” develop such questions.</td></tr>
<tr><td>Vocabulary</td><td>Range
• The candidate has a big enough vocabulary to hold discussions on a wide variety of topics, at some depth. However, for the most difficult Part 3 questions that the examiner may ask, (e.g., testing to see if she might qualify for Band 8), her vocabulary may be insufficient to allow her to answer with complete fluency.
Flexibility and Precision of Meaning
• Generally, she shows quite strong vocabulary flexibility (= knowledge of the wider meanings and usage of a word, beyond a single meaning or usage).
Idiomatic Usage
• She shows good knowledge of several common idiomatic expressions.
• She might use a few examples of less common idiomatic vocabulary but also might use some of these inappropriately.
Paraphrase
• She shows the ability to successfully use other words to convey her meaning when she does not know the exact word that a native speaker would use or when she might need to rephrase a sentence to clarify or amplify her meaning.
Style
• She shows an awareness of appropriate language style (informal/formal usage) but may occasionally choose vocabulary that is unsuitably formal, such as vocabulary that is more suitable for written English rather than spoken English.</td></tr>
</table>

Vocabulary	Collocation ● She shows good knowledge and understanding of collocation (= the most natural and common combinations of different words), although she may make a small number of inappropriate choices of word combinations.
Grammatical Range and Accuracy	Errors ● This candidate makes a few more grammatical errors than a Band 8 for grammar (for example, 5 to 10 errors) but these are usually minor errors, when using the more advanced grammatical structures. ● She might make a very small number of (perhaps 1 or 2) "simple" errors such as when using irregular past tense verbs or omitting the use the past tense when it should be used. Such errors are the result of "old habits" of speech rather than a lack of knowledge. Range ● This candidate "impresses the examiner" with her ability to accurately produce a wide range of grammatical structures, including the most advanced structures. However, a few, mostly minor errors exist. Complex Sentences ● This candidate quite frequently uses complex sentences and shows a good range of connectives used to form these sentences.
Pronunciation	Accent ● The candidate's native accent might still be recognizable, but the accent of a native English-speaker is more dominant than the native accent. Understandability ● The pronunciation is very clear and accurate almost all the time. The examiner never or rarely needs to ask the candidate to repeat anything. ● There might be one or two times when the examiner needs to "think twice" about what word the candidate just said but it is rare for the examiner to need to ask the candidate to repeat herself. ● There should be no "patches" of language or short combinations of words that the examiner does not understand at all. However, the examiner might have to quickly "think twice" about the meaning of one or two "patches of language". Basic Sound Accuracy ● Except for perhaps one or two occasions, the candidate pronounces all letters and diphthongs accurately.

Pronunciation	Sentence Stress • Most of the time, the candidate accurately places the sentence stress on the correct word in order to accurately express or emphasize her meaning. • The candidate might make one or two errors when placing the word stress in noun + noun or adjective + noun combinations but these errors are usually for the lesser-known word combinations. Intonation • The candidate shows good knowledge of how native English-speakers use intonation, i.e., a rising or falling tone, to communicate meaning. Speed of Delivery and Chunking • The candidate frequently shows some knowledge of how native English-speakers vary their speech speed to show meaning. This is mostly shown by her ability to speak in “chunks” of “word groups” faster than other parts of her sentences. However, she probably does not consistently speak in “chunks”. Linked Sounds • As part of her ability to show the skill of chunking, the candidate shows good ability at linking her speech sounds so that these chunks can be spoken faster. These chunks are spoken almost as if they were one long word. • Along with an overall ability to speak linked sounds, the candidate shows a few instances of being able to link and blend her sounds very much like a native speaker does (or some native speakers do), for some short word combinations. For example, she might say, “dɪd'” for “did you”. Word Stress • There might be one or two instances of the candidate mispronouncing a multi-syllable word by stressing the wrong syllable but these pronunciation mistakes do not cause confusion.
Item	**6分**
Fluency and Coherence (& Cohesion)	Fluency • This candidate’s fluency is marked by her willingness to speak continuously (or her lack of fear of continuing to speak, even if it results in some errors). • This candidate shows both the willingness and the ability to seek clarification if she doesn’t understand a question, especially in Part 3. • She also has some ability to start talking immediately following a question, even if to just comment about the question. By doing this, she largely avoids sitting there silently for an unnaturally long period of time before answering a (more difficult) question, as Band 5 and Band 4 candidates tend to do.

Fluency and Coherence (& Cohesion)	Coherence ● Occasionally the examiner momentarily has trouble following the flow of the candidate's ideas. This is a result of the candidate breaking her flow of language a few times in order to self-correct, search for vocabulary or grammatical structures or to search for ideas to talk about. ● The candidate shows knowledge of a few different connective phrases and words and uses a variety of them several times during the test, although sometimes the usage is slightly incorrect or unsuitable. (Again, what marks this candidate's usage of connectives is her willingness to attempt to use them.) ● She shows some ability to extend her answers (e.g., adding an appropriate amount of suitable extra information or extending a discussion topic). But this skill is not fully developed. For example, there are times when her answers should be developed more and her ability to extend a discussion question is somewhat rudimentary.
Vocabulary	Range ● The candidate has a wide enough vocabulary to converse on most topics at some depth. However, some of the more difficult questions in Part 3, or topics that are not familiar to the candidate reveal a lack of enough vocabulary, or a lack of vocabulary flexibility to continue a discussion beyond a rather simple, but still correct answer. Flexibility and Precision of Meaning ● Generally, she is able to express the meaning she wants to express. But she makes a few errors in word choice, although these are usually not severe enough to cause confusion or a lack of understanding in the listener (the examiner). ● Unlike the Band 5 candidate, many of her vocabulary mistakes are a result of her willingness to try to speak expansively, even attempting at times to speak beyond the limits of her vocabulary knowledge. Idiomatic Usage ● She shows only a limited knowledge of the most commonly used idiomatic expressions. Paraphrase ● When needed, she shows the ability to successfully rephrase her sentences for clarification. Similarly, she shows the ability to choose different words to convey meaning when she does not know the most appropriate word to use. However, sometimes her choice of vocabulary is not the most suitable choice when attempting to paraphrase. Style ● At times, she may speak using inappropriately formal language (such as the language in "business English" letters or in academic writing). Collocation ● At times, she might use a few inappropriate word combinations but these are usually not serious enough to cause confusion.

<table>
<tr>
<td>Grammatical Range and Accuracy</td>
<td>
Errors
● This candidate makes more errors than a Band 7 candidate, perhaps 10 to 20 errors, but not as many as a Band 5 candidate.
● Most of these errors are made when attempting the more advanced grammatical structures. However, a small number of the errors are at the less advanced level, such as “old habits” of not using a correct irregular past tense verb or not using the past tense when it should be used.
Grammatical Range
● The candidate shows knowledge of and willingness to attempt to use some of the more advanced grammatical structures, even though she might make several errors when doing this.
She sometimes produces these more advanced structures correctly, or produces them with perhaps one error in the structure, but usually not several errors.
Basically, she shows that she has some understanding of the more advanced grammar but she still has not thoroughly perfected the use of this grammar.
In general, this candidate has knowledge of grammatical structures beyond that of Band 5 and is willing to demonstrate this knowledge, even at the risk of making mistakes. As long as these attempts are mostly correct and do not result in confusion to the examiner or contain many errors, the candidate is given points for showing this knowledge, rather than being penalized for the errors.
● This candidate shows at least some knowledge of, and correctly uses (some of the time), most of the following grammatical points:
—the perfect verb tenses;
—the perfect modal verbs;
—the passive voice;
—reported speech; and,
—the subjunctive mood.
She has at least a basic understanding of the usage of the word, “would” and can (usually) correctly make sentences such as, “If I had more free time, I’d (= I would) go out more often with my friends.”
However, she probably does not even attempt the past unreal conditional, such as, “If I had known they were coming, I would have cleaned my house” or, if she does attempt it, she might make more than one error using this structure.
● When speaking about the future using the verb, “will”, this candidate shows the ability to use adverbs of certainty such as “possibly”, “probably” etc.
● This candidate probably also shows the ability to use “there + be” in other tenses, besides the simple present tense.
● The candidate nearly always answers questions using complete sentences i.e., one-word answers are rare.
</td>
</tr>
</table>

Grammatical Range and Accuracy	Complex Sentences ● She shows some knowledge of complex sentences and a willingness to produce many of these in the test. However, her range of connectives used to produce these sentences may still be a little limited and she might sometimes uses a connective word or phrase inappropriately or incorrectly. ● The candidate shows the examiner, (at least two or three times), that she can correctly use the relative pronoun, "which", as well as other relative pronouns.
Pronunciation	Accent ● The candidate's native accent is possibly quite obvious but it does not interfere with understandability. At the same time, the national accent of an English-speaking country might also be discernable. Understandability ● The candidate speaks clearly most of the time but there might be 2 or 3 times when the examiner does not understand a word and needs to ask the candidate to repeat what she just said. ● Perhaps once or twice the examiner does not understand a "patch" of language such as a short combination of words. Basic Sound Accuracy ● There might be occasional inaccuracy in a few of the vowel, consonant and diphthong sounds but the examiner usually can guess what word the candidate is saying. For example, saying "ship" instead of "sheep". ● Overall, the candidate does not habitually mispronounce any one vowel, consonant or diphthong, although she might randomly mispronounce some of these at times. Sentence Stress ● Overall, she shows some knowledge of correct sentence stress, although she does not use correct sentence stress in every utterance. ● The candidate has some knowledge about which word to stress in noun + noun combinations or adjective + noun combinations but might still make a few mistakes with this. ● The candidate shows some knowledge of how to stress keys words in a sentence for emphasis, such as when contrasting. Intonation ● The candidate shows some knowledge of how to use intonation, for example, when speaking a list, but is not consistent with her use of correct intonation. Linked Speech Sounds ● The candidate mostly links her speech sounds in a natural way but occasionally speaks each word separately, like a robot. Word Stress ● The candidate might stress the wrong syllable in a multi-syllable word a small number of times but the word is usually recognizable to the examiner.

Item	5分
Fluency and Coherence (& Cohesion)	Fluency • This candidate can usually keep talking but, in order to do this, she frequently repeats her sentences or phrases, self-corrects or speaks unnaturally slowly (or a combination of all three of these). • Quite often her slow speech is because she is trying so hard to use correct grammar and choose the correct vocabulary. (This candidate possibly has had little or no experience in speaking English in a communicative situation with other people, not just with English speakers.) • For simple speech in many or most of her Part 1 answers, this candidate can speak quite fluently, with few hesitations or self-corrections or hesitation when searching for words or grammatical structures. But as the test progresses and the questions or the Part 2 task require more complex language, her fluency progressively breaks down. • In Part 2 there may be a few times when the candidate pauses for an unnaturally long period of time, although these periods are usually just for a few seconds. • In Part 3, the candidate pauses for an unnaturally long period before answering several of the questions, except for the simplest questions. Her speech is usually quite slow in answering most Part 3 questions because she doesn't have a big enough vocabulary to express herself. Coherence • The typical Band 5 candidate shows knowledge of only a narrow range of connective phrases. In other words, she does not often attempt to connect her ideas by beginning sentences with connective phrases or, when she does, she repeats the same, sometimes rather simple phrases too often. • The typical Band 5 candidate also does a rather poor job at "developing his or her answer" i.e., at giving extra information. This candidate might not fully understand that almost every question in the test (except for the 4 introduction questions) is actually "an invitation to give information". This candidate thinks the questions are more simple questions. For example, a question such as, "Do you like listening to music?" is really asking you to, a) first answer the question directly and, b) then give extra information about your music-listening habits and tastes. In Part 3, many Band 5 candidates continue to think that the questions are simply basic questions, without understanding that you should not just answer the basic question but answer in a "discussion style", which means expanding your answer quite a lot and/or speaking an introductory statement before you answer the basic question, for example, by saying something such as, "Well, it depends on the situation. For example, if...then... But on the other hand, if...then..." • Some Band 5 candidates, for example, some older candidates who have been working for a few years, tend to speak impersonally in the Speaking test. These candidates think of the test as an "interview" when they should think of it more as a "simulated conversation". If you avoid expressing your feelings or opinion then you will find it harder to speak extensively in some answers.

Vocabulary	Range • The candidate has enough vocabulary to generally hold a limited, short discussion on familiar topics, but unfamiliar topics reveal a lack of vocabulary in these areas. • Her answers to discussion questions in Part 3 usually communicate meaning but are short. • For the more difficult Part 3 questions, she may be at a loss how to answer (or may not understand the question itself.) • She can answer Part 2 topics but there might be a few unnaturally long pauses in her speech when she searches for words. Flexibility and Precision of Meaning • Her vocabulary often shows that she has limited flexibility, i.e., a narrow understanding of the meaning and usage of some words. That is, she may use some words correctly but tends to use these words as if they were newly learned, with only one usage or one translation from her own language. • She may overuse some words. • Even when speaking about familiar topics, she tends to give rather short answers that could be called, "minimum" answers—answers that do usually correctly address the basic question but do not show a wider vocabulary, even when she might know a wider vocabulary. This is often because she is afraid to attempt to speak expansively. Idiomatic Usage • She rarely shows knowledge of the most common idiomatic vocabulary, such as phrasal verbs. Paraphrase • She sometimes attempts to rephrase her sentences for clarification but is not always successful in conveying her meaning when she does this. Style • She shows little or no knowledge of the different levels of formality to use. Collocation • She might make several errors in choices of word combinations and these errors might occasionally cause confusion in the listener.
Grammatical Range and Accuracy	Errors • The candidate makes a grammatical mistake of some kind, big or small, in about one out of every four or five sentences. Grammatical Range • The candidate usually speaks in short, simple sentences and sometimes gives one-word answers. • She might have some knowledge of more advanced grammar (for example, the ability to understand it when reading), but she usually does not attempt to produce it. When she does attempt to produce the more complex grammatical structures, they almost always contain so many errors that she needs to try again to produce that structure. For this reason, most Band 5 candidates simply avoid trying to produce more complex grammatical structures.

Grammatical Range and Accuracy	• The candidate usually correctly makes sentences with verb-subject agreement (i.e., single verb form goes with single subject and plural verb form goes with plural subject) but occasionally makes errors here. • The candidate usually can correctly produce simple, short sentences using the present simple tense. • When using the present continuous tense, she might omit the "be" verb, such as, "I studying…" or, "I'm study...". • When asked past tense questions, the candidate sometimes answers correctly but often makes mistakes, especially with the irregular past tense verbs. Sometimes she answers a past tense question using the present tense. In a past tense Part 2 topic, she sometimes completely omits to use the past tense or only uses it a few times. • When speaking about the future using the verb "will", the candidate rarely or never uses adverbs of certainty such as "possibly", "probably" or "definitely". • The candidate can usually use "there + be" in the present tense but rarely or never uses it in any other tense. • The candidate rarely or never voluntarily shows knowledge of the present perfect tense. However, when directly asked a present perfect tense question such as, "How long have you known her?" she might answer by saying, "I've known her for about two years". But more often than not, she answers with a short statement such as, "About two years", not a complete sentence. When she attempts to form a complete sentence using this tense, she sometimes makes a mistake of some kind. • The candidate does not have a clear understanding of the difference in usage between the past tense and the present perfect tense. • The candidate is confused about the past perfect tense and if she attempts to use it, it is usually used incorrectly and/or formed incorrectly. • The candidate might sometimes make the mistake of using a single noun when speaking in general (for example, "I like dog"). • She often does not use the plural after the words, "one of" or "many". • The candidate is confused about or knows nothing about the subjunctive voice and usually does not understand or correctly use the word, "would". • The candidate rarely or never correctly forms the passive voice when it is needed. • The candidate does not know the difference in usage between the words, "wish" and "hope". • This candidate probably uses "can" and "must" when talking about the future, instead of correctly saying, "will be able to" and "will have to". Complex Sentences • The few times when the candidate speaks a complex sentence, the parts of the sentence are usually joined with such simple words as, "and", "or", "but" or "because". • The candidate rarely, or never, uses the relative pronouns, "which", "who", "that" etc.

Pronunciation	Overall • If the examiner feels that the candidate's pronunciation is better than a Band 4 but not quite as good as a Band 6, the score is Band 5. • To a large extent, it is the number of times that the examiner does not understand things (either a word or a patch of English) that determine whether the candidate is Band 4, 5 or 6. Accent • The candidate's native accent might be strongly evident and may, at times, result in mispronunciation of some sounds. However, the examiner is often able to guess the meaning when the candidate mispronounces a vowel, consonant or a diphthong. Understandability • The candidate speaks clearly most of the time but there are about 4 or 5 times in the test when the examiner doesn't understand the pronunciation of a single word. • There also might be about 3 or 4 times in the test when the examiner doesn't understand a "patch" of language, such as a part of a sentence or a complete, short sentence. Basic Sound Accuracy • There is inaccuracy in a few of the vowels, consonants and diphthong sounds but usually the examiner can guess what word the candidate is saying. For example, saying "ship" instead of "sheep" and saying "maths" so that it sounds like "mice". • The candidate might habitually mispronounce one or more of the vowel, consonant or diphthong sounds. Intonation • The candidate speaks with a natural rising and falling tone at times but at other times speaks in a "flat" or "wooden" monotone. Sentence Stress • She has some knowledge about stressing the key word in a sentence, for example, when speaking about contrasts, but only sometimes does this correctly. • The candidate has little understanding of which word to stress in noun + noun combinations or adjective + noun combinations. When speaking these combinations, she is more or less guessing which word to stress and, in an attempt to avoid an error, often stresses neither word. Linked Speech • The candidate frequently doesn't link her speech sounds or words and, instead frequently speaks each word separately, like a robot. Word Stress • The candidate stresses the wrong syllable in a multi-syllable word a few times but usually the word is recognizable to the examiner.

Item	4分
Fluency and Coherence (& Cohesion)	Fluency • This candidate speaks with noticeable pauses before almost all answers. • She repeats or corrects herself often. • Her speech is unnaturally slow. • The candidate may be very slow to begin speaking in Part 2. • There are long pauses between sentences or groups of sentences in Part 2. Coherence • She can link some basic sentences using simple connectives but these connectives are usually used repetitively. • For more complex answers, or in Part 2, her meaning is often unclear.
Vocabulary	Range • The candidate can give simple answers to most Part 1 questions but the answers are usually very short, often spoken using the least words possible or using one word. • She cannot answer most Part 3 questions unless the examiner deliberately simplifies the Part 3 questions so that they resemble the simpler Part 1 questions. • She does not use adjectives very often and when they are used, they are limited to simple adjectives such as “good”. Flexibility and Precision of Meaning • She might frequently make guesses at the correct word to use, resulting in many incorrect word choices. • She struggles with Part 2, with frequent, long pauses while she searches for words.
Grammatical Range and Accuracy	Errors • The candidate makes a grammatical mistake of some kind, big or small, in about one out of every two sentences. Grammatical Range • This candidate can produce a few simple sentences correctly. • She repeatedly uses some of these simple sentences that she feels she can speak correctly, rather than showing a wider range. • She frequently attempts to answer questions using one-word answers. • The candidate's knowledge of verb tenses is often limited to the simple present tense, and the future tense, both of which she might speak correctly some of the time, but not always.

Grammatical Range and Accuracy	• All of the weaknesses written for Band 5 grammar also apply to this candidate but much more so. For example, the past tense is rarely used correctly or never used at all by Band 4 candidates. • The candidate might frequently make errors in verb-subject agreement and often fails to use a plural noun when needed. • The candidate sometimes alternates between "he" and "she" in her Part 2 monologue, causing confusion in the listener. • The candidate might be confused about which word to use among the pronouns, "he", "him", "his", "she" and "her". Complex Sentences • When she speaks using a sentence, it is nearly always a simple sentence. On the rare occasions when she attempts a complex sentence, the candidate's knowledge of linking words is limited to, "and", "or", and "but".
Pronunciation	Accent • The candidate's native accent is so strong that it interferes to a large extent in her English pronunciation. Understandability • The examiner can understand what the candidate is saying about 70% of the time—the other 30% is unintelligible or very difficult to understand and the examiner might give up asking the candidate to repeat herself after a while. Intonation and Sentence Stress • The candidate might occasionally show some examples of correct rising/falling intonation and stressing the correct word in a sentence but mostly speaks in a monotonic way, like a robot. • She might sometimes attempt to stress one particular word in a sentence but she lacks the understanding of which word to stress, with the result that these attempts are usually random guesses at which word to stress. Word Stress • The candidate stresses the incorrect syllable in a multi-syllable word several times.
Item	**3分**
Fluency and Coherence (& Cohesion)	Fluency • This candidate pauses for a long time before answering almost all questions, including Part 1 questions. • She might not be able to even begin answering some questions, often because she doesn't understand the question.

Fluency and Coherence (& Cohesion)	• She might not even begin to speak at all in Part 2, (usually because she doesn't fully understand the wording on the task card). Or, if she does speak in Part 2, she speaks only a few sentences. Coherence • She has a very limited ability, or no ability to link sentences. • Her answers are often short sentences or utterances that sometimes seem only indirectly related to the question. • It is difficult for this candidate to express her meaning, even when she understands the question.
Vocabulary	Range • The candidate only has enough simple vocabulary to answer the easier personal questions such as her name, where she lives, what she does in life and the simpler questions about her habits. • Her answers are very short, often one-word answers. • She does not understand the more difficult Part 1 questions and Part 3 must be especially adapted by the examiner to resemble the simplest of the questions from Part 1. • She often can only say a few words or just a few short sentences for Part 2 and sometimes cannot say anything at all. • She rarely uses any adjectives.
Grammatical Range and Accuracy	• She answers using one word answers very often. • She has virtually no knowledge or understanding of verb tenses. • She attempts to make some simple sentences but is usually unsuccessful. Except for a few memorized sentences, she only has the knowledge to construct a few very simple sentences correctly.
Pronunciation	Accent • The candidate has a very heavy native accent that severely interferes with her English pronunciation. Understandability • The examiner can only understand the candidate's pronunciation less than 50% of the time. Much of what the candidate says is unintelligible or very difficult to understand. • Virtually everything the candidate says is spoken in a monotonic way, like a robot.
Item	2分
Fluency and Coherence (& Cohesion)	• This candidate is able to speak very little English and pauses for quite a long time before almost every word. • There are long silences because the candidate understands very few of the questions. • It is very difficult for the examiner and the candidate to communicate at all with each other.

Vocabulary	• This candidate only knows a few simple words of English and a few, short memorized phrases or sentences. • She cannot communicate much beyond saying "Hello" and giving her name.
Grammatical Range and Accuracy	• This candidate only knows one or two simple, memorized sentences and phrases. • She usually doesn't fully understand any questions beyond, "What's your name?"
Pronunciation	• The examiner can only recognize a few English words in what the candidate says, and the candidate usually says very little.
Item	1分
Fluency and Coherence (& Cohesion)	• There is no communication possible between the examiner and the candidate. • The candidate says virtually nothing.
	• The examiner can hardly recognize that the candidate is speaking English. This candidate speaks almost nothing, anyway.
Item	0分
	Does not attend.

第2章

轻松搞定

PART 1

- 现状和基本注意事项
- 标准回答结构
- 评分要点详解
- 话题类型总结
- 目标性考核问题的高分回答模式
- 如何快速延展信息（解决该怎么说）
- 如何快速寻找观点和词汇（解决该说什么）
- 官方高频题库及高分参考范文

第1节　现状和基本注意事项

从目前的趋势看，在P1一般有12道题左右，涉及大概3个方面的问题。不过有时候考官心情不好，会问得很少，尤其当他们不耐烦的时候（口语考官每天要面对各种类型的考生，疲惫不堪），这和考生的表现好坏无关，如果你确信自己没有犯太大的错误，不用介意!

在考试过程中，按照剑桥官方规定，考官引入一个新的话题时，一般都会说“Let's talk about...”。你要稍微注意一下，因为这些信息可以让你推测出接下来可能会出现哪些问题，做好预判工作。如果考官不说，不用太在意。

当你回答问题时，考官通常会保持沉默，或者他会说些非常简短的话，例如“Ah!”“Mm!”“OK.”“Thank you.”“Good!”“That's interesting.”之类的话。考官不会也不应该和你就话题展开讨论。记住，请不要问考官问题，诸如“I'm from Xi'an—have you ever been there?”或者“I like basketball. Do you like it?”但是如果你听不清考官问题，你有权让考官重复问题，可以快速地问“Pardon?”“Sorry?”当然你也可以更加有效地提问，像“Do you mean...?”不要害怕为了弄清楚问题而去提问，这也是交流的重要组成部分。不懂装懂、答非所问在雅思口语考试中是非常致命的!

若考官要求你重复你刚才所说的，有可能是因为没有听明白或听清。请不要原词原句重复，最好是换些词，要是能整体改变就更好，避免考官依旧听不懂你在说什么。很多时候，这不仅仅是发音的问题，更可能是不太正确的发音和不太合适的选词共同导致的！换言之，倘若你的发音很清晰准确，你却用了不合适的词，考官一般不会让你重复答案，同样地，如果你的选词合适但发音不太完美，考官也不会让你重复。由此可以看出，如果考官让你重复，你就需要迅速判断出哪个词用得不合适，在重复说的时候一定要换掉。如果考官还不太明白，那就稍微附加个例子辅助说明。另一种策略就是直接换一种表达，如“In other words”或者“What I mean is”。

通常情况下，第一部分答案的时间长度平均要控制在15～20秒左右。询问基本情况的问题答案要简短，5～10秒左右就够了，比如考试开始时的例行问题“What is your full name?”“Where do you come from?”“Are you a student or do you work?”以及每组话题的第一个问题，如话题“cooking”中的第一个问题“Do you like cooking?”个别问题可以说得更久一点，特别是当话题被深入时，时间可以达到30秒。务必记住：在短时间内要尽可能给出更多的信息!

在第一部分考试过程中，遇到考官打断你，请不要感觉受到冒犯或不舒服，剑桥官方规定：控制考试的时间和确保考试合理推进是考官责任的一部分。但是，如果出现考官随意打断的情况，不要太紧张，很多时候是考官自己的问题。

很多考生有时候会抱怨话题很陌生，找信息的时候又不敢瞎编。考官Robert就此发表看法：这是口语考试，不是警察问讯，这意味着你完全可以说一些“white lies”（无恶意的谎言），有时候编一些东西能帮助你更好地表达，尤其是展示运用词汇能力。考官感兴趣的是你的表达能力，无意于分辨内容的真假。当然，在能够回答的情况下，尽可能说实情，这样的话，你就能够更自信地表达，语气也更自然，因为你只需要考虑英文，而不是先去想观点再去思考怎么用英语回答。在中国，目前有不少考生为了更好地应对不熟悉或不太能够答好的话题，采用背答案的方式（市面上风行很多版本的答案素材），千万不要在考官面前成段去背诵已经记好的句子，尤其是表现得特别明显。考官们表示：鉴别考生是否在背答案对他们来说是件非常简单的事情，而且他们将会对这样的考生产生非常厌恶的情绪，然后提出更难的题目。为什么考官对这样的现象如此反感呢？理由很简单：首先，雅思口语考试考查的是考生自由沟通的能力；其次，考生不应该在考前知道雅思口语话题。所以，当你事先知道部分口语话题时（在中国，这是一件SO EASY 的事情），请千万别在考试时表现得太明显！

“烤鸭”们读到这里，肯定会满腹牢骚：不背，我口语又不好，马上就要考试，该怎么办？别急，在此书中，我们在后面章节会详细介绍针对考题快速思考和组织信息的神器，相信大家会大呼过瘾。

对于那些已经深陷“背素材”苦海的考生，考官Robert有以下力挽狂澜的建议，希望大家能够受益！

* Don’t try to repeat or practice that answer 100% exactly the same each time you say it. Instead, vary your answer a little each time you say it, hopefully making it a little better each time. Or, you can paraphrase this idea. Don’t 100% memorize a long answer, instead, memorize just the key points, so that you are memorizing your answer to about 70% accuracy.

* Whenever you repeat or practice an answer, speak it naturally, as if you were really speaking to another human being. Don’t repeat any prepared answers like a robot.

建议

不做百分百重复，力求循序渐进提升；
避免百分百记忆，把握要点七成精确；
无论何时做陈述，表述答案真实自然；
仿佛向人真倾诉，回答杜绝人如机器。

第2节 标准回答结构

对几乎每一个回答，你需要给出两个部分：直接答案＋延展信息。

▶直接答案

要求：在雅思口语考试中，对考官的问题做出自然合理的第一反应。

直接答案并不代表立刻给出的答案，当然更不是间接答案，间接答案会直接降低连贯性。

下面是间接答案的例子：

Question: “Do you work or are you a student?”

Answer: “Oh, I’ve been working for five years.”

这个回答确实告诉考官你目前在工作，但非常间接。这个问题是让你从“A”和“B”中进行选择，所以你必须首先做出选择，然后再适当增加信息，所以更加合适的回答应该是这样的：“I’m working. In fact, I’ve been working for five years.”

考试中个别问题偶尔可以用合适的间接回答进行缓冲，比如说：当问题比较难时，你需要在给出答案前做短暂思考“Let me think about that”，或者先就问题给出一点评论“Good question”。这很正常，即便在日常生活中，你使用中文和别人交流时也会发生。但是要记住，当你需要时间思考时，要用语言示意考官，而不是傻乎乎坐着发愣。换句话说，你必须在考官问完问题后就立刻作答，但没有必要每次都在第一时间给出问题的直接答案。在第一部分，这种缓冲要尽量少发生，毕竟第一部分的话题大多非常简单（这种缓冲方法更加适合P3）。

▶延展信息

要求：考生要非常积极地给考官更多的信息（信息包括你的感受和观点）。

在考官们看来，给出延展信息最好的方式（当然，不是唯一方式）是尽量将信息点包含在同一句话中，通常情况下，你可以使用关系代词做到这一点，例如such as和which等，使你的句子变成复杂句。这种技能的展示对你在语法评分区获得6分以上或整体评分超过6分，都有很大的帮助。

同时，当你给出延展信息的时候，要确保信息是“新”的，也就是说不是每个人都已经知道的信息。举个例子吧：“I study chemistry, which has a lot of experiments.”我们通常都知道化学这门学科肯定包含很多实验，这种回答就如同说“我喜欢历史，它包含很多过去的故事”。然而，如果你这么说：“I study chemistry, which has a lot of interesting experiments.”考官就会“不明觉厉”。

另外，要时刻记得分享你的感受，你的喜欢与不喜欢，你的偏好或你的观点，即使问题没有直接问你的感受。你要尽量放松自己，在给出直接答案后，如果你找不到其他可以补充的信息，就可以选择去谈谈你的感受，或者就算你有很多信息去补充，在里面加一点自己的感受也是考官乐意接受的。谈感受的时候如果能加上理由就更完美了。

第3节　评分要点详解

下面我们来学习评分标准中的四大要点：

语音语调	音准及口音
	语音节奏（单词重读、句子重读）
	语调
	语组、停顿及语流
词汇	丰富性
	精确性
	动词词组
	词语搭配
	高分情感词
	俚语
语法	比较级
	情态动词
	被动语态
	时态
	条件结构
	复杂句型
流利连贯	自然度
	连贯性

▶语音语调：*Pronunciation*

语音语调是雅思口语考试中你给考官留下的第一印象，同时也是同学们在备战中需要打败的第一个“拦路虎”，如果你的语音不清楚或语调不合适，考官会听不懂你在说什么，从而严重影响你的最终成绩，你用再好的词汇和语法也徒劳无功。

在雅思口语考试中，语音语调主要考查以下几个方面：

Sounds and Accent, Rhythm (Word Level Stress, Sentence Level Stress), Intonation, Chunking and Pausing and Speed of Delivery

1. 音准及口音：Sounds and Accent

音准及口音是口语辨识度的一个重要因素，很多考生在口语表达中经常出现单词发音不标准、不饱满或带有地方口音的问题，这些都会影响到考官对考生口语的初步判断和理解。

(1) 音准：

考官主要看的是考生元音发得是否清楚和标准。

Vowels				Diphthongs		
iː	ɪ	ʊ	uː	ɪə	eɪ	
e	ə	ɜː	ɔː	ʊə	ɔɪ	əʊ

个别辅音如吐舌音或咬唇音也是重要音准评分点：

v	θ	ð

(2) 口音：

在雅思口语考试中，美式发音同样被接受，即使你说的是中式口音，虽然有点影响，但是对短期备战来说，可以忽略，因为口音经过长时间训练才可能有所改变。想学习英音的同学，多叔推荐英剧《唐顿庄园》《神探夏洛克》，至于美音，可看的美剧太多，主要推荐《老友记》，但是要记住，一集至少要看5遍才会开始对语音有感觉，否则只是娱乐罢了。

关于如何提高音准和口音能力，考官Robert建议：

* You need to focus on speaking clearly and getting your vowel sounds correct.

* Most of you will have a smart phone or access to a computer. There are many apps and websites now available which will help you with your phonetic sounds. Use them and practice whenever you have spare time, for instance on the bus on the way to work or college. During your lunch and coffee breaks—a few minutes every day will soon pay dividends.

建议

注意说话要清楚，力求元音读准确；

电脑手机多智能，软件网站助语音；

随时随地皆可学，上班上学乘车时，

午饭茶歇均可用，日积月累颇受益。

2. 语音节奏：Rhythm

语音节奏是语音语调评分区的一个重要评分点，它决定着你的口语是否有韵律感，它包括Word Level Stress和Sentence Level Stress。

(1) 单词重读：Word Level Stress

官方解释： Word level stress, which is the stronger pronunciation of a syllable over the others in the word is a crucial factor in generating the right pronunciation.

我们经常会在单词重读上犯错误，这也是雅思口语考试常见扣分点，因此考生对一些不太清楚重读位置的单词一定要通过查字典来确认。考生可能误读一些雅思口语高频单词，如：Repu**ta**tion, Cer**ti**ficate, Pre**fer**, U**ni**que。

单词重读位置规则

① 一个单词只允许存在一个重读（如果单词有两个重音，重读指的是主重音），如果你听到两个重读，那就是两个单词。

② 我们只能重读元音，不能重读辅音。

③ 有些单词，重读位置不同，词性和意思也将随之改变，如 present。

(2) 句子重读：Sentence Level Stress

官方解释： There are also important sentence-level features of pronunciation. With sentence stress in English, you need to give stress to certain words while other words are quickly spoken. For instance, some words in a sentence are emphasized or slightly louder than other words.

句子重读也被称为“口语的旋律”，通过重读句中某些单词来凸显语意的重点，在很大程度上有助于考官理解你整句话表达的意思，特别是当语速较快时。下面我们来看几个简单的例子：

Roses are **red.**

Violets are **blue.**

Sugar is **sweet.**

And **so** are **you**!

下面我们来讲解通常情况下一个句子中哪些单词应该重读：

母语是英语的人喜欢重读句子中的“内容词”（content words），这些词都是一个句子的核心词。

“内容词”的定义：一个句子中可以通过逻辑串联成主体意思的核心词。

它们通常是：

- *Nouns* e.g. kitchen, Peter
- *(Most) principal verbs* e.g. visit, construct
- *Adjectives* e.g. beautiful, interesting
- *Adverbs* e.g. often, carefully

哪些词一般不需要重读呢？这些词被多叔定义为“结构词”。

“结构词”的定义：一个句中即使缺少也不影响主体意思的词。

- *Determiners* e.g. the, a, some, a few
- *Auxiliary verbs* e.g. don’t, am, can, were
- *Prepositions* e.g. before, next to, opposite
- *Conjunctions* e.g. but, while, as
- *Pronouns* e.g. they, she, us

为了帮助大家理解以上理论，我们举个生活中简单的例子，如果你收到你朋友发的一条英文短信：

SELL BIKE GONE BEIJING

我们很容易就知道：朋友准备卖掉自行车，因为他已经去了北京。上面的四个词就属于“内容词”，需要重读。加上一些“结构词”后就可以形成一个完整的句子。如下：

Can you SELL my BIKE because I’ve GONE to BEIJING?

通过这个小例子，相信大家对句子重读又有了更深一步的认识。

关于如何提高句子重读能力，考官Robert建议：

Notice you don’t usually put stresses on words in a sentence that are less important.

Consequently the English rhythm of speech is based not only on word stress but also on sentence stress or accent.

There are clear distinctions between words that are emphasised and words that are not essential to intelligibility.

The stress patterns are important for speech production and listening comprehension.

建议

句中需注意，不要总是强调那些非重点；

口语有节奏，单词句子有重点或者重音；

单词有区别，强调的和不强调的不一样；

强调重方式，影响说话结果和对方理解。

3. 语调：Intonation

官方解释：Intonation in English is an important vehicle for meaning. It helps the listener to get a clearer picture of what the speaker intends to mean. Intonation is the pitch of your voice changing as you talk.

通俗来说，语调指的就是口语表达中的“感情”，我们中国考生在雅思口语表达中经常语调平淡，让考官“累觉不爱”。这是因为在西方语言中，语调也是传达意思的一个重要因素，考官非常不喜欢考生说英语的时候基本没有抑扬顿挫。

如何在短期内学会调整语调？如果采取传统方式去学习，如跟读等，很难见效！多叔告诉你最简单的方式，可以使你的语调很快有感觉！大家都知道，语调是为了表达感情，那么在一句话中通常有哪些词带有感情呢？答案是“形容词”“副词”。同学们只需要在说口语的时候刻意重读“形容词”“副词”，整个语调就会变得完全不同，考官会觉得你在用心和他交流，进而提高语调评分。

举例：I **really** enjoy it.

The Internet can offer you an **efficient** way to learn a foreign language.

关于如何调整语调，考官Robert建议：

If the monotone voice is used in the IELTS test this may result in lower scores.

For you to convey the right intonation, you must first understand what you are saying. This might seem a fairly obvious statement.

But it is the intonation of words that carry your feelings and emotions. It's what gives your talk meaning. However, in terms of the IELTS exam, the examiners are not going to expect perfect intonation.

But it is important that your speaking voice is not monotonous and that you do try to put some "attitude", "feelings" and "emotion" into your voice.

建议

语音单调，在雅思口语中会导致减分；
语调正确，基于理解自身的表达意图；
措辞语调，恰恰传递你的感受与情绪；
言辞达意，尽管考官不期待语调完美；
避免枯燥，声音包括态度情绪和感情。

4. 语组、停顿及语流：Chunking and Pausing and Speed of Delivery

(1) 语组：Chunking

在口语表达中，将句中的某些词顺在一起自然表达，这些词的组合称为"语组"，从而在其后形成自然停顿 (pausing)。这是语音语调能达到7分的必要因素。

官方解释：Chunking and pausing can help package information to help the listener—the examiner (and yourself) understand.

考生要学会将句子自然分割成几个语组，从而更加流畅自然地表达。我们来做个小练习感受下，请大声读下面这句话并同时录音，再听听自己读得是否自然！

I am a professional photographer whose main interest is to take special, black and white photographs that exhibit abstract meanings in their photographic structure.

(2) 停顿：Pausing

停顿的长短不一，要根据语意确定。较为独立的内容之间停顿较长，较为紧密的内容之间停顿较短。

然后，我们通过语组分割的方式，重新朗读这句话：

其中"/"表示短停顿，"//"表示长停顿，大写部分为重读的音节和单词。

I am/a proFESsional photographer/whose MAIN INterest/is to TAKE/SPEcial/BLACK and WHITE/PHOtographs//that exhibit/ABstract MEANings/in their photoGRAPHic STRUCture.

大家读完后会明显感觉到自己的语调和自然度有了极大的提升!

短期内想提高“语组”能力的考生可以先学会一些常见的习惯性语组:

“and all of those kinds of things”

“and stuff like that”

“I'm not really sure but...”

“a lot of people think that...”

“maybe it's something to do with...”

“I guess that it could be because...”

同学们在使用以上表达的时候，要不间断，一气呵成。考官会认为你有基础的“chunking”能力。

(3) 语流：Speed of Delivery

通过合理运用语组分割出重要信息和次要信息，重要信息需要慢读，而次要信息则须轻快，使得口语表达有缓有急。

官方解释： the ability to consistently vary her speed by speaking in “chunks” of word groups.

我们很多考生未曾听过或直接将这个评分点理解成语速，这是不对的。语速是说话的一般速度，对考生来说，自然合适就好，不要太快或太慢。而语流强调的是信息传递的速度变化，讲到重要信息时，考生要降低速度并同时重读，这是一个成熟口语表达者必须具备的能力。

关于如何提高“语组”能力，考官Robert建议:

* You should divide your speech into “chunks”, which may be single words or groups of words to communicate a thought or idea.

* The chunks will focus particularly on information you think is important.

* This is a useful skill for you to practise. If you are nervous you might let your speaking “get away from you”, speak too fast and lose comprehension and thus your final mark will be much reduced.

建议

分解说话内容，拆成单词或者词群片段;

语组用于强调，尤其聚焦特别重要信息;

此为有用技巧，考生可以练习并且实践;

紧张导致偏离，过快影响理解并致减分。

5. 常见的发音错误

1	[æ] in “sad” “bad”
2	[aɪ] in “bike” “like”
3	[t] in “but” “great”
4	When “o” is pronounced as [ʌ].
5	“Mechanism”
6	“Woman” and “Women”
7	“Southern”
8	“Graduated”
9	“Survey”
10	“Industry”
11	“Protect”
12	“Economy”(and related words)
13	“Technical” (and related words)
14	How to say “you know” when introducing a new piece of information?
15	When and when not to emphasize the word, “some”?

(1) [æ] in “sad” “bad”

许多考生发这个音的时候，口形偏小，而且力度不够，具体发音规则及视频请登录www.dsielts.com查阅。

(2) [aɪ] in “bike” “like”

许多考生发这个音的时候非常接近“爱”，这样是不对的，要将口腔打开至最大，具体发音规则及视频请登录www.dsielts.com查阅。

(3) [t] in “but” “great”

许多考生发这个辅音的时候经常过重，类似于“踢”，请一定要轻读，否则听起来很奇怪！

(4) 当“o”读作[ʌ]

有很多单词，考生不太注意就容易发错，下面这些单词中的“o”要发成cut中的元音，大家一定要注意！

Among	Accompany	Company	Month
Monkey	Comfortable	Onion	Oven
Front	Stomach	London	Won
Mom	Monday	Wonder	Ton
Monk	One		

(5) Mechanism

这个单词重音在第一个音节上，不是第二个。

Mechanism ['mekənɪzəm]

但是 mechanical [mə'kænɪkl]的重音在第二个音节上。

(6) "Woman" and "Women"

Woman读作['wʊmə]；Women读作['wɪmɪn]。

(7) Southern

这个单词第一个元音读作[ʌ]，整体读作['sʌðən]。很多考生喜欢将"ou"发成[au]，这样显然是不对的。

(8) Graduated

Graduated这个单词的重音在第一个音节上，应该是['grædʒʊeɪtɪd]，不是[grædʒʊ'eɪtɪd]。

Graduate 这个单词如何发音取决于它的词性。

动词：to graduate ['grædʒʊeɪt]

名词：a graduate ['grædʒʊət]

形容词：a graduate ['grædʒʊət] student（美国人喜欢把graduate用作形容词。英国人经常说postgraduate。两者的意思相同，都表示"研究生的"）

graduation [ˌgrædʒʊ'eɪʃn]（毕业典礼）

(9) Survey

Survey可以作为名词或动词，发音有别。

名词：survey ['sɜːveɪ]重音只能在第一个音节上。

动词：survey [sɜːr'veɪ]重音在第二个音节上，有时候也可以在第一个音节上。

总之，作名词时重音只能在第一个音节上，作动词时两个都可以。

(10) Industry

Industry这个单词的重音在第一个音节上['ɪndəstrɪ]，而且第二个音节应读成[də]，而不是[dʌ]。

与此不同的是，形容词industrial读成[ɪn'dʌstrɪəl]。

(11) Protect

Protect读作[prə'tekt]，重音在第二个音节上，需要注意。

(12) Economy 及相关词

很多考生在使用economy以及相关词时，总会犯很多错误，不论是在口语还是在写作中。通过下面这个表格，我们来系统学习一下economy及相关词的用法。

（需要重读的音节已经清晰标明）

Words	中文	Examples	Pronunciation
Economy	（国家的）经济；经济制度	* China's economy is growing very fast at the moment. * The economy is strong.	[ɪ'kɒnəmɪ] or [ɪ'kɑːnəmɪ]

Economist	经济学研究者；经济学家	She works as an economist with the People's Bank of China.	[ɪ'kɒnəmɪst] or [ɪ'kɑːnəmɪst]
Economise	节省	I really need to economise because I'm spending money faster than I should.	[ɪ'kɒnəmaɪz] or [ɪ'kɑːnəmaɪz]
Economics	经济学	I'm studying economics, which I find quite interesting.	[ˌiːkə'nɒmɪks] or [ˌekə'nɒmɪks]
Economic	经济的；经济学的	I'd say it's both a political and an economic problem.	[ˌiːkə'nɒmɪk] or [ˌekə'nɒmɪk]
Economical	节约的；节俭的	People who live in the desert need to be very economical with water.	[ˌiːkə'nɒmɪkl] or [ˌiːkə'nɑːmɪkl]

(13) Technique 及相关词

technique [tek'niːk]技法，手法，技巧。通常比较具体，如：He has a great painting technique. Technology通常来说比较笼统和抽象，泛指技术。

下面是相关单词的读音及使用举例。

Words	中文	Examples	Pronunciations
Technology	技术；工艺及应用科学（如工程技术）；工艺学；工程学	I think one reason why people are living longer nowadays is the fact that medical technology has advanced a lot in the last few decades.	[tek'nɒlədʒɪ]
Technological	技术（上）的	* a major technological breakthrough (重大的技术性突破) * technological changes (技术上的改变)	[ˌteknə'lɒdʒɪkl]
Technical	技术的；专科的；艺术的；工艺的；技艺的；技巧的	* He's a musician with great technical skill but he doesn't play with much feeling. * I don't really understand the technical language in this report.	['teknɪkl]
Technician	技术人员；技师；工艺师	There's one research student working in this laboratory and he's supported by three lab technicians who help him with the equipment.	[tek'nɪʃn]
Hi-tech (= High-tech)	高技术的	He's got many of the latest hi-tech devices such as an iPod and a new type of mobile phone that allows him to watch films on the Internet.	[ˌhaɪ'tek]

(14) 如何使用"you know"

"You know"有两种使用方式，重音在"you"或"know"上，意思有很大差别。

① 当重音在"you"上时，表示"you already know"，我们在口语交流中经常使用到，尤其是想解释一些东西却找不到合适的词或观点的时候，可以用这种方式，类似于"like" "something like" "what I mean is" "such as"，我们来举个例子。

问题："What's the difference between traditional stories and modern stories?"

回答："Well, traditional stories are usually set in the traditional lifestyle that Chinese people had, which was rural, whereas most modern stories have modern, urban settings. As well as that, most traditional stories are either myths that explain natural phenomena such as how the moon came to be in the sky or stories that teach you a moral lesson, you know, like teaching people what is good and bad behaviour, such as the story of the boy who cried 'wolf'. But most modern stories are not myths or moral tales; they just tell a short story, which is often an adventure story or a mystery story, like what we see in a TV programme or in a movie."

② 当你提出一个考官可能不知道的事实时，重音放在后面"know"上，举例：

"You know, I've only been living in Beijing for the past three years, so I don't know the city as well as I know my hometown."

(15) "Some"何时该重读

这个单词在不同使用环境下有两种意思。

"Some"表示有一些，不是很多。

"Some"表示只是一部分，不是全部。

① 在第一种情况下，some要轻读，其后的词需要重读，举例："What did you see in the park?" "I saw some people, some dogs, some trees, some grass and some flowers."

② 在第二种情况下，some需要重读，强调只是一部分不是全部，形成对比。举例："The topic of climate change is quite controversial at the moment. Some experts even predict that the world is now starting to enter a prolonged cold period."类似的有：someday, somehow, somebody, someone, someplace, something, sometime, sometimes, somewhere，其中"some"表达的是"a certain" or "a particular"，比如"someday" = "a particular day, but I don't know exactly which day"。

▶词汇：*Vocabulary*

"好词"的定义：能够准确表达你的想法并使你能够自然使用的词汇，合适即可，不需要所谓的"高级词汇"。

如何找机会展现"词汇能力"？

展现词汇的使用能力是第一部分重要的评分点，当然对整个口语考试同样如此。在考试过程中，考生要多寻找机会去表现词汇能力，一般来说可以采取多举例的方式，例如"for example/instance"，比如当考生被问及电影时，可以列举电影类型，当被问及家务活时，可以列举家务活，诸如“sweep the floor”“wash the dishes”“take out the garbage”“ironing”等。至于是否有必要使用所谓的“大词”“难词”，考官Robert表示没有必要，雅思口语需要的都是“basic and everyday vocabulary”。很多同学为了炫耀自己的词汇能力，采用剑桥词汇中的高级词汇，殊不知那些词汇主要是为阅读、写作服务的，这样做的结果会使你的表达很不自然，尤其是对口语基础不好的同学，生硬地使用高级词汇会使表达显得非常突兀，适得其反！

如同我们前面所提到的，考生有时候可以适当撒谎，不必要讲真话从而错失展现词汇能力的机会。例如考题：“Do you have anything on the walls of your home (or, your room)?”有可能你怕损伤墙壁，没有在墙上布置任何东西。但如果你真这么说，就错失了一次秀词汇的良机。相反，你完全可以说墙上有幅画，然后简单描述一下，如：a bamboo forest with two tigers lying on some grass，这样你就可以获得更多的词汇分数。同样道理，如果考官问你，从你家或你房间的窗户可以看到什么，也许你没有充分的词汇去描述你看到的真实情况，同样可以采取编造的方式，用你会的词汇去尽可能描述。

在雅思口语考试中，可以通过展现以下要素来提高词汇得分。

1. 动词词组（简称“动组”）：Phrasal Verb

定义：在雅思口语考试中，考官非常看重考生是否具备口语化动词词组的使用能力，这是词汇评分区的重要评分点，“动组”通常由2～3个动词构成，构成方式为“**verb + adverb**”或者“**verb + preposition**”。

举几个例子：“look after” somebody; “come up against” difficulties; “look forward to” something in the future。想考7分或以上的同学要特别留意。

P1高频“动组”举例（括号内为相关话题）：

While away—Spend time doing something because you have nothing better to do: It is a great pleasure of mine to while away some time gift shopping. [Gifts]

Turn up—Appear: If someone is late for a meeting with me then they are likely to find an empty space when they turn up because I will have turned tail and run. [Patience]

Splash out—Spend a lot of money on something that is not essential: It doesn’t help that my parents recently splashed out on a large flat screen TV now I’m really hooked. [TV Programmes]

Cool down—Get cooler: In the heat of the summer, it’s also a place to cool down and relax away from the heat and the hustle and bustle of the city. [Trees/Forest]

Catch up—Get work, etc., up to date: What I do is catching up with the news via the news apps I have on my phone. [News]

Chuck out—Dispose of something you no longer need or want: But actually I soon grew out of it and most of those clothes have either been chucked out or consigned to the bottom drawer of my wardrobe. [Shopping/Clothes/Fashion]

Hang out—Spend time socially: Some days we might just hang out in Starbucks doing our homework, surfing on their free wifi. [Friends and Family]

Put on—Start wearing: Everyone sheds their drab winter clothes and puts on their summer best. [Sunshine]

Bear down on—Move towards: The drivers there are maniacs and even though I always stick to the cycle lane I' m always in fear of my life as I dodge the scooters cars and even lorries bearing down on me. [Bicycles]

Sell out—Have no more of something left because it has been bought: If I get the tickets, and I know they will sell out fast, I'll be over the moon. [Concerts and Music]

更多动组请登录www.dsielts.com，查阅链接“口语动组查询”。

2. 词语搭配（简称“词搭”）：Collocation

定义：所谓“词搭”，指的是使用合适的词去搭配另一个词，从而表达更准确的意思。以英语为母语的人总会有习惯的“词搭”。

举例：我们可以说“fast train”而不说 “quick train”；我们只能说“quick shower”而不说“fast shower”。

在雅思口语考试中，考官要判断考生是否具备使用“less common language”的能力。就“词搭”来说，如果想考到7分或以上，要学会展现“uses less common lexical items with some awareness of style and **collocation**”的功力。

在雅思口语考试中，在谈到个人经历或感受时最容易使用高级“词搭”：

① 我们经常使用一些含有副词的高级“词搭”来表达强烈感受、极端情况或个人事件，特别是负面经历，这些副词有absolute, complete, total, utter等。

举例：

absolute agony	complete astonishment	total bliss
(an) utter catastrophe	absolute despair	total ecstasy
utter fury	(a) complete idiot	utter loathing
total madness		

② 在雅思口语中，great是一个常见的高级“词搭”要素，通常用来表达情感。

举例：

great admiration	great anger	(a) great disappointment
great enjoyment	great excitement	(a) great failure
great fun	great happiness	great joy

当然了，除了表达个人经历或感受时经常使用到高级“词搭”，在雅思口语中还有其他如由heavy构成的高频高级“词搭”。

heavy drinker/smoker	heavy traffic	heavy rain
heavy duty	heavy heart	heavy meal
heavy weight	heavy breathing	heavy eyelids
heavy feet	heavy handed	heavy snowfall
heavy artillery	heavy thinker	heavy dose

更多“词搭”请登录www.dsielts.com，查阅链接“地道词搭查询”。

3. 高分情感词：Emotional Words

定义：高分情感词指的是在英语口语中能够精确体现表达者情绪和判断的词汇，主要有“高分形容词”和“高分副词”。

(1) 要学会使用能更加丰富地表达感受的高分形容词。

举例：disappointed, embarrassed, fascinated, annoyed, inspired, thrilled, exhilarated, overwhelmed, delighted, disillusioned, astonished, appalled, mystified, relieved...

(2) 学会使用能更加丰富地表达个人品质的高分形容词。

举例：talented, ambitious, co-operative, aggressive, driven, warm-hearted, open-minded, even-tempered, easy-going, analytical, introverted, extroverted, outgoing, empathetic, creative, imaginative, loquacious, philosophical, sophisticated, naïve, loyal, trustworthy, determined, motivated, persistent, goal-oriented...

(3) 要学会使用表意更加丰富的高分副词，这些副词可以用来开始一个句子，也可以用在句子中间，它们可以帮助你更加精确地传递你的意思，很多都是以“ly”结尾。

举例：hopefully, strangely, luckily, unfortunately, usually, rarely, frankly, seriously, actually, certainly, definitely, surely, probably, possibly, scarcely, hardly, barely, frequently, normally, absolutely, entirely, perfectly, virtually, merely, simply, distinctly, specifically, substantially, exactly, vividly, explicitly, consistently, reluctantly, deliberately, accidentally, (e)specially, personally, drastically, slightly, positively, moderately, fairly, utterly, apparently, theoretically, realistically, obviously, roughly, approximately, logically, typically, thoroughly, considerably, significantly, ultimately...

更多高分情感词请查询www.dsielts.com，点击雅思口语中“口语词汇”。

4. 俚语：Slangs

在雅思口语考试中，俚语是词汇评分区的一个高分要素，官方明确要求高分考生必须具备“Uses some less common and idiomatic vocabulary”的能力，但是如果使用不当或不熟练，则会影响最终分数。

官方解释：They are phrases, words or expressions that do not have the same meaning as the actual words used in the phrase.

P1高频俚语举例（括号内为相关话题）：

Pipe dream—a wish or an idea that is impossible to achieve or carry out (derived from the dreams or visions induced by the smoking of an opium pipe): So maybe one day I would like to live in a house like they do. But maybe that's a pipedream because I'm such a city boy/girl I'll never leave. [House/Flat/Apartment]

Live and let live—believing that other people should be allowed to live their lives in the way that they want to: So we all need to live together and help each other, live and let live is what I say. [House/Flat/Apartment]

Hang out (some place)—to spend time in a place habitually: Is this where you guys hang out all the time? I love being near the shops and hanging out at my regular haunts, having coffee, chatting with my friends. [Your Hometown]

Buckle down (to something)—to settle down to something; to begin to work seriously at something: I'd prefer to be a party person but I have to buckle down and do the work. [Work or Studies]

The world is your oyster—you have the ability and the freedom to do exactly what you want: The world is becoming our oyster too. [Work or Studies]

Rose-tinted glasses—(British, American & Australian) if someone looks at something through rose-tinted glasses, they see only the pleasant parts of it: I might be looking at the past through-rose tinted glasses, but I can't remember it being like this, even in my young life. [Advertisements]

Mad as a hatter and/mad as a march hare—crazy (alludes to the crazy characters in Lewis Carroll's *Alice's Adventures in Wonderland*): This makes us laugh because she totally reorganises his kitchen, which drives him as mad as a hatter. [Food and Cooking]

Clean up your act—to improve your behaviour: I even miss breakfast and don't have time for a shower, so I'm a mess when I get there. In the future I am really going to try to clean up my act. [Time management]

As a token (of something)—symbolic of something, especially of gratitude; as a memento of something: It's basically just a token of our affections for each other. [Gifts]

本书P1高分范文中有大量地道俚语出现，请考生在理解的基础上合理使用！

更多俚语请登录www.dsielts.com，查阅链接"地道俚语查询"。

几点建议：

* 避免使用俗套谚语，尤其是那些中国学生经常说的，比如："All work and no play makes Jack a dull boy.""Every coin has two sides.""No pains, no gains."这些已经不能够打动现在的考官了，他们更想听到的是接地气的日常沟通语句。

* 现在的考生喜欢从市面上买素材，每当看到里面的高大上词汇就心动不已，这里要提醒大家，有些词你看得懂但未必会灵活使用，在考试的时候强行套用会给考官留下不好的印象，所以尽量使用自己很有把握的词汇！口语交流最重要的是自然顺畅！

* 考生可以准备一个单词本，把平时接触到的一些和口语话题相关的"好词"记录下来，因为这些词通常来自带有语境的材料，如视频或听力材料，所以更加容易去合理使用！

* 避免使用太正式的词汇。在雅思口语考试中，有些同学分不清哪些词对雅思口语来说太过正式，不宜使用。以下表格中，考官Robert列举了雅思口语中经常会出现的"过正式"词汇以及相对应的"合理"词汇，其中标明"有点正式"的词汇可使用在第三部分（第三部分偏学术讨论风格）。

(1) 常见的“过正式”的动词

Table 1a

Verbs to use	Verbs to avoid	Comments
Buy	Purchase	
Leave/Go	Depart	
Help	Assist	
Need	Require	
Ask for	Request	
Start/Begin	Commence	
Live	Reside	
Get	Obtain	
Get/Gain	Acquire	
Watch	Observe	
Please	Gratify	“Gratify” and the noun, “gratification” are unnecessarily formal in speaking. For example: “She accepted the gift with much gratification.” Just say, “She was very happy to accept the gift.” or, “She was very pleased to accept the gift.”
Own	Possess	To say, “I possess a computer and many books.” sounds much too formal. But the noun, a “possession” is normal, not formal sounding.
Fix	Repair	“Repair” is a little formal. For example, “I’m going to repair this broken chair.” sounds unnecessarily formal but, “I got my shoe repaired.” doesn’t sound too formal. Why? “Fix” is probably more suitable when the item to be fixed is composed of simple, solid parts, like a chair and one part is “broken”. In other words, if something is “broken”, it’s suitable to talk about “fixing” it. But if, for example, your shoe is losing some of its stitching, we don’t normally say it is “broken”. In this case, it sounds normal to say, “I got my shoe repaired”.
Want	Desire	
Stop	Cease	

Let	Permit	For example, "My parents don't permit me to stay out late at night." sounds too formal.
Tell	Inform	The noun, "information" is not overly formal.
Answer/Reply	Respond	

Table 1b

Verbs to use	Verbs to avoid	Comments
Write to	Correspond with	
Start again	Resume	
Seem	Appear (a little formal)	For example: "You appear to be tired today." sounds a little formal. It is better to say, "You seem to be tired today."
Ask	Enquire/Inquire	For example: "I enquired if there was a room available." sounds unnecessarily formal. It is better to say: "I asked if there was a room available."
Try	Endeavour	
Think	Deem	The word "deem" is very old-fashioned. It is not even suitable for the writing test and is definitely unsuitable for most spoken language.
Would like to/ Want to	Wish to	For example, "I wish to study in Britain." sounds too formal. Avoid that usage of "wish". But in the following sentence, "wish" is used normally: "I wish I could speak better English." (Don't use "can" in that sentence.)
Will/Let's/ Should	Shall	In England, "shall" is used in everyday speech with "I" or "we" but for other English speakers, the word "shall" is only used in formal situations or situations when one is trying to be exceptionally polite. If you know your examiner is from Britain, using "shall" to mean "will", "Let's..." or "should" is OK. But if you know your examiner is not from Britain, I suggest not using it.
(If... +) would	(If... +) should	For example, "I should say so" when used to mean, "I'd say so" (= I would say so) is overly formal. Similarly, "I should be worried if I were you." is too formal. Instead, it is more normal to say: "I'd be worried if I were you."

(2) 常见的"过正式"的名词及被动语态

Table 2a

Nouns to use	Nouns to avoid	Comments
Some help	Some assistance	
A home	A residence	
The beginning/ The start	The commencement	
A drink	A beverage	
High school	Secondary school	The words, "secondary school" might be used by the examiner but unless the examiner first uses it, you should use "high school". ("Middle school", a term sometimes used in the USA is unfamiliar to most British and Australian examiners.)
People	Persons	Saying something such as, "five persons..." sounds like "officialised writing" (公文体). It is best to avoid this word. Of course, the singular noun, "person" is normal.
People	Individuals	The word, "individual" is normal to use as an adjective or when we are talking about a single person and emphasizing the uniqueness of the person or the character or personality of that person. For example, "He's a very strange individual." But I suggest not using it as a substitute for "person" when not emphasizing the individualistic or unique nature of that person. Using "individuals" to mean "people" is unnecessary and it sounds like "officialised writing" (公文体).

Table 2b

Use	Do not use	Comments
(Mang) people say that...	It is said that...	The example here, ("It is said that...") is an example of using the passive voice (被动语态) of a "reporting verb" to indicate a generally held belief or opinion. Other examples are, "It is believed... " and, "It cannot be denied... "

		These expressions are used in very formal writing and are not suitable for speech, even educated speech. In general, English speakers try to avoid the passive voice (被动语态) whenever possible when speaking everyday language because it can sound too impersonal. (However, as shown below, there are occasions when the passive is suitable in everyday speech.) Instead of using the passive voice, you should try to speak personally, especially when you are talking about yourself. For example, the following sentence sounds unnecessarily formal: "I live near an airport and passing planes can be heard night and day." (From *New Concept English*) A much more natural way to say that is: "I live near an airport and I (can) hear passing planes night and day." "Speaking personally" does not just mean using, "I" or "my"—it means saying who did the action of the verb and includes using, "you", "he", "she", "they", the actual name of the person or, as in the example shown here, "people" or "many people" etc. When you are talking about someone who you know personally, you should especially try to speak personally, not impersonally. When the Passive Voice is Suitable: The passive voice is most suitable to use when you don't know who did the action, or when who did the action is not important, such as when talking about when something was built. For example, it's suitable to say, "It was built during the Ming Dynasty, about four hundred years ago." It is also quite suitable when you do know who did the action but when the verb is a creative activity such as "build", "make", "invent", "compose" or "write". For example, the following sentences are normal spoken English: "It was composed by Mozart." "It was invented by Thomas Edison." And, "It was written by Lu Xun." However, if the person is someone close to you, it is much more suitable to speak personally. For example, the following sentence sounds a little too impersonal when talking about your grandmother: "It was made by my grandmother." It is better to just say: "My grandmother made it."

Table 2c

Use	Do not use	Comments
I've got to.../ I have to.../ I must...	It is necessary for me to...	This is similar to using the passive voice. Even though this includes the word "me", it sounds too impersonal.

(3) 其他常见的“过正式”词汇及句型

Table 3a

Use	Do not use	Comments
Yes	Of course	For example, when the examiner says, "Could I see your identification please?" don't reply with, "Of course!" This sounds falsely formal and besides, it is not a true "Yes/No" question.
While	Whilst	
When	Upon	For example, "When she entered the room, she..." sounds much better than, "Upon entering the room, she..."
Interesting places	Places of interest	"Places of interest" sounds like a written advertisement. (It's also overused in China.) Just say, "interesting places" or "tourist sites" if that's what you mean.
It's immense.	It is of immense size.	Saying, "be verb" + "of" + "adjective" is formal. For example: "It's of great interest to me." Better sentences are: "I find it interesting." Or, "It's interesting."

Table 3b

Use	Do not use	Comments
A lot of/Lots of/A large amount of	Much	The sentence, "There was much snow on the ground after the heavy snowfall" sounds too formal. That is, avoid speaking "much" in an affirmative sentence (肯定句). I even suggest avoiding this usage in your writing test because the writing test is not as formal as many people think. "Much" used this way is suitable for a formal speech or formal writing. For example, here is a suitable but formal usage of the word "much": "We have made much progress in the past year." This sentence is suitable to use in a situation such as when a company CEO is making a speech to a meeting of company shareholders or when the president of a country is giving a speech to the whole nation.

		Your high school teachers told you there were only two choices, "many" and "much" but your high school teachers were not really teaching you spoken English—they were mostly teaching you written English because the College Entrance Exam has no English speaking test. "A lot of" is quite natural in spoken English and, "lots of" is also used although it is a little more informal. Although this usage of "much" sounds formal, the following are normal in everyday speech: Used in questions: "How much?" "Do you have much food at home?" "Is there much snow on the ground?" Used in Negative Sentences (否定句): "I don't have much food at home." "There's not much snow on the ground."

Table 3c

Use	Do not use	Comments
On top of that.../ As well as that.../ In addition (to that)... (a little formal)	Moreover	It is best to only use, "Moreover" in academic (i.e., formal) writing.
So...	Consequently... (a little formal)	Those examples I have labelled as "a little formal" are suitable to use when you are speaking about deeper, more serious topics, using language that is a little more formal than when talking about more "everyday" topics. For example, in the following sentence, "so" is better to use than, "consequently". Too formal = "I've been playing football ever since I was seven years old and consequently I'm very good at it now." More natural = "I've been playing football ever since I was seven years old so I'm very good at it now." But in the following example, "consequently" is suitable: "Many new factories have opened up in China in the past few years and these factories play a crucial role in reducing unemployment, which is a serious problem here. Consequently, people tolerate the pollution that the factories produce because they think it's an acceptable price to pay."

Table 3d

Use	Do not use	Comments
For that reason.../ That's why.../So...	Therefore... (a little formal)	"Therefore" is best used when speaking about more serious topics and especially when you have used the language of logic to come to a conclusion. Here's an example of an unsuitable use of "therefore": "I love singing, therefore karaoke is my favourite way to relax." A better way to say that is: "I love singing—that's why karaoke is my favourite way to relax." Or, "I love singing so karaoke is my favourite way to relax."
After that	Thereafter	
Immediately	Forthwith	
As a result... / In this way...	Thus...	"Thus" is too formal for most spoken English and even too formal for most written essays. It is used mostly when coming to a logical conclusion when writing mathematics.

Table 3e

Use	Do not use	Comments
So.../ As a result...	Hence...	"Hence" is very formal and old fashioned, even too formal for your writing test (in most cases).
That's to say...	That is to say...	Not using the contracted form makes the expression, "That is to say..." sound like written English, not spoken English. The same comment applies to the four examples below, in most cases. Use contracted English as much as possible.
What's more...	What is more...	As above.
It's...	It is...	As above.
I can't	I cannot	As above.
I don't	I do not	As above.

Table 3f

Use	Do not use	Comments
Because	As/For/Since (a little formal)	For example, "I'm sitting for the IELTS exam as I want to study in Australia." Or, "I'm sitting for the IELTS exam for I want to study in Australia." It's more natural to say, "I'm sitting for the IELTS exam because I want to study in Australia." "Since" is used more in written English than in spoken English and is therefore formal. However, it is not too formal-sounding when used in speech at the beginning of a sentence such as: "Since I'm still a student, I don't have much money for travelling." But when "since" is used in the middle of a sentence, it does sound unnecessarily formal. For example: "I don't have much money for travelling since I'm still a student." It is better to use "because" instead of "since" in that sentence. This is a rather unusual case of the shorter words being more formal than the longer word.
I've got a new computer.	I've a new computer.	Using "got" with the contracted form of "have" is more natural spoken English and better, in my opinion, although some English speakers do use, "I've a new computer" in everyday speech.
From where	Whence	"Whence" is very old fashioned and formal and not even suitable for your writing.

Table 3g

Use	Do not use	Comments
Don't need to + verb	Needn't + verb	As with the "I've a..." example above, some people do use "needn't + verb" in everyday speech but for many English speakers, including me, it sounds a little formal. Using, "don't need to..." sounds better.
And these are: ... (or similar words)	As follows: ...	"As follows" is best used in rather formal writing, when listing or giving examples.
Specifically say which one you mean, even if you have to repeat what you just said.	"The latter" and "the former"	These are best reserved for rather formal writing, not speaking.

Better to use words such as, " (or) you could say" or, "I'd even say..."	...if you will.	The expression, "if you will" is used in formal writing. It means something like, "or this word, if you prefer to use it". For example, "My mother is my best friend, my source of strength, if you will." A better way to say that is, "My mother is my best friend—I'd even say, my source of strength."

Table 3h

Use	Do not use	Comments
Who...with	With whom	For example, "She's one of the people with whom I live." is too formal sounding. It is better to say, "She's one of the people who I live with." Even better is to drop the word "who" completely and just say, "She's one of the people I live with."
Who...to	To whom	Similarly, "She's the person to whom I spoke." is too formal. A much better way to speak is: "She's the person who I spoke to." or, even better, "She's the person I spoke to."
Who...for	For whom	
Or omit the word "who" completely		Natural spoken English is like this. We can omit the relative pronoun (关系代词)when that pronoun is used as the object, not the subject. But in the following sentence, we must use "who" because "who" is the subject: "I know a man who has five children." In this sentence, "who has five children" = "he has five children" = "the man has five children".
Just omit, "that"	that (a little formal)	As in the example above ("who"), the relative pronoun "that" is often omitted in informal speech. However, it does not sound highly formal to include "that" when speaking. For example: "Being a vet is something that I've dreamed about all my life." A better way to speak is: "Being a vet is something I've dreamed about all my life." Even better is to speak more directly, "I've dreamed of being a vet all my life." Another example: "It's the type of film that I like the most." A better way to speak is: "It's the type of film I like the most." Or, more directly, "I like this type of film the most."

Table 3i

Use	Do not use	Comments
Which...in/ Which...with	In which/ With which	This is similar to the use of "by whom" and "with whom". For example, the following sentence sounds too formal: "That is the city in which I was born." It is much more normal speech to say, "That's the city which I was born in."
Regarding/ Concerning	As regards	This is written business English.
Happy	Sanguine	The word, "sanguine" has a formal, literary (文学的) feel to it. When speaking, the word, "happy", "optimistic" or a similar everyday word is much more natural.
My hometown is on the banks of the Yangzi River.	My hometown lies on the banks of the Yangzi River.	When the word, "lies" is used this way, it has a literary (文学的) feel to it. It's suitable in a book but doesn't sound very natural in everyday speech.
You	One	For example: "One feels more relaxed when sitting in a quiet park, away from the hustle and bustle of the city." It is much more natural to say: "You feel more relaxed when sitting in a quiet park, away from the hustle and bustle of the city." Even more natural in spoken English is to change the words, "when sitting" to, "when you're sitting" or, "when you sit": "You feel more relaxed when you're sitting in a quiet park, away from the hustle and bustle of the city." Or, "People feel more relaxed when (they're) sitting in a quiet park, away from the hustle and bustle of the city."

Table 3j

Use	Do not use	Comments
Do/Work (or other simple words)	Be engaged in (a little formal)	For example: "I'm engaged in international trade." sounds unnecessarily formal. It is better just to say, "I work in international trade." This is another example of using the passive voice when it is more suitable to speak personally.
Pardon?/Sorry?	I beg your pardon?	

Alright/OK	In order	For example: "Everything was in order" sounds like "officialised writing" (公文体). Just say, "Everything was alright" or, "Everything was OK" or some other everyday words to describe the specific situations such as, "Everything was just as I had left it."
I was very surprised by the news.	I was most surprised by the news. (a little formal)	Using "most + adjective" or "most + adverb" sounds unnecessarily formal. Use "very" or, "very much", "extremely" or "really".
(Very) many/Several	Numerous	

P1题库高频真题词汇

(1) Dance 舞蹈

• Jazz 爵士舞	• Striptease 脱衣舞
• Folk dance 民族舞	• Ballet 芭蕾
• Tap dance 踢踏舞	• Belly dance 肚皮舞
• Ballroom dance 交谊舞	• Latin dance 拉丁舞
• Hula 草裙舞	• Rumba 伦巴
• Tango 探戈	• Samba 桑巴
• Waltz 华尔兹	• Foxtrot 狐步
• Flamenco 弗拉门戈	

(2) Wedding 婚礼

• Growing old together 白头偕老	• Groomsman/Best man 伴郎
• Bride's maid 伴娘	• Betrothal gifts/Bride-price 彩礼
• Celebrating at the wedding feast 吃喜酒	• Get engaged 订婚
• Engagement ring 订婚戒指	• Go-between 红娘
• Bridal sedan chair 花轿	• Bridal veil 婚纱
• Wedding banquet/Wedding dinner 婚宴	• Marriage registration 结婚登记
• Marriage ceremony 结婚典礼	• Marriage certificate 结婚证
• Matchmaker 媒人	• Honeymoon 蜜月
• Teasing the bride (on wedding night) 闹洞房	• Spouse 配偶
• Proposal/Courtship求婚	• Everlasting love 天长地久
• Evening gown 晚礼服	• Fiance 未婚夫
• Fiancee 未婚妻	• Wedding candy 喜糖
• Wedding feast 喜宴	• Marriage interview 相亲
• Newly weds 新婚夫妇	• Bridegroom 新郎
• Bride 新娘	• Bridal dress 新娘礼服

• Fetching the bride 迎亲	• Mother-in-law 岳母
• Life companion 终身伴侣	

(3) Architecture 建筑

• Gothic cathedral 哥特式教堂	• Garden architecture 园林建筑
• Unique shape 独特的外形	• Architecture style 建筑特色
• Architectural complex 建筑群	• Ancient architectural complex 古建筑群
• Architectural art 建筑艺术	• Ancient architectural art 古建筑艺术
• Architecture history/History of architecture 建筑史	
• Ingenious layout 精心的布局	• Arch bridge 拱桥
• European classical architectures 欧洲古典建筑	
• Cantilever bridge 悬臂桥	• Suspension bridge 吊桥
• Floating bridge 浮桥	• Seventeen-arch bridge 十七孔桥
• Upturned eaves/Cornice 飞檐	• Glazed tiles 琉璃瓦
• Beam 梁	• Pillar 柱
• Balustrades 栏杆	

(4) Scenic Spot 景点

• Summer resort 避暑胜地	• Picturesque landscape 风景如画
• Lovely scenes 佳境	• Wonderful example 绝妙的典范
• Noted sights 名胜	• Idyllic landscape 田园风光
• Natural spectacle 自然奇观	• Symbol of history 历史象征
• Snow-covered landscape 雪景	• Exquisite workmanship 做工精巧

(5) Weather 天气

• Humid 潮湿的	• Dry 干燥的
• Foggy 多雾的	• Rainy 多雨的
• Cloudy 多云的	• Windy 多风的
• Sunny 晴朗的	• Gloomy 阴郁的
• Chilly 寒冷的	• Stuffy 闷热的
• Torrid 炎热的	• Agreeable/Pleasant 宜人的

(6) Art 艺术

• Sketching 素描	• Graffiti 涂鸦
• Field trip 实地考察	• Artifact 手工艺品
• Rich culture 丰富的文化	• Art exhibit 艺术展览
• Modern art 现代艺术	• Ancient art 古代艺术

• Cultural art 精美艺术	• Performance art 表演艺术
• Structural art 建筑艺术	• Delicacy 精品
• Human expression 人类表达方式	

(7) Internet 网络

• Easy access to information 易获取信息	• Stay up to date with 与时俱进
• Reliable source 可靠来源	• At your finger tips 唾手可得
• Chat room 聊天室	• Map quest 地图查询
• Social life 社交生活	• News headlines 新闻头条
• Horoscope 星相运程	• Do evil things 做坏事
• Hacker 黑客	

(8) City and Countryside 城市和乡村

***City*城市**

• Traffic jam 交通阻塞	• Rush hour 高峰期
• Easy access to news 易获取消息	• Soaring crime rate 急剧上升的犯罪率
• Worldly-wise 世故的	• Telecommunication 通信
• Culturally diverse 文化多元化的	• First-rate health care 一流的医疗保健
• Recreational facilities 娱乐设施	

***Countryside*乡村**

• Quietness 安静	• Longevity 长寿
• Low crime rate 低犯罪率	• Cheap living expenses 低生活成本
• Backward 落后的	• Uninformed 消息闭塞的
• Free from a contaminated environment 远离受污染的环境	
• Tedious 乏味的	• Monotonous 单调的
• Idyllic 田园的	• Economic gap 经济差距

(9) Types of Music 音乐类型

***General*普通**

• Band music (incl. marching bands) 管弦乐	• Children's music (incl. nursery rhymes) 童谣
• Latin dance music (e.g., Flamenco, Tango) 拉丁舞音乐	
• Electronic/Digital music 电子音乐	
• Ethnic & national music (incl. traditional Chinese music, Chinese opera, folk songs) 民族音乐	
• Film music电影音乐	• Religious music宗教音乐
• New Age Music (= Meditation music. This is music that is meant to relax the listener. It often includes sounds from nature such as a running stream, bird calls etc.) 新世纪音乐（也称冥想音乐）	

***Classical European Music*传统欧洲音乐**

• Baroque music 巴洛克音乐	• Chamber music 室内乐
• Orchestral music (such as composed by Mozart, Beethoven etc.) 管弦乐	
• Opera 歌剧音乐	• Ballet music芭蕾音乐
• Waltz music (esp. Johann Strauss) 华尔兹音乐	

***Modern Popular Music*现代流行音乐**

• Bluegrass 蓝草音乐	
• Blues (mostly sung by American black singers) 蓝调	
• Country & Western music 美国乡村音乐	• Disco music (techno, trance) 迪斯科音乐
• Hip-hop 嘻哈音乐	
• Jazz (e.g., modern jazz, big band, ragtime) 爵士乐	
• Rock 'n' roll (incl. rockabilly, heavy metal) 摇滚乐	
• Rap music 饶舌音乐	• Reggae/Ska (Jamaican music) 雷鬼音乐
• Rhythm & Blues 节奏布鲁斯	
• Pop music (This is a general term for the young people's music that is played most often on the radio. It includes most of the types of music listed under "Modern Popular Music". In China, most of this music consists of love ballads and light rock and roll.) 流行乐	

(10) Types of Movies 电影类型

英国人通常喜欢用“film”，但同时也会使用“movie”；美国人通常喜欢用“movie”，同时也会使用“film”。

• Action films 动作片	• Adventure films 冒险片
• Animated Cartoons 卡通片	• Comedy films 喜剧片
• Horror films 恐怖片	• Martial arts films 功夫片
• Musicals 音乐剧	• Romance films 爱情片
• Romantic comedy films 爱情喜剧片	• Science fiction films 科幻片
• Silent movies 默剧	• (Suspense) Thrillers 惊悚片
• Teen movies 青少年电影	• War movies 战争片
• Westerns 西部片	• Documentary films 记录片

(11) Types of TV Shows 电视节目类型

注意：在口语中，一般情况下“show”等同于“programme”。

• Cartoon programmes (showing a series of cartoons) 卡通节目
• Children's shows (e.g., programmes for children under the age of 6) 儿童节目
• Documentary programmes 纪录片节目
• Travel and tourism programmes (showing a traveller visiting a different place in each episode) 旅行节目

• Science and technology documentaries 科技纪录片
• Nature and wildlife programmes 自然和野生动物节目
• Dramas (e.g., police dramas, historical dramas based on the three kingdoms period) 戏剧节目
• Game shows (including quiz shows) 游戏节目
• Musical video shows (e.g., MTV, programmes showing a series of pop music videos) 电视音乐节目
• Reality TV shows 电视真人秀
• Comedy shows (incl. situational comedies/sitcoms) 喜剧节目
• Soap operas 肥皂剧
• Sports programmes (e.g., live broadcasts of sports events) 体育节目
• Talk shows (= chat shows) 脱口秀
• Variety shows (e.g., the Chinese Spring Festival Gala showing a variety of different performances) 综艺节目
• The news 新闻节目
• Special news programmes (focusing on an important current topic) 特别新闻节目
• Current affairs & news analysis programmes (incl. interviews and discussions between panellists) 时事政治及新闻分析节目

(12) Advertising 广告

*Types*类型

• TV & radio advertisements (= TV & radio commercials) 电视和电台广告
• Newspaper & magazine ads (incl. the classified ads) 报纸和杂志广告
• Billboards (next to main roads, railway lines, on subway station walls etc.) 户外广告
• Mobile-phone text messages 手机短信广告
• Flyers & handouts (e.g., on the street, put into letterboxes etc.) 传单广告
• Internet advertisements (e.g., pop-up ads) 网络广告
• Posters (e.g. wall posters, bus stop posters) 海报广告

*Visible Logos*可见徽标

• On professional athletes' clothing 职业运动员服饰上	
• On signs in front of shops etc. 店门前标志上	
• On T-shirts, hats, jackets & other clothing T恤、帽子、夹克等衣服上	
• On handbags and other accessories 手提包和装饰品上	
• On Formula 1 cars F1赛车上	• On hot-air balloons 热气球上

*Advertisements in other prominent places*其他醒目位置的广告

• On the side of buses and trains 公交车和火车侧身广告	
• Cinema advertising 电影广告	• Sports stadium advertising 体育场广告

(13) Things to Read 阅读材料

*News*新闻

• Newspapers 报纸	• News magazines 新闻杂志
• Company & organization newsletters 公司和组织简讯	
• The Internet. The Internet includes copies of the printed newspapers and news magazines but also has news pages that are especially written for the Internet. One important sub-group of Internet news pages consists of independent journalists. These independent journalists usually include their commentary and opinion with their reporting of factual information. 网络新闻。网络新闻包括纸质报纸和新闻杂志的复本，也包括专门为互联网撰写的篇章。网络新闻的一个重要组成部分是独立记者。这些独立记者在报道事实信息的时候常常加入自己的评论和观点。	
• Scandal 丑闻	• Reader's interest 读者兴趣
• Quality paper 高级报纸，严肃报纸	• Fast update 更新（新闻内容）快
• Sidebar 花絮新闻	• Readability 可读性
• Hot news 热点新闻	• Human interest 人情味
• Profile 人物专访，人物特写	• In-depth reporting 深度报道
• Timeliness 时效性，时新性	• Sensational 耸人听闻的，具有轰动效应的
• Sex scandal 桃色新闻	• Hearsay 小道消息
• News value 新闻价值	• Suspended interest 悬念
• Highlights 要闻	

*Magazines*杂志

• Fashion magazines 时尚杂志	• Movie magazines 电影杂志
• Computer magazines 电脑杂志	• Sports magazines 运动杂志
• Hobbyist magazines 业余爱好杂志	• Technical & professional journals 技术类专刊
• Art magazines 艺术杂志	• Home decoration magazines 家庭装修杂志
• Women's magazines女性杂志	

*Literature*文学

• Autobiographies自传	• Biographies 传记
• Novels (Historical novels, Thrillers, Mystery stories, Romance novels, Detective Stories, Science Fiction) 小说	
• Poetry 诗歌	• Plays 戏剧
• Short Stories 短篇小说	• Essays 随笔
• Literary Criticism 文学评论	

*Education*教育

• Textbooks 教科书	• Reference books 参考书
• Encyclopaedias 百科全书	• "Self-help" books 自助书（如旅游指南）

*Entertainment*娱乐

• Comic books 漫画书	• Puzzle books 谜语书

(14) Types of Clothing 衣服

*Casual Wear*休闲服

• A pair of jeans 牛仔裤	• A pair of slacks 宽松裤
• A T-shirt T恤	• A sweater 毛衣
• A pair of shorts 短裤	• A cardigan 羊毛衫
• Pyjamas (= pajamas) 睡衣	

*Formal Wear*正装

• A business suit 西装	• A waistcoat 马甲
• A tie 领带	• A bow tie 领结
• A wedding gown 结婚礼服	• A ballroom gown 舞厅礼服
• A tuxedo 无尾礼服	• An overcoat 大衣
• A fur coat 皮大衣	

*Sportswear*运动服

• A tracksuit 田径服	
• Clothes for football, basketball etc. 足球服、篮球服等	
• Ski clothes (a ski vest, a pair of ski trousers, a ski jacket) 滑雪服	
• A pair of swimming costumes (= a swimsuit)泳装	
• Golf clothes 高尔夫服	• Sports fishing clothes 运动钓鱼服

*Footwear*鞋类

• Dress shoes (= formal shoes) 皮鞋	• Sandals 凉鞋
• House slippers 室内拖鞋	• Thongs (= flip-flops) 人字拖
• Gym boots/sneakers 健身鞋	• Dancing shoes 舞鞋
• Martial arts slippers 武鞋	
• Sports shoes (e.g., football, golf, track & field shoes) 运动鞋	
• Work boots 工作靴	• Rain boots 雨靴
• Fur-lined winter boots 皮毛冬靴	• High-heels 高跟鞋
• Platform shoes 厚底鞋	• Casual shoes 便鞋
• Hiking shoes/Travelling shoes 旅游鞋	• Slipper 拖鞋
• Canvas 帆布鞋	• Boots 靴子
• Axido 沙滩鞋	• Pumps 低跟轻便舞鞋
• Climbing shoes 登山鞋	• Football shoes 足球鞋

• Jogging shoes 慢跑鞋	• Basketball shoes 篮球鞋
• Leisure shoes 休闲鞋	• Tennis shoes 网球鞋
• Baseball shoes 棒球鞋	• Aerobic shoes 有氧运动鞋

***Hats*帽类**

• Baseball caps 棒球帽	• Cowboy hats 牛仔帽
• Straw hats 草帽	• Panama hats 巴拿马帽
• Stetson hats 斯泰森毡帽	• Arctic weather hats 北极帽
• Cloth/towelling hats 布帽	• Berets 贝雷帽
• Fur hats 皮帽	• Ski masks 滑雪帽
• Hard hats/safety hats 安全帽	• Motorcycle helmets 摩托头盔

(15) Electrical & Electronic Appliances电子、电器设备

***Home Appliances*家用电器**

• Refrigerators 冰箱	• Microwave ovens 微波炉
• Electric stoves 电炉	• Rice cookers 电饭煲
• Coffee makers 咖啡机	• Toasters 烤面包机
• Blenders/food mixers 搅拌机	• Washing machines 洗衣机
• Clothes dryers 干衣机	• Electric Irons 电熨斗
• Air conditioners 空调	• Electric heaters/radiators 电暖器
• Humidifiers 加湿器	• Electric fans 电扇
• Kitchen exhaust fans (above the stove) 抽油烟机	
• Vacuum cleaners 吸尘器	• Electric shavers 电动剃须刀
• Electric toothbrushes 电动牙刷	• Hairdryers 吹风机
• Reading lamps 台灯	• Electric drills 电钻
• Electric sewing machines 电动缝纫机	
• Remote control devices, such as for a TV or an air conditioner 遥控器	
• A battery charger 充电器	• A voltage adapter 电源适配器

***Entertainment*娱乐**

• DVD/VCD players DVD/VCD 播放器	• Televisions 电视机
• Radios 收音机	• CD players CD 播放器
• Tape players/tape recorders/cassette players/cassette recorders 卡带机	
• Stereo systems 立体音响	• Speaker(s) 喇叭
• A headset/a set of headphones/a pair of headphones/a pair of earphones 耳机	

• A microphone (for making recordings on the computer) 话筒	
• A walkman 随身听	• An MP4 player MP4 播放器
• An iPod 苹果音乐播放器	• Karaoke machine 卡拉OK机

***Communication*交流**

• Telephones 电话	• Cellphones (= mobile phones) 手机
• Fax machines 传真机	

***Computer Appliances*电脑设备**

• Computers (including laptop computers/notebook computers) 电脑	
• Monitors 显示器	• Scanners 扫描仪
• Printers 打印机	

(16) Methods of Storing Memories保存记忆的方法

• Photographs (in a photo album) (相册中的) 照片	
• Photographs (stored as digital photos on a computer or an electronic storage device) (电子) 照片	
• Diaries 日记	• Videos 视频
• Tape recordings 录音	• Keeping old letters 保留旧信件
• Storing emails 保存邮件	
• Making backup (CD's of digital photos, videos, audio recordings, written documents, scanned documents etc.) 备份	
• Keeping souvenirs and mementos 保留纪念品	

(17) Things That Some People Collect (as a Hobby) 收集 (作为爱好)

• Stamps 邮票	• Coins 硬币
• Rocks 岩石	• Shells 贝壳
• Insects 昆虫	• Antiques 古董
• Artwork (paintings, calligraphy etc.) 艺术品	
• Comics, magazines, old books 漫画、杂志、旧书	
• Music CDs 音乐CD	• Film DVDs 电影DVD
• Postcards 邮票	• Dolls 玩偶
• Models (model cars, model trains, model ships, model planes etc.) 模型	
• Matchboxes 火柴盒	• Cigarette packs 香烟盒
• Beer cans 啤酒罐	
• Items with a special motif (toys, models & pictures of dogs, cats or horses etc.) 卡通玩具	
• Telephone cards 电话卡	• Souvenirs of places visited 旅游纪念品

(18) Environmental Problems环境问题

The Problems问题

• Pollution: air pollution, water pollution (incl. oceanic pollution), soil pollution, noise pollution 污染：大气污染、水污染（包括海洋污染）、土壤污染、噪声污染	
• Species loss物种灭绝	• Deforestation森林砍伐
• Desertification沙漠化	• Waste disposal废物处理
• Water shortage水资源短缺	

Other Related Vocabulary其他相关词汇

• Pollution 污染	• Fertilizer 肥料
• Factory waste 工厂废物	• Rivers and streams 河川
• Heavy metals 重金属	• Sulphur dioxide 二氧化硫
• Fossil fuels 矿物燃料	• Hydrogen 氢
• Wind power, solar power, solar cells 风能、太阳能、太阳能电池	
• Vehicle exhaust 汽车废气	• Power station 发电站
• Waste disposal 废物处理	• Recycling 回收利用
• Incineration 焚化	• Landfill 垃圾掩埋

Desertification沙漠化

• Sand storms/dust storms 沙尘暴	• Overgrazing 过度放牧
• Goats (one of the major causes of desertification) 山羊（沙漠化的主要原因之一）	
• Grasslands 草原	• Reforestation 重新造林
• Land regeneration 土地再生	

Species Loss物种灭绝

• Habitat loss 栖息地消失	• Ecological balance 生态平衡
• Genetic diversity 遗传多样性	• Genes, genetic engineering 基因、基因工程
• Natural compounds (from living organisms) 天然化合物	
• Medicinal uses 医疗用途	
• Genetically produced medicines (from the use of the genes of other species) 基因药物	
• Improved/higher food production (from the use of original crop genes) 提高的/更高的食物产量	

(19) Housework家务

• Washing the dishes 洗碗	• Sweeping the floor 扫地
• Mopping the floor 拖地	• Making the bed铺床
• Preparing meals 准备饭菜	• Washing vegetables 清洗蔬菜

• Cooking 烹饪	• Tidying 收拾
• Ironing 熨烫	• Dusting 打扫
• Taking out the garbage 扔垃圾	• Doing the laundry/washing clothes 洗衣服

(20) Secondary Schools中学

Secondary schools 比较正式，通常说high schools。

• Physics 物理	• Chemistry 化学
• Geography 地理	• Politics 政治
• Mathematics [Math (U.S.); Maths (Br.)] 数学	• P.E. (Physical Education) 体育

(21) Leisure Time & Relaxing休闲时光、放松

• To relax (Don't add "myself" or any variation of "self" after this word.) 放松 (后面不加 "-self")	
• To wind down 放松	• To take it easy 从容
• To take a stroll; to take/have a walk 散步	• To meditate 冥想
• Massage 按摩	• Sauna 桑拿
• Sofa 沙发	• Soft, soothing music 舒缓音乐
• Holidays (Br.) = vacation (U.S.) (A "holiday" (singular) usually refers to a public holiday, i.e., a day or small number of days when most people take time off work.)假期	

***Public holidays*公共假日**

• A weekend 周末	• Go on a trip/take a trip/to travel 旅行
• To go sightseeing 观光	• A hobby 爱好
• An interest 兴趣	• A pastime 消遣
• To pass the time (Do not say, "to kill time" except when you are talking about situations when time seems to be moving particularly slowly because you have nothing to do such as waiting for two hours at the train station to catch your train.) 消磨时光	

(22) Rain雨

• Humid 潮湿	• Sticky 粘的
• Uncomfortable 不舒服的	• Refreshing 提神的
• Cooling 冷却的	• A storm 暴风雨
• A thunderstorm 雷雨	• Thunder 雷
• Lightening 闪电	• A deluge 洪水
• To pour 倾泻	
• To "rain cats and dogs" = to rain very heavily 下倾盆大雨	

• A flood 洪水	• An underpass 地下通道
• To inundate 淹没	• The rainy season 雨季
• The monsoon season 季风季节	• The tropics 热带
• A drought 干旱	• Parched 干渴的
• To sprinkle 洒	• A drop 滴
• A dry spell 干旱期	• Irregular 不规律的
• A trickle 细流	• To dry up 干涸
• A reservoir 水库	• A dam 水坝
• To irrigate 灌溉	

(23) Restaurants & Food饭店与食物

• A menu 菜单	• A hotpot 火锅
• Seafood 海鲜	• Cantonese style food 粤菜
• Sichuan style food 川菜	• American-style fast food 美式快餐
• A pizza 比萨饼	• A vegetarian 素食者
• Take-away food (= food to go) 外卖	• Hot (= spicy) 辣
• Salty 咸	• Sour 酸
• Sweet 甜	
• A cafe (this is a small restaurant, not a coffee shop such as Starbucks) 小餐馆	
• A restaurant 饭店	
• A cafeteria (this is usually a self-serve eating place such as in a school or factory) 自助餐厅	
• A snack bar 小吃店	• Instant noodles 方便面

(24) Letters信件

• Business letters 商务信件	• Personal letters 私人信件
• Postcards 明信片	• Love letters 情书
• Spams 垃圾邮件	• An attachment 附件
• To download 下载	• Computer viruses 电脑病毒
• To keep in touch with someone 和某人保持联系	
• To hear from someone 收到某人来信	

(25) Daily Routine日常生活

• Usually, always, often, frequently, sometimes, rarely, seldom, never 等频率词汇	
• Alert 警觉的	• Fresh 新鲜的
• Tired 疲惫的	• To take a break 休息

• To go online 上网	• To check my email 查邮件
• Warmed-up 热身了的	• In the evening(s) 在晚间
• In the afternoon(s) 在下午	• In the morning(s) 在上午
• In the middle of the night 在午夜	• During the day 在白天
• During working hours 在上班时间	

(26) Animals动物

① Major Biological Classifications of Animals主要动物的生物学分类

• Mammals 哺乳类	• Reptiles 爬行类
• Amphibians 两栖动物	• Birds 鸟类
• Fish 鱼类	• Insects 昆虫类

② Domesticated Animals家畜

***Pets*宠物**

Dogs狗	
• Pekinese 哈巴狗	• Chihuahua 吉娃娃
• Poodle 狮子狗	
• Dachshund/sausage dog 达克斯猎狗/腊肠狗	
• Collie 柯利牧羊犬	• Puppy 小狗
• Dalmatian 斑点狗	• German Shepherd 德国牧羊犬
• Labrador 拉布拉多	• Golden Retriever 金毛犬
Cats猫	
• Long-haired cats 长毛猫	• Short-haired cats 短毛猫
• Burmese cats 缅甸猫	• Tabby cats 斑猫
• Alley cats (feral cats, street cats) 巷猫（如野猫、街猫）	
• A kitten 小猫	
Birds 鸟类	
• The Asian mynah bird 亚洲八哥	• The canary 金丝雀
• The budgie (= the budgerigar) 虎皮鹦鹉	
• The parrot 鹦鹉	• The pigeon 鸽子
• Sparrow 麻雀	
Fish 鱼类	
• Goldfish 金鱼	• Tropical fish 热带鱼
Other Pets其他宠物	
• Rabbits 兔子	• Guinea pigs 豚鼠
• Hamsters 仓鼠	• Ferrets 雪貂
• Tortoises 乌龟	

***Farmed animals*养殖动物**

• Chickens 鸡	• Ducks 鸭
• Geese 鹅	• Pigs (= hogs) 猪
• Sheep 羊	• Beef cattle 肉牛
• Dairy cows 乳牛	• Goats 山羊

***Work Animals*劳力动物**

• Water buffalo 水牛	• Horses 马
• Donkeys 驴	• Mules 骡子
• Camels 骆驼	• Elephants 大象
• Yaks 牦牛	

③ Wild Animals野生动物

***Endangered Animals in China*中国濒危动物**

• Pandas 熊猫	• Tigers 老虎
• Black bears 黑熊	• Wolfs 狼
• Mongolian wild horses 蒙古野马	

***Other Wild Animals in China*其他中国野生动物**

• Snakes 蛇	• Foxes 狐狸
• Deers 鹿	• Wild horses 野马
• Monkeys 猴	• Squirrels 松鼠

(27) Parks公园

• An entrance 入口	• An entrance fee 入场费
• A statue 塑像	• A sculpture 雕塑
• A fountain 喷泉	• A pool 池子
• A lake 湖	• A pond 池塘
• A river 河	• A bridge 桥
• A rockery 假山	• A bamboo grove 竹林
• A fish pond 鱼塘	• Lawns 草坪
• Gardens 花园	• Flowers 花
• Plants 植物	• Trees 树木
• Vines 葡萄藤	• A park bench (= a park seat) 公园长凳
• In the shade 树荫	• In the sun 在阳光下
• A pathway (= a path) 小路	• To stroll 漫步

• To walk 散步	• To jog 慢跑
• To do exercises 做些运动	• To do stretching exercises 做伸展运动
• To do aerobics 做有氧运动	
• to do tai ji = to practice tai ji 打太极 (拳)	
• To chat 聊天	• To dance 跳舞
• To play a musical instrument 弹奏乐器	• To perform 表演
• To sing 唱歌	• To entertain 娱乐
• To play chess 下棋	

(28) Describing People 描述人

以下形容词可以使用在这些表达中："She's very ________." "She's a very ________ person." "She's a very ________ type of person."

其中very 可以换成：quite, rather, somewhat, really and extremely.

• Friendly 友好的	• Easy-going 随和的
• Laid-back (= habitually very relaxed; not easily excited or angered) 懒散的	
• Relaxed 放松的	• Mellow 成熟的
• Warm-hearted 热心的	
• Hospitable (describing a very welcoming host towards guests) 热情的	
• Generous 慷慨的	• Helpful 乐于帮助的
• Co-operative 合作的	• Humorous 幽默的
• Funny 好玩的	• Interesting 有趣的
• Unique 独一无二的	• Special 特别的
• Impressive 令人印象深刻的	• Kind 善良的
• Sympathetic 同情的	
• Honest (= does not lie, cheat, steal etc.) 诚实的	
• Considerate 周到的	
• Thoughtful (= considerate = thinks about the feelings and welfare of other people) 体贴的	
• Caring 有同情心的	• Selfless (the opposite is, "selfish") 无私的
• Down-to-earth 脚踏实地的	• Idealistic 完美主义的
• Extroverted (the opposite is, "introverted") 外向的	
• Outgoing 活泼外向的	• Sociable 喜欢社交的
• Shy (This means, "a little fearful" of other people) 害羞的	
• Sensitive 敏感的	• Quiet 安静的
• Studious 好学的	• Traditional 传统的
• Conservative 保守的	• Old-fashioned 落伍的

• Fashionable 时尚的	• Modern 现代的
• Fashion-conscious 赶时髦的	• Stylish 时髦的
• Well-groomed 被小心照料的	• Well-dressed 穿着考究的
• Attractive 吸引人的	• Good-looking 好看的
• Handsome 帅气的	• Pretty 漂亮的
• Elegant 优雅的	• Graceful 优雅的
• Gentle 温和的	• Statuesque (usually for tall women) 雕像般的
• Well-mannered 有礼貌的	• Cultured 有教养的
• Sophisticated 世故的	• Open-minded 思想开放的
• Confident 自信的	• Competitive 有好胜心的
• Fearless 无畏的	• Independent 独立的
• Individualistic 个人主义的	• Adventurous 冒险的
• Rebellious 叛逆的	• Persistent 坚持的
• Industrious (= hard-working) 努力的	• Motivated 有上进心的
• Single-minded 专一的	• Goal-oriented 以结果为导向的
• Determined 坚决的	• Ambitious 有雄心壮志的
• Strong-willed 意志坚强的	• Passionate 有激情的
• Enthusiastic 热情的	• Positive 积极的
• Fit (= healthy, especially with strong muscles, a healthy heart and healthy lungs: Someone who can walk up a high mountain without resting is very fit.) 健康的	
• Health-conscious 热衷健康的	• Artistic 艺术的
• Talented 有才华的	• Capable 有能力的
• Musical 精通音乐的	• Expressive 善于表现的
• Intelligent 聪明的	
• Smart (informal) (= intelligent, in U.S. = well-dressed, in Br.) 聪明的（美），穿着考究的（英）	
• Bright 聪明的	• Analytical 善于分析的
• Erudite = well-read (usually for older people) 博学的	
• Well-educated 受过良好教育的	• Well-informed 见多识广的
• Devoted 专注的	• Knowledgeable 知识渊博的
• Skilled/skilful 娴熟的	• Professional 专业的
• Careful 细心的	• Neat 灵巧的
• Meticulous 一丝不苟的	• Reliable 可靠的
• Punctual 准时的	• Curious 好奇的
• Far-sighted 有远见的	• Insightful 富有洞察力的

• Intuitive 有直觉力的	• Wise 智慧的
• Mature 成熟的	• Responsible 有责任心的
• Sensible 明智的	• Imaginative 有想象力的
• Creative 有创造力的	• Playful (usually children) 贪玩的
• Rambunctious (e.g., a 2-yr-old child) 闹腾的	• Energetic 精力充沛的
• Adorable (Don't say "very adorable". But "really adorable" is OK.) 可爱的	
• Cute 伶俐的	• Loveable 惹人爱的
• Lovely 可爱的	• Loving 有爱心的

(29) The Sections of a Newspaper报纸板块

• The local news section 地方新闻板块	• The international news section 国际新闻板块
• Letters to the editor 读者来信板块	• The business section 商业板块
• The entertainment section 娱乐板块	• The sports section 体育板块
• The classified advertisements section 分类广告	
• The comics/comic strips 漫画板块	• The travel section 旅行板块
• The modern living section 现代生活板块	• The fashion section 时尚板块
• The home decoration section 家庭装修板块	

(30) Water水

• Consume/consumption 消耗	• Water used in agriculture 农业用水
• Water used in industry 工业用水	• Trickle irrigation 滴灌
• Water for domestic uses (= household uses) 家庭用水	
• Watering public lawns and gardens 浇灌公共草坪及花园	
• Taking/having a bath 洗澡	• Taking/having a shower 淋浴
• Cleaning/brushing your teeth 刷牙	• Flushing the toilet 冲厕所
• Washing the dishes 洗碗	• Washing the car 洗车
• Turn off, turn on 关闭、打开	• A tap (= a faucet) 水龙头
• A running tap 流水的水龙头	

(31) Games 游戏

***Adult games*成人游戏**

• Chess下棋	• Mah-jong麻将
• Weiqi (I suggest you use the Chinese name, not the Japanese name, "Go") 围棋	
• Card games (e.g., poker) 纸牌	• Pool/8 ball/billiards/snooker 台球
• Computer games 电脑游戏	• Drinking games 喝酒游戏
• Guessing games 猜谜游戏	

*Children's Games*儿童游戏

• Marbles 弹珠	• Hide and seek 捉迷藏
• Hopscotch 跳房子游戏	• Scissors, rock and paper 剪刀石头布

(32) Playgrounds操场

• A swing 秋千	• A slide/a slippery dip 滑梯
• A carousel 旋转木马	• A see-saw 跷跷板
• A jungle-gym/a set of monkey bars 儿童攀爬架	

(33) Cooking烹饪

• Recipe 食谱	• Fried food 油炸食物
• Western-style food 西餐	• Chef 大厨
• Sweet and sour pork 糖醋里脊	• Gourmet 美食家
• Cuisine 菜肴	• Nutrition 营养

(34) Sports Facilities体育设施

• A swimming pool 游泳池	• A basketball court 篮球场
• A badminton court 羽毛球场	• A tennis court 网球场
• A squash court 壁球场	• A volleyball court 排球场
• A football field 足球场	• A baseball field 棒球场
• A hockey field 曲棍球场	• A running track 跑道
• A cycling track 自行车道	• A golf course 高尔夫球场
• A golf driving range 高尔夫球练习场	• An archery range 射箭场
• A shooting range 射击馆	

(35) Time Management 时间管理

• Punctual 准时的	• To procrastinate 耽搁	• Phone diary 手机时间表
• Punctuality 准时	• To postpone 推迟	• A timetable 时间表
• To plan ahead 提前计划	• Overdue 到期	• A schedule 计划表
• On time 准时	• The due time 到期时间	• To fritter away one's time 浪费某人时间
• On schedule 准时	• The due date 到期日期	• A short-term goal 短期目标
• A deadline 期限	• Prompt 立刻的	• A long-term goal 长期目标
• Timely 及时的	• To fall behind 落后	• Goal-setting 目标设定
• A rush job 急活	• To be behind 落后	• A priority 优先处理的事
• At short notice 临时通知	• To rush 抓紧时间	• High priority 特别优先处理的事
• To be behind time 落后	• To hurry 匆忙	• Low priority 稍后考虑的事

• To delay 推迟	• Urgent 紧急的	• Efficient, inefficient 有效率的、低效率的
• To put off doing sth. 推迟做某事	• To cram (for an exam) 临时抱佛脚	• Organized 安排有序的
• To leave sth. till the last moment 把某事拖到最后	• To be pressed for time 时间紧迫	• Flexible 灵活的

(36) Tradition传统

Adjectives	Nouns	Verbs
• Traditional 传统的	• A tradition 传统	• To observe a custom 遵守风俗
• Customary 习惯的	• A custom 风俗	• To follow a custom 遵循风俗
• Ceremonial 仪式的	• A ceremony 仪式	• To bow 鞠躬
• Religious 宗教的	• A ritual 仪式	
• Superstitious 迷信的	• A rite 仪式	
• Formal 正式的	• A practice 惯例	
• Conventional 惯例的	• A convention 习俗	
	• Folklore 民俗	
	• A superstition 迷信	
	• A belief 信仰	
	• A myth 神话	
	• A legend 传说	
	• A festival 节日	

(37) Change改变

Adjectives	Nouns	Verbs	
• Better 更好的	• Progress 进步	• To grow 增长	• To restrict 限制
• Worse 更坏的	• A development 发展	• To increase 增多	• To suppress 抑制
• Former 之前的	• A metamorphosis 蜕变	• To rise 提升	• To abolish 废除
• Current 现在的	• A transition 过渡	• To expand 拓展	• To renew 更新
• Modern 现代的	• A rate of change变化率	• To extend 延伸	• To rejuvenate 使恢复活力
• Fashionable 时尚的	• A radical change 剧烈改变	• To broaden 扩大	• To renovate 改革
• Up-to-date 最新的	• A gradual change 逐渐改变	• To widen 加宽	• To revamp 改进
• Contemporary 当代的	• An imperceptible change 细微改变	• To lengthen 加长	• To streamline 使合理化

		• To intensify 增强	• To recondition 修补
		• To magnify 放大	• To refurnish 重新装备
		• To decrease 减少	• To rehabilitate 恢复
		• To fall 下降	• To regenerate 使再生
		• To contract 缩短	• To reform 改革
		• To shorten 减短	• To reverse 逆转
		• To reduce 减少	• To improve 改进
		• To fluctuate 波动	• To develop 发展
		• To vary 改变	• To mature 使成熟
		• To move 移动	• To modernize 使现代化
		• To relocate 迁移	• To enhance 加强
		• To transport 运输	• To advance 前进
		• To shift 改变	• To ameliorate 改善
		• To divert 转移	• To alleviate 减轻
		• To substitute 替代	• To relieve 减轻
		• To transform 转变	• To correct 改正
		• To replace 取代	• To deteriorate 恶化
		• To convert 转变	• To worsen 使恶化
		• To build 建立	• To age 老化
		• To construct 建设	• To decay 衰减
		• To demolish 拆除	• To degenerate 退化
		• To fix 修理	• To aggravate 使加剧
		• To repair 修复	• To exacerbate 使加剧
		• To update 更新	• To impair 损害
		• To alter 改变	• To corrupt 腐败
		• To modify 修改	• To discontinue 中止
		• To limit 限制	• To abandon 放弃
		• To contain 包含	

▶语法：*Grammar*

回答完整性

考生给出直接答案的时候，句子一定要完整，尤其不要用一个词来回答问题，举个简单例子，如果考官问你："Do your work or are you a student?" 不要只回答："Student." 或者回答 "Do you like sports?" 时，不要给出残缺的直接答案："I like it."

注意时态

本书中列举了P1高频问题类型，你可以发现有些问题类型中包含了不同的时态，因此，在回答此类问题的时候，要直接给出相应时态的回答。有时在你紧接着补充的信息里，你需要改变时态，但通常情况下，时态基本上和前面保持一致。举个例子，当问题中包含“did”(或者“was”“were”)时，你给出直接答案时需要体现过去时态，过去时可以贯穿整个答案。比如问题：“When did you first start reading newspapers?”直接答案是先回答什么时候，然后在延展信息中依然可以使用过去时，补充为什么或者怎么得到及在哪儿得到新闻报纸。如果问题中包含了现在完成时，你的直接答案必须是完成时，但是延展信息最好是过去时。举例说明：“Have you received any training at work?”直接答案可以说“Yes, I have.”延展信息也使用完成时“I have been trained to give presentations to my customers.”但是，考官希望延展信息使用过去时，这样能体现出你语法使用的灵活性。高分答案里的延展信息要使用过去时，指出该培训在什么时候发生，这样又可以体现你的细节表达能力：“Yes, I have. I was trained how to give presentations to my customers when I started this job.”

当谈到过去情况时，考生可以寻找机会说出一些更能体现语法深度的表达，比如“Because I thought it was very challenging.”而不是像众多考生一样说“I think it is very challenging.”尽管很有可能你现在依旧这么认为。两者的显著不同是前者是间接引语，是高分语法的要素。再举个例子，“Why did you choose your major?”你应该回答“I chose that major because I thought it would suit my interest.”而不是“I chose that major because I think it suits my interest.”大家注意一下，前者，即高分答案中有一个非常加分的词“would”，在这里它是“will”的虚拟语气形式。

中国考生可能会觉得口语中的重点是少犯语法错误或多用几个从句。诚然，这两点很重要，但是在雅思口语中，还有其他很多重要的语法评分点，下面我们来系统学习一下：

1. 比较级：Comparative Structures

I like watching movies **more than** watching TV.

I think banks are **as much** to blame as governments on this issue.

2. 情态动词：Modal Verbs

The government **has to** be more open.

Many people think we **should** be doing more for the environment.

3. 被动语态：Passive Voice

The movie **was directed** by a first-timer.

These buildings **are being designed** by American architects.

4. 时态：Tenses

时态是考官最敏感的语法评分点，也是最容易影响考生语法得分的要素之一。

除了过去时需要注意以外，我们来学习下可以获得语法高分的时态：

- Past perfect tense
- Present perfect tense
- Future tense
- Future perfect tense

我们通过P1的三个常见问题来看看具体如何去使用这些高分时态：

Hometown

Q.Where is your hometown? How long have you been living there?

- **I am from** XX which is in XX province. **I have lived** there since 2005. (Present perfect tense)
- **I had lived** with my grandmother in another city **before I moved** there. (Past perfect tense)
- Soon **I will move** away to go to university. (Future tense)

Work

Q. What job (or what work) do you do?

- **I work in** an office. **I have worked** here since June. (Present perfect tense)
- **I had worked** in a phone shop before, but **they had closed** the shop because of money problems. (Past perfect tense)
- **I will soon** move to university. But **I will** have to look for another job. (Future tense)

Study

Q. Do you like your major?

- **Now I really** love my major. **I have been** doing it for one semester. (Present perfect tense)
- At the beginning **I did not** like it. This is because **I had not** really understood what it was about. (Past perfect tense)
- I know that by the end of this semester **I will have really got** to grips with the subject matter. (Future perfect tense)

5. 条件结构：Conditional Structures

条件结构一般由“if”引导，通常有3种情况：

① 常常发生的真实事件：Real events that always happen (first conditional)

② 想象中的事件：Imaginary events (second conditional)

③ 想象中过去的事件: Imagined past events (third conditional)

举例：

- If we finish early, we will go out for lunch. —first conditional—possible situation
- If we had time, we would visit our friends. —second conditional—imaginary situation
- If we had gone to New York, we would have visited the exhibit. —third conditional—imagined past situation

6. 复杂句型：Complex Structures

① 了解复杂句

考生在作答时，要寻找机会展现使用复杂句型的能力，但没有必要像写作那么复杂。这是语法得到6分以上的另一个重要因素。这其中有个重要的关系代词“which”（或“that”）。考生通常在给出延展信息时喜欢堆积信息，但考官想看的是你能够通过使用“which”更好地组织语言。举个简单例子“I enjoy swimming in summer time, it is a lot of fun and it can cool my body.” 应该改成“I enjoy swimming in summer time, which is a lot of fun and it can cool my body.” 本章第6节会通过神器详细告诉大家如何形成这种表达习惯。

下面我们来具体地说下P1中的复杂句型构成方式和典型案例：

复杂句型的定义是：一个句子由几个子句构成，每个子句都包含一个动词，这些子句由连词进行连接。比方说：两个简单句，“I like Edison, he has 9 girlfriends.” 可以改成通过关系代词“who”连接的一个复杂句：“I like Edison who has 9 girlfriends.”

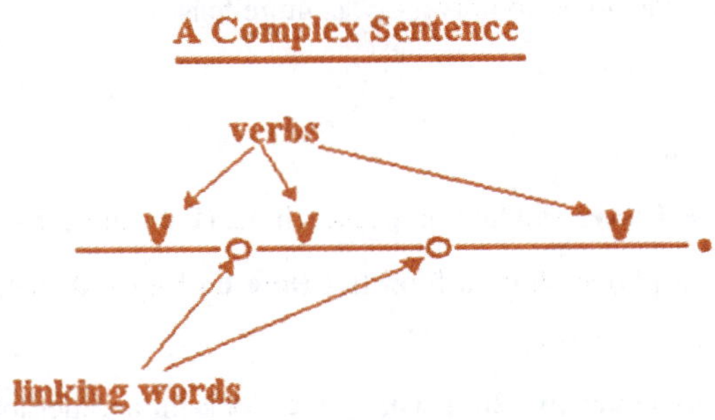

在口语考试中，能够使用不同的词来连接句子是非常重要的，这样可以形成更长更复杂的句子，考官非常看重这个，这也是你语法获得6分以上的重要因素。考官必须严格遵守此标准。下面提供几种好的方法来塑造标准的复杂句型。

* 首先，除非必要，否则尽量不要重复名词，可以用代词来替换，如：he, she, it, we, they, this, that, the one, the ones

* 学会使用关系代词：which, who, whom, where, when

* 要尽量学会使用以下词汇：if, although/though, even though, apart from, as well (as), at the moment, even, while, whereas, either, neither (+nor), unless, rather than, instead of, as soon as, when, once, after, while, meanwhile, besides, in spite of, despite, yet, still, provided/providing that, except, in order to, in case, depending on, because, but, and, as, or, for example, for instance, like, such as, by

* 学会使用以下副词，它们同样可以帮助构成复杂句型：mainly, chiefly, especially, particularly, predominantly, primarily, specially, especially, specifically, mostly（如：I love singing very much, especially singing in the Karaoke bar with my family members.）

特别注意：

* “although”后面千万不要跟着“but”，相信大家都知道，但是在口语考试中却经常犯错，因为在紧张的情形下，考生会犯一些无意识的错误，所以我建议考生尽量不要使用这个表达，可以尝试使用“even though”。
* 如果你想表达“因为”，可以使用“because”，但是我发现很多机构老师教考生用“for”“as”来替换。这两个词在日常口语交流中稍显正式，最好不要在第一部分这么用，比如：“I'm sitting for the IELTS exam as I want to study in Britain.” 就显得不太自然。另外，since也是一个用来表示原因的词，应该使用在复杂句的开头，例如：“Since I'm not interested in cycling, I don't want to learn it at all.” 但是如果使用在句子中间，就如同“as”“for”一样，有点太正式了。
* 在复杂句中表示并列关系时，不要过度使用“and”，可以用其他表达方式进行替换，如“as well as that”“apart from this”等。

②复杂句型专项训练

Example 1

"I need to learn English. English is very important. English will help me get a good job. I want to work in international trade. I'm studying international trade right now."

"I need to learn English ________ is very important ________ it'll help me get a good job in international trade _______ I'm studying right now."

Answer

"I need to learn English, which is very important because it'll help me get a good job in international trade, which I'm studying right now."

Example 2

"I work in a software company. I'm a computer programmer. My work is quite challenging. Our clients usually want us to write programs in a short period of time."

"I work in a software company _______ a computer programmer _______ is quite a challenging job _______ our clients usually want us to write programs in a short period of time."

Answer

"I work in a software company as a computer programmer, which is quite a challenging job because our clients usually want us to write programs in a short period of time."

Example 3

"I like watching films. Watching films is my favourite pastime. I like comedy films. I don't like violent films. I don't like horror films."

"Watching films, _______ comedy, is my favourite pastime _______ I don't like films with a lot of violence _______ horror films."

Answer

"Watching films, especially comedy, is my favourite pastime although/but I don't like films with a lot of violence or horror films."

Example 4

"I don't ride my bicycle very often. I take the bus to university. It's faster. I do use my bicycle on the weekends. At that time I have no classes."

"I don't ride my bicycle very often _______ it's faster to take the bus to university _______ I do use it on the weekends _______ I have no classes."

Answer

"I don't ride my bicycle very often because/since it's faster to take the bus to university although/but I do use it on the weekends when I have no classes."

Example 5

"Yes, Chinese people do like growing flowers. Many people live in apartments in cities. It's not easy to grow flowers in an apartment. Some people have a balcony. People sometimes grow flowers on their balcony. Retired people sometimes grow flowers on their balcony."

"Yes, Chinese people do like growing flowers _______ _______ many people live in apartments in cities, it's not easy to grow flowers, _______ people _______ have a balcony, _______ retired people, sometimes grow flowers on their balcony."

Answer

"Yes, Chinese people do like growing flowers but since/but because many people live in apartments in cities, it's not easy to grow flowers, although people who have a balcony, especially retired people, sometimes grow flowers on their balcony."

Example 6

"Would you say the place where you live is good for families with children?"

"Well, not really, no, because _______ the apartments are all modern and clean, there are very few places for children to play outside."

Answer

"Well, not really, no, because although/even though/despite the fact that the apartments are all modern and clean, there are very few places for children to play outside."

Example 7

"I'm interested in sport. There are many other things that I'm interested in. I'm interested in computers and music."

"I'm interested in sport _______, _______, there are many other things that I'm interested in, _______ computers and music."

Answer

"I'm interested in sport but, besides that/as well as that, there are many other things that I'm interested in, such as/like/for example/for instance computers and music."

Example 8

"Three years ago, my father gave me some good advice. This advice was very useful. It saved me from making a very unsuitable career choice."

"Three years ago, my father gave me some good advice _______was very useful _______ it saved me from making a very unsuitable career choice."

Answer

"Three years ago, my father gave me some good advice which was very useful because it saved me from making a very unsuitable career choice."

Example 9

"When I was in second year of high school, I had a maths teacher. His name was Mr. Wang. He really changed my life. He inspired me to love mathematics."

"When I was in second year of high school, I had a maths teacher _______ Mr. Wang _______ really changed my life _______ inspiring me to love mathematics."

Answer

"When I was in the second year of high school, I had a maths teacher named Mr. Wang who really changed my life by inspiring me to love mathematics."

Example 10

"To tell you the truth, I don't play much sport. I don't walk much. I drive my car everywhere. I drive my car to my office. My office is near my home. I sometimes play table tennis. I'm quite good at table tennis. I know more exercise would give me more energy. I just don't seem to find the time for exercise. I'm too busy with my work."

"To tell you the truth, I don't play much sport ________ do I walk much ________ I drive my car everywhere, ________ to my office, ________ is near my home ________ I sometimes play table tennis, ________ I'm quite good at. I know I'd have more energy ________ I did more exercise ______ I just don't seem to find the time for exercise ______ I'm too busy with my work."

Answer

"To tell you the truth, I don't play much sport nor do I walk much because I drive my car everywhere, even to my office, which is near my home although I sometimes play table tennis, which I'm quite good at. I know I'd have more energy if I did more exercise but I just don't seem to find the time for exercise because I'm too busy with my work."

▶流利连贯：*Fluency and Coherence*

连贯性是P1的一个重要评分点，考官主要看重的是考生的表达中逻辑关系是否合理，我们来看看考官Robert 对连贯性的解读：

* "Coherence" refers to the degree of understandability of several ideas that are presented together; "cohesion" refers to the linkage of the ideas. For long or detailed utterances, cohesion is one of the most important ways to achieve good coherence.

* For Coherence, the examiner is not allowed to give a sub-score of 6 or more if the candidate does not show knowledge of a range of connective words and phrases (to show connection between sentences or ideas, and usually placed at the beginning of sentences).

* For the "Fluency and Coherence" sub-score, the examiner needs to assess a sub-score for each of Fluency and Coherence. If the two sub-scores are different, the lower of the two scores is the final sub-score. For example, sometimes a candidate gets 5 for the Coherence sub-score even when he or she is as fluent as a Band 6 or even a Band 7 candidate. She usually fails to qualify for a 6 for this sub-score because she does not show a wide enough knowledge of connective phrases.

* To repeat: If a candidate is a 7 for fluency but only a 5 for coherence (as shown by a limited usage of connectives), then that candidate gets a score of 5 for this sub-score, not the average of 7 and 5, which is 6. The sub-score here is the highest score that "satisfies" both fluency and coherence—a score of 6 would satisfy the description of this candidate's fluency but would not satisfy a description of this candidate's coherence.

(Remember, "fluency" just refers to the flow of words from the mouth, i.e., the continuity and speed of this flow. But coherence is largely based on the choice of language spoken—mostly the words and phrases that are used to connect ideas so that "the ideas flow".)

建议

"连贯"：若干观点总体易懂；

"衔接"：观点之间有机连接；

话语，不论多长，亦不论多具体，

最佳方法之一，"衔接"展现"连贯"。

连接词语常在句首，显示句子或观点间的关系；

要求考生展示一定使用连接词语的能力；

禁止考官给未使用连接词语者高于6分的子分；

"流利连贯"子分基于考官对每一项的评估，

若子分不同，选取最低值作为最终结果。

举例说明：有时"流利"可达6分甚至7分，

"连贯"为5分，结果实际分数常常不到6，

一切皆因连接词语使用不足。

重申：如果"连贯"为5分，因连接词语使用有限导致，

结果分数通常为5分，即使"流利"可达6分甚至7分，

并非5和7取平均值。

"流利"表示语流和语速。

"连贯"多仰赖连接词语的使用。

下面我们来系统学习一下重点"逻辑关系"的表达方式，从而有效提升连贯性（所用例句均可用于P1相关话题）。

1. 提出两种对比观点，但并不强调差别

(1) On the other hand (另一方面)

It really depends. A big house can give you a large space to enjoy the good life, for example, you can have a small gym in the sitting room. On the other hand, if you live in a flat you don't need to worry about a lot of cleaning.

(2) Alternatively (作为一种选择)

I usually stay at home reading my favourite books, alternatively I may watch a lot of TV especially variety shows.

(3) Then again (然而) (Used when an alternative idea suddenly comes to mind)

Yes. I would like to because I am already familiar with everything around my house, then again I might move out a couple of years later.

2. 提出两种对比观点，强调差别

(1) However (然而，但是) (A little formal)

We can enjoy better food in the restaurant, however hygiene sometimes is a big problem.

(2) Nevertheless (不过，虽然如此，然而，仍然) (A little formal)

I wouldn't say that all advertisements are a bad influence on children—some of them are quite informative and entertaining. Nevertheless, I think some advertisements might be detrimental to children.

(3) Having said that/That said (即便如此) (A little formal. Stress on the word, "said". Meaning = "Even though I just said 'A', an alternative or opposing idea, 'B' is also true.")

Yes. I do think so. Learning English isn't easy; it needs hard work and practice. Having said that many people do become quite fluent after a few years of study.

(4) At the same time (但是，然而)

I think good teachers have to be quite strict in order to keep the class under control. At the same time, teachers should be warm and friendly so the students can relate to them as human beings.

(5) Mind you (你要知道) (Esp. British English. Stress on the word, "you". Informal. Meaning = "Even though I just said 'A', don't forget this important opposing or contrasting point, 'B'.")

To tell you the truth, I don't really like my major very much. Mind you, the teachers are excellent.

(6) Still (还是，然而)

Honestly speaking I want to be famous, still it may bring me a lot of trouble.

(7) Yet (还是，然而)

Cycling can offer you a lot of benefits like keeping you fit or you can appreciate the wonderful scenery along the way, yet you would feel very exhausted after you had finished it.

(8) Instead (相反)

I don't read newspapers very often, instead I either watch the news on TV or I read it on the Internet.

(9) In spite of (this/that) /Despite this/Despite that (尽管如此)

I know talking on the phone can be much more convenient, in spite of this, I enjoy texting to my friends through which I can express different kinds of feelings.

(10) Even so (尽管情况如此)

I hardly have anytime to walk every day, even so I try to make some time to walk with my wife after dinner.

(11) In contrast (相反)

Young people like films that are full of excitement and romance reflecting how they feel about things. In contrast, older people prefer more subtle and thoughtful films.

3. 表明相似或类似

(1) Likewise/Similarly (也，同样)

Yes, I think there should be a little more emphasis on practical skills, especially in primary school. Similarly, in high school and university, there should be more emphasis on the practical application of what students learn at school.

(2) In the same way/In a similar way(同样)

My grandmother taught my mother how to cook when she was just a child. In the same way, my mother taught me when I was about ten years old.

(3) By the same token (相应地，基于同一理由)

Yes, I think we should try to follow the advice of our parents. By the same token, parents should consider what their children really want, not just what they themselves want.

4. 表明反驳

"On the contrary" 有两种用法，大多数中国学生都不太了解。

* "恰恰相反，那不对"

Many people think travelling abroad is very good, on the contrary I think it is much better to travel in my own country.

* "in fact" "as a matter of fact" "actually" 没有转折的意思，有种强调的意味。

I don't think it is very important for children to learn how to cook, on the contrary I believe it is not necessary.

5. 表明承认某事属实、有效、合理等(后面通常跟有转折意味的词)

Of course/Admittedly/Naturally/Obviously/Clearly/Undeniably/Undoubtedly

Of course, online shopping may have a lot of benefits but sometimes you could get some fake goods.

Admittedly, some older people do like music with a quick rhythm but I think the majority of them dislike that type of music.

Naturally, I hope to find a job that's both interesting and well paid like being a lawyer, but I know that such jobs are hard to find.

Obviously, there'd be fewer cars on the roads if they were much more expensive to buy.

Undeniably, he was the fastest runner in the race.

Undoubtedly, this car proved to be the best value of them all.

6. 表明强烈事实

After all (毕竟，终究，归根结底) /You have to admit

I think I will not leave my hometown in the future after all it is the place where I was born and raised.

7. 表明前语无效(意思是前面说的你就当没听见)

Anyway/Anyhow (无论如何) /At any rate (无论如何，不管怎样) /In any case (无论如何，总之)

当考生在表达细节上突然感觉吃力时，可以采用此方式来直接告诉对方你的总体想法，作为自然收尾。

My hometown is a wonderful place for travelling. For example there are many historic buildings like the Lei Feng Tower and the library. Anyway they are very famous, each year a lot of tourists come to my hometown for a nice trip.

8. 表明增加信息

(1) 除此以外

As well as that/Not only that (Informal; good for speaking)

I like swimming very much simply because it can help me to lose my annoying weight as well as that it is a perfect way to make new friends who have the same interest as me.

On top of that (Informal; good for speaking)

Well, firstly, emails are much faster and cheaper than handwritten letters. On top of that, they're much more convenient—you can read or write emails with just a few strokes of the keyboard, without worrying about paper, envelopes and stamps and going out to mail your letters.

Another thing is

I think the latest video technology is in many ways superior to books in educational value because this technology has written words but also has information in audio and video form. Another thing is, it's easier to store and carry around a disc than a book that holds the same amount of information.

What's more

Yes, I think the Internet has changed people's reading habits—for the better. I say that because now we can tap into a much larger range of, and volume of reading material than we could when we just relied on our collection of books at home. What's more, topics such as current events are being updated daily so we can always be up to date with the news.

Furthermore (A little formal)

Actually, I think academic skills are more important than practical skills because, if you have highly developed academic skills you can usually get highly paid work. Furthermore, I think in the future, society will value those who have brainpower more than those people who can do practical things with their hands.

In addition (A little formal)

Reading allows people to become aware of their society and, in fact the whole world. In addition, reading is the main way that people increase their education and we all need to continually learn in order to make progress in our careers.

Besides

I don't like eating in restaurants. Actually there's a restaurant near my home but I don't often go there because it's too expensive and, to be quite frank, I don't like their service—they're much too slow. Besides, right now I'm too busy to eat out very often.

注意："besides"有别于"in addition"，因为"besides"后面跟的是一个不同类型的理由。简单来说吧，在上面例子中，前两条原因是对饭店的批评，但是besides后面跟的原因和饭店缺点无关。

(2) 就此而言

For that matter (Similar to "as a matter of fact", "in fact" and "actually")

To tell you the truth, I'm not very interested in basketball. For that matter, I'm not very interested in any sport.

9. 表明举例

For example/For instance/As an example/To begin with/To start with/For a start

I am fond of doing many kinds of sports, for example playing tennis and football.

There are a lot of benefits associated with swimming; to start with, swimming can help you to shape your figure.

10. 表明细节

Specifically/To be more specific/In particular/As a matter of fact/ In fact/Actually

Cycling can make me feel relaxed, specifically, when I am riding along the road in the countryside, I can forget all the troubles from my work.

I like painting animals, lovely ones in particular.

Old people might choose to watch TV to entertain themselves, as a matter of fact, they are more interested in some programmes about health.

11. 表明重新阐述

I mean/What I mean is/To put that another way/What I'm trying to say is/My point is/In other words/That is (A little formal)/That is to say (A little formal)

My hometown is very attractive for tourists, I mean, there are a lot of scenic spots in my hometown which interest people from outside the area.

12. 表明总结

Overall/On the whole/Basically/Fundamentally

Overall, if you visit my house, you will feel that you were in a gallery.

13. 表明整体或典型

Generally/In general/Typically

Generally, people in China do not travel as much as Western people.

Typically, we often send gifts on some formal occasions, like celebrating a birthday.

14. 表明除外

Otherwise/Except (for)

Weekends should be the best time for me to go boating, otherwise, I can't find any time to do that.

I enjoy all different kinds of music, except rock music.

15. 表明目的

(In order) to (+ verb)

Our government has invested a lot of money in cleaning the air in order to make people healthier.

16. 表明强调

Above all

The Internet brings people a new world to share information and emotion. Above all, the Internet provides people with some useful apps which enable them to lead an easy life.

Indeed (A little formal)

Indeed, online shopping can offer people much cheaper goods.

17. 表明原因

The main reason why/One of the reasons why/One reason why/The main reason why

The main reason why children should do some housework is that they can develop their independence by simply washing dishes or sweeping the floor.

18. 表明结果

As a result/As a consequence/Consequently/So/Because of this/In this way/Therefore (A little formal) (Avoid using "hence" or "thus"; they are too formal, even in writing)

I have spent a lot of time learning cooking, as a result, now I can cook great food.

19. 表明同步发生

At the same time/Simultaneously/Meanwhile/In the meantime

Reading can greatly broaden children's horizons, at the same time, it can cultivate their curiosity towards the world.

20. 表明突然插话

By the way

I enjoy reading a lot especially some novels. By the way I have just bought a new novel written by Mo Yan.

21. 表明回到前话题

As I was saying/As I mentioned before

As I was saying, writing emails can save me a lot of time.

22. 表明思考性停顿(合理避免长的停顿，减少Fluency的扣分)

Let me see/Let's see/Well/You know

Let me see, planting trees, to a large extent, can prevent soil erosion.

23. 表明开始

First/Firstly/First of all/To begin with/In the first place（第一）

Avoid using, "first and foremost" in the speaking and writing tests because it usually sounds like a cliché (陈腔滥调).

Firstly, advertisements can help you decide what to buy.

At first/Initially/Originally/In the beginning/At the beginning（当初，开始）

At first, I had no idea about how to take nice photos.

注意："At first" 不能表达 "First" or "Firstly" 的意思。

24. 表明结尾

Last/Lastly/Finally（最后）

These three are used for listing several things that happen in sequence: "First...Next...Then... Last/lastly/finally."

Lastly, museums can provide people with a good place to find out about history.

下面是考生经常犯的理解错误：

很多考生使用 “at last” 表达 “last” (最后)，这其实是个错误。“At last” 表示某人等了你很长时间，你终于来了。此处，At (long) last = Finally，意为“终于”。

注意：有的考生喜欢在延展信息结尾使用 “last but not least”，这在口语中是非常适合的。但是由于该表达方式被中国考生滥用（甚至在写作中），所以考生应尽量避免使用，可以替换成 “And last, but still very important, is...”

第4节 话题类型总结

P1的话题都是围绕“you”展开的，考生需要尽可能地表达个人观点。基于此，P1话题可以分为9大类（附加高频问题类型及举例）：

1. Personal facts

What is...?

(What is your major/your full name?)

Where...?

(Where do you come from? Where are you living now?)

Is it...?

(Is it a big city or a small place?)

How long...?

(How long have you been living there?)

Do you...?

(Do you ever use the Internet?)

Can you...?

(Can you drive?)

2. Personal likes or dislikes

Do you like.../to do...?

(Do you like sports?)

What do you like most about...?

(What do you like most about your hometown?)

Is there anything you dislike about...?

(Is there anything you dislike about travelling?)

Are you interested in...?

(Are you interested in painting?)

What's your favourite...?

(What is your favourite flower?)

3. Personal habits or experiences

Do you often...?

(Do you often read newspapers?)

How do you...?

(How do you organize your time?)

How often do you...?

(How often do you watch TV?)

When/Where do you (often)...?

(When do you listen to music?/Where do you often walk?)

What do you use...for?

(What do you use a computer for?)

What do you like to do + during a period of time?

(What do you like to a do on weekends?)

How do you spend + a period of time?

(How do you spend your evenings?)

In what situations do you...?

(In what situations do you take photographs?)

When did you.../was the last time you...?

(When did you start using mobile phones/when was the last time you went to see your relatives?)

How did you do...?

(How did you learn to cook?)

Did you do...?

(Did you have any special clothes to wear when you were a child?)

Have you ever...?

(Have you ever been to a musical performance?)

4. Personal preferences

Do you prefer A or B?

(Do you prefer sending emails or writing letters?)

Do you like A or B?

(Do you like travelling alone or with friends?)

Would you prefer A or B?

What kind/part of...do you...?

(What kind of music do you like to listen to/What part of your home do you like the most?)

Which do you think is better, A or B?

(Which do you think is better, watching movies in the cinema or at home?)

5. Personal ideas

Do you think...is good/necessary/important?

(Do you think rain is good?)

Do you think it's important to...?

(Do you think it's important for a person to have a good relationship with their neighbours?)

What (do you think) are the benefits of...?

(What do you think are the benefits of travelling by train?)

Would you say...?

(Would you say it's suitable for children to do some housework?)

6. Personal judgements (comparison)

What are the differences between A and B?

(What are the differences between paper dictionaries and electronic dictionaries?)

What do you think are the advantages and disadvantages of...compared to...?

(What do you think are the advantages and disadvantages of bicycles compared to cars?)

Do you think A and B feel the same about...?

(Do you think boys and girls feel the same about sports?)

Has...changed in the past...years?

(Has your hometown changed in the past 10 years?)

How/In what ways have...changed in the past and now?

(How/In what ways have TV programmes changed in the past and now?)

Is...the same in the past and now?

(Is the traffic problem the same in the past and now?)

7. Personal explanations

Why do you...?

(Why do you want to know the latest news?)

What are the reasons why...?

(What are the reasons why people ride bicycles?)

8. Personal plans

What are your...plans?

(What are your future work/study/travel plans?)

Do you plan to...?

(Do you plan to learn cooking in the future?)

Would you like to...?

(Would you like to move to another city in the future?)

9. Personal observations (group behaviours)

Do people in your country...?

(Do people in your country like planting flowers?)

What kinds of people...?

(What kinds of people most often use the Internet for work?)

How do people in your country...?

(How do people in your country celebrate birthdays?)

Do Chinese people...?

(Do Chinese people often go to museums?)

Do children...?

(Do children also like riding bicycles in your country?)

第5节 目标性考核问题的高分回答模式

雅思口语考试P1中有70%左右的问题为“目标性考核问题”，旨在检测考生针对特定问题是否具备合理表达“function of language”的能力，这是被绝大部分学生和老师所忽视的！所谓“function of language”指的是对某种问题有其特有反馈方式，举个简单例子吧，你被问到“why”的时候，回答“because”是正常反应，对P1来说，“function of language”比这要复杂很多，而且富含评分点。考生在回答过程中如果没有合理的“function of language”会被认为不自然，同时失去很多分数。

下面列举的是P1中考生必须掌握的“目标性考核问题”及相应的“function of language”。

1. Talking about “do/is/can/would” (DICW)

在P1中经常会出现以“do/is/can/would”开头的提问方式，与此类似的有以“did/were/are/could/have/has”开头的提问方式，遇到此类考题时，考生的第一反应就是“是”或“否”。首先要注意的是如果题目中包含“or”，该考题成为选择疑问句，如“Do you prefer to watch movie at home or in the cinema?”就只能做出选择，不能用“是”或“否”来回答。

回答方式：Yes/No

Absolutely

Certainly

Definitely

Not really

Unfortunately

有些考题必须灵活处理，不能只给出肯定或否定回答，否则你很难继续延展信息而且言之成理。比如最近的考题“Are there any traditions to name children in your country?”如果说有，你找不出具体的传统，如果直接说没有，考官又觉得你语言能力很有限，表达不好。这个时候我们要考虑如下回答：“Unfortunately, we may not have any traditions to name children, at least I don’t know.”

2. 表达喜欢和厌恶

Example question: What kinds of sports do you like?

I like...

My favourite...is...

I enjoy...

I just love...

I absolutely adore...

I’m crazy about...

I’m (quite/rather) keen on...

I'm addicted to...

I'm really into...

I don't mind...

As far as...is concerned, I can take it or leave it.

I don't care too much for... = I'm not really into...

My least favourite...is...

I dislike...

I can't stand...

I hate... (extreme expression)

注意：当表达个人感情尤其是喜欢和厌恶时，要使用脸部表情配合表达，更显真实！

表达强烈感情时，需要格外重读关键词。

仅在表达某件你经常做而且几乎无法自拔的事情时才能够使用"I'm addicted to..."

千万不能说"very like"，这是典型的4分表达。我们可以这样使用："verb + very much" or, "very much + verb"。

3. 表达偏好

Example question: Do you/Would you prefer to send emails or written letters?

My preference is...because...

I prefer A to B because...

I prefer...because...

If I had the choice, I'd + V...because...

If I had the choice, I'd rather + V...because...

If I have the choice, I'll + V... (a real possibility for the future)

注意：V = 动词原形。

为了表达更加丰富，你也可以说："I (very) much prefer...", "I certainly prefer..." and "I definitely prefer..."

不要给出"I like both of them"或者相似的答案，举个例子吧，如上面的问题，同时喜欢发邮件和写信对很多人来说的确很正常，但是题目问的是你更喜欢哪个，如果你直接回答两个都喜欢，就不太符合我们前面所说的"直接答案"，你完全可以说"I have no preference, really—I like both of them equally."

在上述表达后面延展信息的时候，需要将两个对象进行对比，这样的话，你要使用表示"比较关系"的语言，例如比较级，这样可以提高语法分数。

4. 给出喜欢或厌恶的原因

...because...

...since...

The main reason I like...is that it's...

What I like best about...is...

The thing I like best about...is...

The best/worst thing about...is...

I don't like that very much because it's too...

That's because I find it...

5. 表达个人习惯

Example question: What do you usually do on the weekends?

I often...

I usually...

Sometimes I...

As a rule, I...

While I'm studying I usually...

Whenever I can I...

回答此类问题不要说"I will"，除非你的表达信息中含有"if"或者类似的意味，如果你对："What do you do in the evenings?" 这一问题给出如下回答，就是大错特错了"Well, after I have had my dinner I will usually watch some TV and chat with my parents." 但是，一旦含有"if"或类似的意味在表达中，情况就不同了："I usually get my news from the TV or the Internet but sometimes, (if there's some special news that I'm interested in,) I'll buy a newspaper and read more about a topic (that) I'm especially interested in."

有同学回答此类问题时喜欢用"always"，这个词表达的是"总是"，不是"经常"，所以要考虑清楚。如果你说" I always dine out with my parents on the weekends." 考官就可能会觉得不太可能，从而断定这是用词错误。

6. 比较

Example question: What are the differences between modern art in China and traditional Chinese art?

合理使用比较级来表达（这是重要语法评分点）

拿"big"举例：

A is bigger than B.

B is not as big as A.

更多表达方式：

A is much better/worse than B.

A is not nearly as good as B.

B is nowhere near as big as A.

A is not quite as important as B.

A is almost as important as B, but not quite.

In comparison to B, A is quite big./A is quite big in comparison to B.

Compared to B, A is a lot bigger.

使用对比方式来表达

____ is _____ but _____ is ____

Example: A is big but B is small.

例子中的形容词前可以添加副词，表达效果更好：A is quite big but B is rather small.

可以使用 “while” 或者 “whereas” 去替换 “but”，表达更加多样化。

该表达方式的语法评分绩点不及“比较级”，但是可以在语音语调评分绩点上有所斩获，同学们在说的时候要重读其中个别单词，给考官留下你有 “sentence level stress” 的好印象。例如（斜体字部分需重读）：*A* is quite *big* while *B* is rather *small*.

7. 表达最近改变

Example question: Has your hometown changed much in the past few years? (e.g. 20 years)

Yes, it has. For example...

表达结构及例句

______ is more ____ than it used to be

The air pollution is much worse/much better than it used to be.

...there are/is more_____ than there were/was...

Today there are many more cars on the roads than there were thirty years ago.

Compared to thirty years ago, _______ has + 过去分词

Compared to thirty years ago, the population of the city has increased by about two million.

______ has + 过去分词 + in the last thirty years

The population of the city has increased by about two million people in the last thirty years.

More _________ today + 现在时 + than was the case thirty years ago

More people today own a car than was the case thirty years ago.

Today ______ are + 现在分词 + whereas thirty years ago + 过去时

Today, more and more people are living in high-rise apartment buildings whereas thirty years ago, we had very few high-rise apartments buildings in our city.

More and more ________ are being + 过去分词 + nowadays but + 过去时 + thirty years ago

More and more large-scale supermarkets are being built nowadays but there were very few of them in my hometown thirty years ago.

8. 表达建议

Example questions: What would you suggest a visitor to your country see and do?

What do you think the government could/should do?

I'd (suggest, recommend, say, tell him/her/them)...

Maybe/Perhaps/Possibly... + could/should...

It might/may help if... + 动词过去式

It would probably + (be a good idea, be useful, help) if + 动词过去式

I suggest/recommend...

需要注意的是"would"经常用在此类问题及回答中，所以切记不要去使用"I will"来回答，要用"I'd..."

在suggest, recommend 后面可以跟动词原形：I'd suggest they visit... 也可以跟动名词：I'd suggest visiting...不需要代词。

注意I'd say只能用于第一种情况。

第四种表达方式比较难，举例说明如何使用：

What do you think the government could do about the pollution problem?

It would definitely help if the government encouraged alternate forms of electricity generation, such as wind farms and solar-power.

注意：后面要使用动词过去式，表示虚拟。同时"definitely"可以换成其他词，如"possibly", "probably", "certainly"。

有的时候考官在题目中不用"would"，这是在检测我们是否会合理使用"would"，你不用关系不大(如第五种表达方式)，用了更彰显语法实力！

举例说明：

Do you have any suggestions for foreigners who are thinking of visiting China?

a. I'd recommend/I'd suggest they visit the Great Wall and see the Terra Cotta Warriors in Xi'an.

b. I'd recommend/I'd suggest visiting the Great Wall and seeing the Terra Cotta Warriors in Xi'an.

9. 表达观点

Example question: Do you think that children should do some housework?

I think...

I feel...

I believe...

Personally, I (think/believe/feel)...

I tend to (think/feel/believe) that...

In my opinion...

In my view...

I've always (thought/believed/felt) that...

I maintain that...

I've always maintained that...

It seems to me that...

I'm convinced that...

As far as I'm concerned...

My view is that...

From my point of view...

To my mind...

The way I see it...

As I see it...

避免重复性表达“personally in my opinion”。

避免中式英语“in my eyes”，应该改成“in my view”。

在使用“maintain”表达观点的时候请注意，只有当你和别人就某观点进行过多次讨论之后，该词才有用武之地。也就是说，如果你头一次就某问题发表观点，最好不要使用“maintain”，比如“I never thought about it before, but I maintain...”这样的表达就不太合理，类似的有“I firmly believe”。

在表达中使用“strongly”“firmly”“honestly”“really”“personally”，效果更好。

同学们喜欢在表达观点的时候使用“frankly (speaking)”，但其实有时候并不太合理。在考官看来，这个词只适合用在当考生的答案让他觉得有点不太符合常规或者令人稍许意外的时候。如：“Who's your favourite film star?”“Frankly, I don't have a favourite film star because I don't often watch films.”类似的表达有“To bet honest”。不正确的情况是：“Frankly, I like living in a big house.”这种表达可能让考官觉得莫名其妙，因为喜欢住大房子很正常。

10. 给出某观点的原因

...because...

...since...

The main reason I say that is because...

One of the reasons I say that is because.../One reason I say that is because...

不要使用“as”“for”，这些词有些正式，而且说起来你会感觉非常不自然。

11. 解释

Example question: Why do Chinese people like riding bicycles?

One reason why...is because/is that...

One possible explanation (for that) is...

The reason why...is because/is that...

The main reason why...is because/is that...

To understand why...you first need to (understand/know/be aware that)...

Well, it's like this...

You could look at it this way...

如果表达确信的理由，可以在上面回答范例中的"is"前加上肯定副词，如"certainly is""definitely is""surely is"。

如果表达不太确信的理由，可以在上面回答范例中的"is"前加上猜测副词，如"possibly is""probably is""might be""may be""could be"。

12. 表达对现在或过去的推测

Example question: Do old people in China have opportunities to attend any forms of classes?

Well, I'm not sure but...

Well, I've never thought about that before but...

I imagine...

I guess...

I suppose...

I'd say...

既然不能确定，考生也可以使用这些表达："maybe""perhaps""possibly""probably""it's quite likely that...""it's quite possible that...""it's quite probable that...""may + V""might + V""could + V"（V = 动词原形）。

13. 表达对未来的推测（通常是相对于现在所发生的变化）

Example question: How do you think the way of communication (in China) will develop in the future?

I predict... + 名词

I (can) foresee... + 名词（+ 现在分词）

I imagine/suppose/guess...

...will + 副词（+ will）

...be (现在时) likely to...

...be (现在时) bound to...

...be (现在时) + going to + V (动词原形) = ...will + V (动词原形)

There'll probably/possibly be...

We might see/have...

...will be + 现在分词...

...might be + 现在分词...

I'd be surprised if + 过去时/过去进行时

I'll be very surprised if + 现在时/现在进行时

I expect...

上面回答范例中标注的"副词"指的是：definitely/certainly/probably/possibly等。

同学们在使用"will"的时候需要注意，它仅能用在特别确信的时候，举例："China's population will be bigger than it is now, thirty years from now." 以英语为母语的人在日常生活中使用will时一般是种承诺，如："I'll give you the money I owe you tomorrow." 所以，建议考生为了表达更加自然，可以考虑加上肯定副词："will definitely" "will certainly"，也可在表达前加上"I think" "I'm sure" "In my opinion" "I believe" 等。举例："I believe that twenty years from now, China will have no people living in extreme poverty."

"Be bound to" 意思是"必然"，已经表达出非常强烈的肯定意味，因此，在表达的时候不需要加上肯定副词如"absolutely"，否则会显得多余。

在表达将来的时候要尽量使用比较级，这是一个重要的高分语法要素，举例："In twenty or thirty years, people will almost certainly be living longer than they do now, due to advances in medical science."

"I foresee" 表示"我预见"，后面通常跟名词 + 现在分词或直接跟名词，举例："I foresee people working fewer hours per week in the future." 或者 "I foresee a decrease in the number of hours people work per week." (注意：是"people work"，不是"people will be working")

"I predict"和"I foresee"意思一致，但是后面经常跟上"will"，举例："I predict people will be working/will work fewer hours per week in the future." "I predict"后面也可以跟上名词，举例："I predict a decrease in the number of hours people work per week." ("people work" "people will be working" 在这里都是可以的)

回答范例使用了将来进行时，这是高分语法要素，举例："In twenty years, some people might be travelling to the moon for holidays."

回答范例："I'd be very surprised if people were still driving petrol-powered cars thirty years from now." 第13条的回答范例和第12条的回答范例可以互用，举例："I'll be very surprised if people are still driving petrol-powered cars thirty years from now." 这两种回答方式可以帮助考生在语法上获得高分。

当你在推测未来时，以下5条建议可以帮助你组织观点：

思考网络如何改变未来，举例：People will probably be buying many things on the Internet in the future and people will be studying more on the Internet.

发挥一下科学幻想能力，举例：flying cars or travelling to the moon for a vacation。这个方法对推测未来是非常有用的，但是同学们要记得使用"possibly" "maybe" "might"，而不是"will"。

思考最新的科技进步，然后推测未来，举例： cloning, genetic engineering, organ transplanting, wind and solar power, hydrogen-powered cars, electric cars, nanotechnology, robots, brain-wave controlled devices等。

思考"全球化"如何影响和改变未来，举例：As the world becomes more of a "global village", people will be interacting with foreigners a lot more, leading to probable changes in international law, politics, language, social customs, business etc.

14. 表达计划、打算及对未来的希望

Example question: What are your future work plans?

I hope to...

I'm going to...

My plan is to...

I plan on + V-ing (动名词)

I intend to...

My ambition is to...

My immediate goal is to...

My ultimate/final goal is to...

Ultimately...

Hopefully...

Ideally...

I expect to...

I'd like to... /I want to...

As an alternative, I might...

If all goes well, I'll/I should...

If everything goes according to plan, I'll/I should...

My dream is to...

It's always been my hope/plan/ambition/dream to...

My heart is set on + V-ing (动名词)

注意：不要说"I wish to"，太过于正式，如："I wish to study in the UK." 应该说："I hope to study in the UK." 或者用更为简单的表达："I'd like to study in the UK." "I want to study in the UK."

"going to" 和 "will" 有差别。"going to" 表达的是两层含义："I intend to" + "it almost certainly will happen"，如果不是特别肯定，就最好不要使用，比如这样的表达就欠妥："I'm going to get a degree in Accountancy in Australia." 因为很多事情都可能导致你拿不到学位。你可以说："I'm going to start my university studies in

Australia in February.” “will” 只有一层含义，就是“几乎肯定会发生”，但是没有“打算”的意思。

最好不要使用 “I want to” 表达计划或打算，因为它只能体现你的主观愿望，但不一定是客观计划安排。其次，这样的表达被很多考生过度使用了，影响词汇得分。

同样，在谈论未来时，不要使用 “can” 和 “must”，它们仅用于现在时，应该是“will be able to” 和 “will have to”。错误举例：“After I go to Canada I can practice more English.” 正确表达是：“After I go to Canada, I’ll be able to practice more English.” 同样道理，“When I arrive in Australia, the first thing I must do is finding a place to live.” 是不正确的，应该是：“When I arrive in Australia, the first thing I’ll have to do is finding a place to live.”

15. 阐明

My point is that...

What I mean is...

My meaning is...

In other words...

That is to say...

Let me put that another way...

To put that another way...

What I’m trying to say is...

More specifically...

For example...

For instance...

有同学喜欢使用 “that is to say”，但这个表达用在P1中稍显正式。这种表达一般在比较严肃的讨论环境下使用，所以更适宜在P3中使用。

16. 解释某词

I can’t remember the word but...

It’s something like...

It’s a thing that...

It’s a type of...

It’s something you...

He’s a person who...

It’s similar to...

It’s kind of like a...

例如，考试时你不知道该如何说榨汁机时，你可以采用此类表达方式：“It is a thing that you can use it to make juice.”

17. 表达“总体来说”

On the whole...

As a rule...

In general...

Generally...

Generally speaking...

For the most part...

Typically...

Usually...

使用此类表达时，记得使用现在时。

尽量在表达时使用复数名词，举例：“Usually, boys like to play computer games but girls prefer to go shopping.”

如果表达“我喜欢狗”，说“I like dog”是不对的，意思是“我喜欢吃狗肉”。应该是：“I like dogs.”再举例：“In general, dogs are friendlier than cats but cats are cleaner than dogs.”需要特别提醒的是，狗分很多种，所以在表达“总体来说”的时候需要加复数，但是你不可以说“I love pandas”，因为熊猫只有一种，可以说“I like the panda”(= “I like the panda species”)。

同学们在表达“总体来说”的时候，会习惯性地使用“有人说”，正确的表达是“(many) people say...”，而不是“someone said”，也不能使用“it is said”(过于正式，不适合雅思口语的自然交流环境)。

第6节　如何快速延展信息（解决该怎么说）

中国考生通常情况下在给出直接答案之后就不太清楚如何去延展信息，更别谈在延展信息的时候顾及评分点，多叔仔细研究分析以英语为母语的人的思维方式，总结出最适合中国考生的“四大黄金法则”，该“四大黄金法则”是四条思维通道，可以迅速激活考生的思维，让考生知道回答的方向，如果能够灵活使用，可以所向披靡。当然不否认还有其他延展信息的方式。

▶黄金法则之一：介绍

我们先来看看中国考生的普遍回答方式：

Do you like walking? Yes, I like it very much, because...

中国的雅思考生已经养成了一个习惯，延展信息的时候喜欢用“because”，这个词本身没有问题，但是如果频繁使用该词，则会显得思维单一，很难得到理想分数，特别是6.5分及以上。

下面我们来说明“介绍”这一黄金法则，它指的是在给出直接答案之后，可以采用进一步演绎的方式进行信息补充。首先，既然是演绎，那么描述主体会被重复，则要使用“which”或“this”等进行指代，这样同时就获得了语法绩点。然后我们来说明如何进行演绎。

1. 第一种介绍方式：修饰

其实考生脑中有很多想法，但是没有找到思路的突破口去激发这些想法。在很多情况下，考生面对陌生对象的时候（在考试中，考题中的主体对考生来说就是陌生对象，尽管有时候题目很熟，但是紧张会导致大脑一片空白，和碰到陌生话题无异），考生最容易想到的就是形容词。

(1) 表达模式：which is + (*adv.*) + *adj.*

Do you like walking? Yes, I like it very much, which I think is a gentle way to exercise my body.

（这是激活思维的一种方式，答案不一定总是这么短，后面会介绍四大黄金法则组合使用所锻造出的漂亮的句子）

Do you prefer texting or talking on the phone? My preference is texting, especially to my girl friend, which is more suitable for expressing my love.

(2) 专项练习

请用以下10个修饰词填空，使句子的意思合理且完整。（括号内为相关话题）

- Enjoyable
- Useful
- (More) Convenient
- (More) Economical
- Important

- Funny
- Helpful
- Picturesque/Eye-catching
- Awesome
- Meaningful

① A computer is an indispensable item in my life, which is fairly _____for me to deal with the school assignments. (Computer)

② I assume that protecting trees is our responsibility, which is extremely ______for maintaining an ecological balance. (Trees)

③ For children, cooking is a basic living skill, which is quite ______ for them to lead a better life in the near future. (Cooking)

④ Indeed, you do not need to go outside and can easily find a lot of goods with a lower price by shopping online, which is so _____for some young people who prefer staying at home almost all day long. (Shopping)

⑤ I often hang out shopping with my friends on weekends, which is very _________. (Spare time)

⑥ I love my hometown a lot, which is always ______ in every season. (Hometown)

⑦ For me, cycling is my favourite way to relax, which is also ______ for me to exercise my body. (Cycling)

⑧ I feel very interested in some TV commercials like the advertisements for KFC, which are always very______. (Advertisement)

⑨ I'm keen on watching comedies, for example "Mr Bean", which are entirely _____. (Movie)

⑩ I would like to take a bus to my workplace instead of driving my car, which is absolutely ______. (Transport)

参考答案

① useful ② meaningful ③ important ④ convenient ⑤ enjoyable ⑥ picturesque ⑦ helpful ⑧ funny ⑨ awesome ⑩ more economical

2. 第二种介绍方式：功能

在10余年雅思教学过程中，我发现考生在碰到话题后的高频反应是"功能"，举个简单例子，如果我问"Do you like sports?"一般都会说功能，比如对自己有什么好处。既然考生有这样的潜意识，那不妨在考前把这种潜意识练熟，并且总结出最可能成为答案的万能功能，这样考试时就会思维清晰，会减少语法错误（很多时候考生在考试时仍在想该怎么说，导致一些语法上的无心之错），而且会更有精力去思考比较好的词。

表达模式：which/this/these can enable/help/encourage/stimulate/push/allow me to do..., which/this/these (can) bring/give/offer/provide me...

举例：

Do you like travelling?

Yes, I do like travelling, particularly in modern cities like Shanghai or London, which enables me to see many kinds of skyscrapers.

What are the advantages of train travel?

Honestly speaking, the first good point is that train travel cannot be easily affected by weather; this helps me to carry out my plans smoothly.

更多例子：(括号内为相关话题)

I would recommend this job to people who majored in accountancy. This helps them to put their knowledge into practice. (Job)

I was very happy to choose my major. This gave me many chances to see a different world. (Major)

I am surrounded by all kinds of advertisements every day. Many of which can offer me a lot of reasons to buy something. (Advertisement)

Cooking programmes in my country are very interesting. These can provide you with many good ways to cook nice food. (Cooking)

I have a timetable in my mobile phone. This can allow me to make my schedule clear and reasonable. (Time management)

I use email almost everyday. This brings me a lot of new information from others. (Email)

I like receiving gifts from my family members. This encourages me to work harder and to have a better life. (Gift)

I used to be so fond of painting especially sketching animals and trees. This stimulated me to love nature. (Painting)

Being patient is absolutely important. This can enable me to calm down when something urgent happens. (Patience)

More and more trees are being cut down every minute and our environment is getting worse and worse which pushes us to protect trees in order to have a greener world. (Tree)

▶黄金法则之二：举例

1. 第一种举例方式（特征/分类举例）

特征/分类举例常用词语：especially, particularly, in particular

我们先看个例子：

Do you like flowers?

Yes, I love them very much, for example, roses and lilies.

中国考生一般都会这么回答，问题也不大，但是逻辑上并不是特别完整，如果想获得更高的分数，可参考下面回答：

Yes, I love them very much, especially those with a strong fragrance, for example roses and lilies.

这样的回答可以直接让考官看出你喜欢花是因为被花的某些具体特征吸引。逻辑上更加完整，更体现细节。

现在我们来学一学如何进行“分类/特征举例”，其实很简单，就是通过寻找题目主体的某一类特征，从而表达“你为什么喜欢，在什么情况下喜欢，在什么场合更适宜”等，使回答更体现你的个人看法，毕竟雅思P1考题绝大部分考查的都是你自己的信息。

举例：

Did you climb a tree when you were a child?

Yes I did. I used to love it so much especially in the summer time when trees were flourishing, so I can enjoy being cool in them.

Do you like watching TV programmes?

Yes, I do like watching TV programmes, I like variety shows in particular, like the “Chinese Talent Show”, because I really admire the humour of the TV presenter in it.

更多例子(括号内为相关话题)：

Do you like being busy? (Being busy)

Well, it really depends. Sometimes, I like being busy especially when I have low spirits, because I want to stop myself thinking bad things.

How do you get the news? (News)

My favourite way of getting the news is listening to the radio, especially when I am driving in the car.

Do you like the clothes you wear? (Clothes)

Yes, I love the clothes I wear, especially as someone told me they looked good on me.

Is it important to be polite? (Politeness)

Yes, I do believe it is very important, especially on some formal occasions, such as meetings or ceremonies.

When do you spend time with your family? (Family)

I usually spend time with my family members late in the day, especially after dinner. We often watch TV together.

Do you prefer to walk in the countryside or in the city? (Countryside)

I very much prefer walking in the countryside, especially those places with good scenery, and then I can feel totally relaxed.

What do you like to do in the sunshine? (Sunshine)

I like playing football or badminton in the sunshine, particularly with my best mates, simply because we all enjoy it.

Do you think it is important to relax? (Relaxation)

Yes, I do think so, especially when you feel quite tired. Without proper relaxation, you would feel very uncomfortable.

Do you ever ride a bicycle? (Cycling)

Yes I do, I ride bicycle almost every day, especially on the weekends.

Do people in your country like using mobile phones? (Mobile phone)

Yes, they do, in fact, a mobile phone has become a necessity in people's daily life, young people are especially fond of using mobile phones, mainly because they use mobile phones not just for contacting friends and family, but also for playing games or watching movies.

2. 第二种举例方式：回忆

考生在P1中很少使用过去时，主要是因为考生没有这样的意识，考官会觉得考生灵活使用时态的能力比较欠缺。"回忆"这种举例方式既可以激发思维，又容易获得语法评分绩点。为了能够做到这一点，考生要学会常见的表达过去的词组，如"used to""when + past tense""once"等，通过不断练习来形成习惯性思维。

举例：

What kind of music do you like best?

Now I'm very keen on rock music, actually I used to be addicted to classic rock bands.

Do you like birthdays?

Certainly. Last year, I had a wonderful birthday, because I received a car from my dad.

更多例子：(括号内为相关话题)

How do you take photographs? (Photograph)

I used to take photographs using cameras and I had to spend a lot of time developing films to get the photos. But now, I usually take photos on my phones, which is more convenient.

Do you think it is important to preserve memories? (Memory)

Yes, I think so, memories are always valuable and sweet, from which I often get happiness. When I was much younger, I liked writing diaries. Now, looking at them, I can feel the old days coming back to me.

What do you usually do with your relatives? (Relative)

I usually play chess with my relatives indoors, especially with my cousins, but, when we were children, we enjoyed playing outside, doing such things as catching dragonflies or climbing trees on sunny days.

Do you like toys? (Toy)

Absolutely, I like them; I still remember I got a big teddy bear from my auntie about 5 years ago, which made me jump for joy at that time.

Do you think the Internet is very helpful in learning history? (History)

Yes, it helps me a lot especially in terms of providing me with old pictures. Once I wanted to get some information about an important historical event and a good website gave me a lot of real pictures.

Which do you think is a more relaxing place to live, the city or the countryside? (Countryside)

Maybe the countryside, I grew up in the city and I find it too noisy sometimes, on the other hand the countryside is more peaceful. Once I spent a summer holiday with my grandpa in a small village, where I felt everything was very quiet. What's more, unlike the city, I did not see a lot of traffic there.

Do you prefer advertisements on TV or those in magazines? (Advertisement)

My preference is for watching advertisements in magazines especially those about sports. Once I saw a great picture in a magazine, which was advertising a brand of sport shoes. Compared with TV adverts I felt it was more real and I liked reading the words below it.

Who usually does cooking in your family? (Cooking)

Honestly speaking, my dad does most of cooking in my family. My mum cooked several times before, but after we tasted the food made by her, we all said we had had enough.

Are you ever late for anything? (Being late)

Yes, sometimes I sleep over in the morning. The last time it happened, I missed my flight. This was a good lesson for me.

How do you feel when you receive a letter or email? (Email)

I always feel very happy. Just because I know there is someone who remembers me. About 2 months ago I received a letter from my classmate who I haven't contacted for a long time. That letter made me feel very happy.

▶黄金法则之三：原因

很多同学在表达原因的时候习惯用“because”，如果频繁使用，表达就会显得非常单调，从而影响词汇丰富性的得分。

我们要学会以下丰富的表达方式，本书在前面function of language中也提到过。

Simply because...

Mainly because...

Partly because...

...since...

The main reason I like...is that it's...

What I like best about...is...

The thing I like best about...is...

The best/worst thing about...is...

I don't like...very much because it's too...

That's because I find it...

举例：

Do you think people will still write letters in the future?

Yes, I think they will simply because emails have no way to replace the emotion in a handwritten letter.

Is the Internet very popular in China?

Certainly the Internet is very popular in China now mainly because people are more willing to use the Internet for shopping or entertaining themselves. For example we have a famous website "Alibaba", where people are able to buy almost everything.

更多例子：(括号内为相关话题)

What is your favourite gift? (Gift)

I have received gifts before like toys and dolls. Among these the one which I liked best was a cute teddy bear. I liked it simply because I can cuddle it when I am sleeping at night.

Do you think children should learn drawing? (Drawing/Painting)

Yes I think so, mainly because drawing is a perfect way for them to develop their imagination. This is very useful in the process of growing up.

Is it important to be patient, and why?（Patience）

Absolutely. It is important partly because people can't get success easily without patience. For example, many students have had experience of making mistakes in a maths test, simply because they were not patient enough to read the questions correctly.

Do you often watch TV? (TV)

Not really, I don't have so much time to watch TV since I have to work overtime almost everyday.

Do you like swimming? (Swimming)

Yes I do. The main reason I like swimming is that it's very beneficial for shaping my figure which is so important for bigger girls like me.

Do you like to go to the forest? (Forest)

Well, I would say yes. What I like best about forest is that I can relax in that green world and enjoy the company of wildlife. Also I really fancy camping in the forest where you can see lots of stars in the night sky.

Do you like the news? (News)

Yes I like reading the news very much, especially international news. The thing I like best about the news is its constantly updating information, which helps me to catch up with the fast developing world.

What kind of clothes do you like? (Clothes)

I particularly like casual clothes like T-shirts and jeans. The best thing about them is that they make me feel more comfortable than wearing formal suit.

Do you like singing? (Singing)

No, I don't like singing very much because it's too difficult for me. It seems that I can't carry a tune.

What qualities make good friends? (Friendship)

It must be honesty. That is because honesty is very important at the start of a new relationship with other people, otherwise there will be a lot of misunderstandings.

▶黄金法则之四：曲折

很多考生在延展信息的时候，总是顺延着说下去，没有任何“曲折”，在逻辑上显得不是非常丰富。下面我来告诉大家如何使你的信息“曲折”，从而获得更多逻辑分数。

1. 假设

假设分成两种：

正假设：if I + 过去时 + I would (not)...

Do you live with your family?

Yes I do, now I am living with my parents, but if I had enough money I would like to rent a new house and live alone.

逆假设：without...I would (not)...

Are your friends very important to you?

Yes they are. Without them I would feel very lonely mainly because they are very nice and we have spent great times together in the past.

2. 转折

这里说的是广义转折：but/however, even though, otherwise, although/though, still, while, whereas, unless, in spite of/despite, except。

举例：

Do you like driving cars?

Absolutely. It is my favourite hobby even though I cannot drive well.

What do you like to do on sunny days?

I'd like to play sports on sunny days but when I have low spirits I prefer staying at home simply watching some TV.

更多例子: (括号内为相关话题)

What do you do in your spare time? (Spare time)

I often read my favourite novels that I can't spend any time on when I am very busy. Otherwise I would not have anything else to do.

Do you like taking photos? (Photograph)

Yes I do like taking photos especially scenery, even though I am not so good at it.

What kinds of news do you often read? (News)

I enjoy reading news about stories of people most of time, but sometimes if there are some important events like the Beijing Olympic games I will change my habits for a while.

Can you give advice to your friends about choosing clothes? (Clothes)

Yes, I think I can. Although I am not good at selecting my clothes I can sometimes give my friends some good advice.

Do you think family members should live together? (Family)

Yes, I think so. Family members should live together to take care of each other. However, I prefer to live by myself but relatively close to my family members.

Do you prefer to spend time with your family or your friends? (Family)

My preference is spending time with my friends simply because we have a lot of things in common. On the other hand it is not bad to have some time with my family. I can feel the love from them that makes me happy.

Do men and women relax in the same way? (Relaxation)

No, I don't think so. Men prefer to do some sports like playing football or basketball whereas women like to go shopping or travelling.

Do you often ride a bicycle? (Cycling)

Not really. I don't ride my bicycle very often unless I have to do a short trip to the countryside with my friends. We often choose to cycle rather than go by car.

When did you get your first mobile phone? (Mobile phone)

Actually I got my first mobile phone when I was a first year student in college despite it was very expensive. I bought it without any hesitation, because I liked its design.

Do you like dancing? (Dancing)

Honestly speaking no. I don't like it at all. I almost never dance except on some special occasions like at a ball or a party.

第7节　如何快速寻找观点和词汇（解决该说什么）

很多考生在雅思考试前针对话题准备了大量的观点和词汇，结果到考试的时候脑子经常一片空白，究其原因，主要是考生记观点和词汇的时候，脑子并没有真正去吸收。那我们如何在备战雅思口语的时候迅速找到合适的观点和词汇，并且能够在考场上自由发挥呢？下面来介绍两个神器“人本论”“人存论”，可以帮考生搞定这个难题。

人本论：我们可以通过人类的感官作为寻找观点的思维端口：“眼睛”“耳朵”“鼻子”“嘴巴”“手脚”“头脑”“心灵”。

拿一道雅思考题举例：Do you like living by sea?

从视觉角度考虑：I really like the spectacular beauty of the sea.

从嘴巴角度考虑：If I lived by sea, I would be so excited that I could eat a lot of seafood.

从手脚角度考虑：I would like to jog along the coast with my lover.

通过该种思维方式，很多话题之间是相通的，不用再准备大量的观点和词，如近期考题：“Do you like going to the forest?”将上面观点稍加改变就可以形成这道题的延展信息，如：“I really like the spectacular beauty of the forest.”

人存论：通过“人所在乎的东西”这个思维角度激活大脑：我们在乎“美丽”“健康”“环境”“情谊”“效率”“金钱”“意义”。

以一道较难的考题为例：Do you like fashion?

从美丽角度考虑：It can make me look more attractive to others.

再举个例子：Does your name have any special meaning?

从意义角度考虑：It stands for brighter future, which is fairly auspicious.

当然了，在寻找观点的时候，“人本论”“人存论”可以混合在一起使用，这样容易使答案变得丰富。

举例：Do you like parties?

从人本论“嘴巴考虑”：I especially like parties with great food.

从人存论“情谊考虑”：It can perfectly strengthen our friendship.

考生在使用的时候，可以结合前面的“四大黄金法则”，这样延展信息将会变得丰富精彩，饱含得分点。

如何结合“四大黄金法则”“人本论”及“人存论”？

在学完第6节、第7节之后，考生应该非常清楚“该怎么说”和“该说什么”，下面我们通过高频难题“rain”为例，来进一步说明如何高质量完成P1问题的作答。

Do you like rainy days?

Yes, I like rainy days. I love the smell of the ground after it rains (嗅觉) and I can see the rain sparkling on the leaves of the trees (视觉) which (修饰) is so enjoyable (心灵).

What do you often do in rainy days?

On rainy days, especially (特征) when I am free at home，I love to curl up (手脚) on the sofa with a good book by my favourite author Samor and listen to (听觉) some soft music. But thinking back to my childhood，I used to (回忆) like playing with my classmates in the rain and doing something like running and catching (手脚) .

第8节 官方高频题库及高分参考范文

▶Name

Do you like your name?

Yes. I like my name very much. It's a very traditional Chinese name which was given to me by my parents. My name means "Good Luck". In China we like to give names that have special meanings.

Does your name have any special meanings?

Yes. My name means "Happy" in Chinese. My parents chose this name, hoping I would have a happy life. I really like my name very much and I think it helps me to smile every day.

Who gives names in China? What's the tradition of giving names?

In general the parents choose names for their baby. But, of course, sometimes the grandparents want to get involved. This is probably the same all over the world.

Are you willing to change your name? Why?

No. I love my name and I don't want to change it. My name was a gift from my parents so it is important to me. Even though my friends call me by the short version or my nickname, my mum always calls me by my full name. How could I change it?

What meanings do the nicknames of Chinese children have?

Most children in China have a nickname. Sometimes our parents or relatives might give us one or our classmates at school might give us a nickname. Sometimes they can be funny or affectionate although some like "Fatty" might be hurtful. Despite this some nicknames can bestow blessings on the child.

In your country, do people feel that their name is very important?

Nearly every Chinese name carries a meaning, so in our tradition names are very important. A name may bestow blessings on a child or be given in order to influence his or her personality and demeanour. Like my name means "Happy" and I think I am a happy girl because of it.

Is it easy to change your name in your country?

Well I have never heard of anyone changing their name unless they haven't told anyone about it. I think I would have to talk to my mum and dad about it and I'm sure they would want to dissuade me from going down that road. Then I would have to go to the police station to change my registration. I think it would be very difficult to do.

What names are most common in your hometown?

Well, let me see. A lot of boys are called Da in my hometown. This means they will achieve things very well. But many boys will probably not live up to their name. Whereas a lot of girls are called Fang which means they have a nice smell or fragrance. So this is a most appropriate name for a girl.

▶ *House/ Flat/ Apartment*

Do you live in a house or a flat?

I live with my parents in a rented apartment in downtown Nanjing. We have lived there for about three years now and I must say it's very convenient for work and of course for shopping. I'm a shopaholic so its great to live so close to the malls.

Do you prefer to live in a house or a flat?

Well. I have never lived in a house so I can't really say. Although my grandparents live in a house at the moment with a nice garden and I really enjoy it when I am there. So maybe one day I would like to live in a house like they do. But maybe that's a pipe dream because I'm such a city girl. I'll never leave the city.

Why do you like your home?

Oh my home is so nice. My parents buy such nice things and I have my own bedroom. They even allow me to choose my own decorations. Also it is downtown so I can always go out to meet my friends and go shopping. I am such a shopaholic that it's great to be so close to the malls. But it is always nice to get home to relax in my comfy room.

Which room do you like best in your home?

My bedroom is by far my most favourite room in my home. It's so comfy. My parents have allowed me to decorate it to my own taste. So I have everything that I need, a TV, an iPod, my games machine and my computer. So in fact I can work, rest and play there.

Do you have a plan to move to a new house or flat in the future?

Well, of course, my mother and father will make that decision as I still live at home. But at the moment my father and mother work in the downtown area and as far as I know they have no plan to move. Anyway I love living in the downtown area, it is so convenient.

What do you think could be added to your flat?

If I had a million dollars, a swimming pool could be added to our flat because I love swimming so much. But that is a bit of a pipe dream. However, at the moment, we could do with a second bathroom. In the morning we are all busy getting ready and running in and out of the bathroom which often makes us late.

Do you know your neighbours? Is it good to know your neighbours?

Our neighbours are the best of the lot. We've known them since we moved in. On the day we moved in they came around to welcome us to the apartment block and since then they have been our firm friends. The main reason I like them is that they are always dropping tasty snacks off for me. So yes, it's good to know our neighbours.

Do you prefer young or old neighbours?

I think the best places are where there is a mix of young and old people. Even though some people might think young people might be noisy and loud provided they respect the other neighbours, as they need somewhere to live too. So we all need to live together and help each other, live and let live is what I say.

▶ *Your Hometown*

Where is your hometown? How long have you been living there?

I'm from XX which is in XX province. All my family are from this province. I lived there until 20XX when I moved away to go to college. When I go back I look forward to seeing the old familiar places and hearing the joyful sounds of my town/city. They say home is where the heart is and you know, they are right.

Is your hometown famous for anything?

Yes, my hometown is famous for the local food/scenery/attraction. People come to my hometown just to enjoy eating the food/enjoying the scenery/visiting the attraction. So most weekends the streets are buzzing with tourists and locals enjoying themselves and bringing the streets alive.

No. I must say my hometown isn't famous for anything in particular. But that doesn't matter to me. Actually I prefer it that way. I like to go out to meet my friends at the places we like. Nobody bothers us. So personally, I think my hometown is famous so no matter what anyone thinks it's famous enough for us.

What do you like most about living in your hometown (or, about living where you are living now)?

When I am in my hometown I love catching up with my friends and family. But when I am back in my own home in XX I love being near the shops and hanging out at my regular haunts, having coffee, chatting with my friends. But on balance I would say my hometown is the best.

Do you like your hometown?

Yes. Of course I love my hometown. I have lived most of my life there so it has many special memories for me. They say home is where the heart is and it's true. Whenever I can I try to get back there. Even though it's a bit of a trek on the train, it's worth while just to be able to see my parents and friends.

Would you say it's an interesting place?

If you came to my hometown you would find plenty of places to keep you occupied. I might be a little bit biased having been born there but it is an interesting place. There are many popular restaurants in the downtown area and some beautiful parks and lakes where you can take a stroll. Then you can visit some of the old buildings and temples and hang out there for a while. I don't think you will be bored.

What would you say are the good points and the bad points of your hometown?

In my town the people are always so friendly. If you have a problem you will always be helped with a smile and a laugh. So in my opinion that's always a good point. As for the bad points, well the air pollution is worse than it was, compared to when I was a kid.

Did your friends grow up in the same place as you?

My oldest and best friends all grew up in my hometown with me and we went to school together, played together, laughed and cried together. Some of my oldest friends are now even going out or are getting married but such is life. But of course I have moved away to college and here I have also made good friends who I like very much.

Would you like to live there in the future?

That's a difficult question. Obviously I am taking this test because I want to study abroad. After completing that study I don't know what the future might hold for me. My life might take me to many places both abroad and here. But I do know, that like millions of other Chinese people, I will always come back to my hometown and parents for the Spring Festival because after all home is where the heart is.

▶ *Work or Studies*

Do you work or are you a student?

I'm currently a university student. I'm studying at XX and my major is XX. Obviously as I'm taking this test I want to continue my studies at a foreign university. So it would seem like I will be a student for many years to come yet. So I hope to work things out here and get my future started.

I'm still a high school student and I'm at XX high school in XX. I'm hoping to continue my studies in a foreign university which is why I'm taking this test. Although I will have to leave home and my parents I really do want to get a good education so that I can get a good job later in my life. So I know I will have to work like a dog to get what I want, but I'm ready.

I am currently working. I have been working for the last XX years. But now I want to continue my studies. This is why I am taking this test so that I can gain entrance to a UK university to get my Master's degree/PhD. So my work is cut out for me. Then hopefully I can get a better job and who knows where the experience will take me.

▶ *Your Work*

What job (or what work) do you do? What do you do in that job?

I am currently working as a marketing manager for an Organic Farm in Changzhou. My job is to promote organic vegetables and to help sell the produce in boxes which are delivered to the customer's homes. It is a challenging job and I have to work my fingers to the bone, but I love it.

Why did you choose to do this kind of work (or job)?

First I wanted to work in marketing. I though I would be able to use my flair for photography and art. So I chose this as my degree major. Then I became more and more interested in healthy living and healthy food. Then I found this position at the organic farm and I have worked hard and become a manager. I think I am really cut out for this work as I love it.

Would you recommend the job to other people?

Yes. I think marketing is fascinating. To sell products you have to be aware of current trends, how people react to things. You have to have a creative and arty side too. So it's a very good set of skills to develop. Plus the work is always changing and it's always very interesting. I never really work up a sweat but it is demanding.

▶ *Your Studies*

Do you like your major?

Do I like my major? No! I love it! I really do love my major and in particular the subject matter and I really like the new friends I have made at university/college/school. But I'm afraid I don't like the work. We are just so busy all the time. I'd prefer to be a party person but I have to buckle down and do the work. Even though I know it's a student's job to be busy and to work hard, sometimes I would appreciate just a little bit of downtime. I can remember being a high school student and thinking how life would be easy at university. What a mug I was. But I know that if I work hard then my future will be good and I will be able to enjoy my life more.

Is that a popular major in your country?

I think as the country has developed, marketing has become much more popular. Everything we buy is now marketed to the max. So it's a very big industry which is getting bigger and bigger so more and more students are doing it as a major. So when I graduate I think anything will be possible.

Is it difficult to learn your major?

I don't think it's particularly difficult to learn the nuts and bolts of marketing. But you also need to have some flair, some artistic skills and to be able to think creatively. I think if you do not have these then you might find the marketing major difficult.

Do you think it's important to choose a subject you are interested in? Why?

Of course. I think if you were not interested in a subject then why would you do it? For example if your parents pushed you into a particular course, say law or medicine, you might just lose interest and be bored silly. Then you might become a very bad doctor or lawyer and be unhappy all of your life. Why do you waste your time? Do something you enjoy.

What's the most enjoyable part of being a student?

I have to say that the most enjoyable part of being a student is making new friends. I have met many nice new people and we can hang out, have dinner, or go for coffee and chat. You know we are students and we want to change the world so sometimes we chat very late into the night. I love chatting. It makes me feel so special.

For you, what's the most interesting part of your course/subject/class?

I have to say the most interesting part of my subject is the photography option. I love taking photos and I have my camera with me always. In fact I always carry two, sometimes, three cameras. When I was a kid I was fascinated with my dad's camera. He gave it to me when he got a new one. I became a bit of a shutterbug. Now if I see something interesting then I can take the shots and maybe use them in my course work. So I can use my hobby to benefit my course work. In the future I am sure I will continue to take photographs, even if by then it's no longer part of my chosen career.

What's the most interesting subjects at school?

The most interesting subjects for me at school have been my ESL classes. We have a great foreign teacher from the UK. He is so funny but he is a good teacher and he always teaches us some interesting things. So apart from English, of course, he also teaches us a thing or two about the World and the West.

What are your future work plans?

Do I have any idea about my future work plans? Well that's a difficult question to answer completely. Obviously I am trying to go to a foreign university and who knows where that will lead me, which in itself is very exciting. When I was at high school I was pretty sure about what I wanted to do after my university studies. But now, so many doors seem to be opening and I have so many choices. Things are available that I didn't even know about back then. Nevertheless, I think my parents would like me to work back here in China and raise a family and do those traditional things. But you know China is changing and so are we—the young people. The world is becoming our oyster too.

Who do you think is more important the, the students or the teacher?

I think students and teachers are both important, but in different ways. For instance I had very good classmates back in my high school. And now my student friends influence my social life. I look forward to being friends with them probably for all of my life. I had a wonderful teacher at high school who really helped me and showed me the ropes. He really encouraged me to work hard. Now, at the moment, I have to say some of the university teachers are not so encouraging. I hope that in the coming years, if I'm lucky, I will get different and better teachers.

Is there anything special about your teachers and classmates in this major?

Some of my teachers and classmates are very special. Some of my teachers have been high-flying professionals before they came to this university to teach us. At the moment a few of them have books being published and are big shots in this area. This is really exciting for me. My classmates are special too. Many are great talents in themselves. I hope that in the future I will still be friends with them. We can meet up in say five years and see if we have been as successful as we think we will be.

How should teachers teach?

I think teachers should teach by example. A good teacher will shape the students' life. When I was at high school I had a teacher who shaped my life before I had even thought about university. Now my teacher is a great influence. I can sit all day and just listen to her talk. I think I am a bit star-struck to be honest. I hope that, after my graduation, I will become a good teacher like her and help to improve my student's lives, like she has mine.

Will children tell their parents if they face difficulties in their studies?

If children have difficulties in their studies they should tell their parents. But I can remember when I had some difficulties in Maths at high school, I was so embarrassed. I just couldn't tell my parents. I felt like a dunce. Then of course it was the teacher who told my parents I had a problem so the result was a million times worse of course. Now I think children should tell their parents their difficulties right away. But kids will be kids and they will keep these things secret. I hope that when I have children they will feel safe and loved enough to come and talk to me about their problems at school. But that might just be a pipe dream.

Do you think it is good for teachers to praise the students when they do something good and point it out when they do something wrong?

Surely it is the main point of being a teacher to praise good work done by students and help them when they go wrong. I can remember at high school there was a teacher who always pointed out my mistakes. He never praised me. I didn't want to go to his class—I was wilting under his constant criticism. Now my teachers at university are quick to praise us to the skies but also quick to help us when a problem arises. Even though I had such a bad experience at high school I still respect teachers for what they do for us. I hope that in the future, my children will have an encouraging teacher, unlike the teachers who did me down.

What subjects are you studying?

The subject I am studying is Business and Marketing. I am mainly focusing on the marketing aspect of the course. I have been fascinated by adverts and how brands market themselves since I was a little kid. At the moment, as the media explodes around us and brands jostle for a market position it's a bit of a cash cow. This is a very exciting field to be in. I can see myself, in a few years, having a very good job from studying this course. I hope it will bring me success in my life.

Why do you choose to study that?

I chose to study Marketing because since I was a kid I have been fascinated by the adverts on TV. They drew me in and to be honest I was a bit hypnotised by them. I can remember always hassling my mum for brand-name clothes and shoes. I was a little devil in that way. Now I can understand the psychology behind the adverts and I can see how they entrance me. In the future I hope to work for a big advertising agency and hopefully one day I will see my adverts on the TV too.

What school or university do you go to now?

The university I go to now is XX. It is considered to be one of the best visual arts universities in the country. I can remember reading about it when I was at high school and asking the teachers opinions about it. They thought it was out of my league but I really wanted to get here. So now I am really glad that I worked so hard and proved those teachers were wrong. In the future if some young person asks me for my opinion about a place I will be encouraging and tell them: "Look at me, I did it, I got to a good university when no one believed I could do it."

How long have you been going to that school/studying your subjects?

I've been going to my school for three years now. I have almost completed my studies. I can't really believe it, the time has flown by and soon I will have to leave. I can remember my first day here; it just seems like yesterday when I stepped through the front door. But now I have to consider my future. I am studying hard to try and pass this IELTS test so that I can go abroad to study. If I pass I know that I can go to London to the University of my choice and hopefully get my Master's degree.

Do you like studying at that school/university?

Do I like studying at my university? No. I love it! I can remember the first day I got here I felt like a little kid. I was just a small fish in a big pool. Perhaps I was a little out of my depth too. But now I am so happy to be here. My life is great and I have some great friends. I know that in the future my classmates will also be my best friends. We will keep in touch via electronic media and I am sure that we will bump into each other professionally too.

What's the most important thing/part of your study life?

The most important part of my study life is the ability to do my own thing. I can remember at high school being so frustrated by the teacher's inflexibility. You had to do it in his way or nothing. It was like talking to a brick wall sometimes. Now the teachers give us free rein to allow us to explore our creativity. It is so liberating. In the future I will remember these lessons and the freedom these teachers gave us. I know it will influence my work a lot and I hope to be able to pass on those values too.

▶ *Advertisements*

Are there many advertisements in your country?

Yes there are many advertisements in my country. They surround us and the social media bombards us daily nonstop. I am totally fed up with the number of advertisements that pop up on my phone and computer. I might be looking at the past through rose-tinted glasses, but I can't remember it being like this, even in my young life. As I go home daily there are even adverts on the side of the road, huge billboards. In the future, I believe it will be worse, especially if the government doesn't stop it. We will just get swamped with so many adverts.

Why do you think there are so many adverts now?

I think there are so many adverts now because the market in China has exploded now. There are literally pots of money to be made and everyone wants a slice of the pie. I can remember when it wasn't like this. Of course consumerism hadn't really taken off when I was a kid. Now there's so much stuff to buy and the manufacturers need to sell it to make a profit. In the future I can see it getting worse. Adverts might even be fed straight into your brain through some strange high-tech device. That's a really terrible thought.

Where are the various places we can see adverts?

Adverts are everywhere. They are not just in "various places" they are simply everywhere, in my pocket, on my phone, on the big screens downtown, popping up on my computer, they are like a deadly virus infecting our lives. I don't think it was like this when I was a kid. I can remember adverts on the TV and some of them were even funny. But now there's a sort of clinical feel to them.

Just walking through the downtown area I am stuck by the visual and noise pollution that these big screens create. I think in the future it will be worse. We will not be able to stop adverts from ruining our lives. It will be like some sci-fi hell.

How do you feel about advertisements?

How do I feel about advertisements? We have a saying in China—mǎma hū hū which means something like “it’s tolerable” or “so so”. So I think in the main adverts are tolerable. At best they are just noise, at worse they are a pain in the butt as they pop up all over my computer or phone screen. I am sure that when I was a kid there were not so many adverts. I just saw a few on TV. But now you cannot get away from them. They infect my life like a bad virus. In the future it will just get worse. Like on some movies when the adverts start to talk to you as they recognize your face. That will be some sort of hell.

What kinds of advertisements do you like the most?

Well if I have to choose which adverts I like the most I would have to say the ones with pretty girls/handsome boys! When they come on I’m caught like a fish in the net and I just have to watch. I can’t help myself. When I was young I used to like some breakfast cereal adverts, some of them were so funny with cartoon animals and stupid kids. They were fun. Now I can take them or leave them, apart from the ones with beautiful people in. I know that I will never have a lifestyle like they portray—fast cars, holidays and jets. But for three minutes maybe I can just dream a little.

Do advertisements (ever) influence your choice about what to buy?

I guess that adverts do influence what I choose to buy although I’m reluctant to admit that. I like to think I stand out from the crowd and am not one of the herd but at the end of the day sometimes I go with the flow. I am sure I never used to be this conscious of what I should be buying or not buying. But I guess when I was young adverts were not so powerful and truthfully there just wasn’t so much choice either. So sometimes adverts make choosing something easier. Like just today I needed a new phone and you know iPhone is advertised heavily here so I got one. I am so gullible. Maybe in the future I will try to think about what I should buy and not let the adverts make my mind up for me.

Do you like adverts on TV?

Sometimes the adverts on TV are so funny that they are better than some programmes. So yes I do like them. I prefer them to be funny or have good-looking girls/boys in them. That makes me a bit shallow, right? But I can remember when I was a kid liking the cereal adverts on the TV. Some of them were like crazy cartoons or had wacky kids in them. Just today I saw some cool adverts for cars on my TV over breakfast. But for me that’s in the future. I won’t be buying a car until I’ve graduated and been in work for a while. So it will be interesting to see what the adverts are like then when I consider buying a car for real.

Do you prefer advertisements on TV or those in magazines?

If I have to state a preference for adverts on TV or in magazines I guess I would have to plump for those on TV. When I was younger I would occasionally look at some magazines but now I really don't read much printed media. Whereas now, I probably watch TV every day. Just this morning I watched TV over breakfast. Some of the adverts on TV nowadays are as funny as TV programmes. Some day I will even look forward to going home, switching on the TV and hoping my favourite ad will come on. But I can take it or leave it really.

What do you think is the purpose of advertisements (or advertising)?

Clearly the purpose of advertising is to sell products and make money. But I think it's all got a bit out of hand now. Everywhere you go there is advertising, it's on my phone, on the Internet, it's everywhere. You can't escape it. In the past it wasn't so bad. I can't remember being so bombarded with messages. Every day I have to clear my phone of many spam messages. I think that it will get worse in the future. Who knows how bad it will get.

What sorts of adverts leave the deepest impression on people?

The types of adverts that leave the deepest impression on people are often those which don't seem like adverts at all. I think the cleverest adverts are those which we actually wear. Sometimes I feel like a walking billboard. All my clothes are branded. So my Nike trainers are really a free advert for the company. I never realised this when I was young. I used to pester my parents for these branded goods without realising that because my mates had them. I was being advertised to. Now, of course, I know what's happening, but I can't seem to break free of the influence. In the future I will try and resist this temptation and if I can I will buy some non-branded goods.

▶ *Major*

What is your major?

The major I am studying is Business and Marketing. I am mainly focusing on the marketing aspect of the course. I have been fascinated by adverts and how brands market themselves since I was a little kid. At the moment, as the media explodes around us and brands jostle for a market position it's a bit of a cash cow. This is a very exciting field to be in. I can see myself, in a few years, having a very good job from studying this course. I hope it will bring me success in my life.

Do you like your major?/Are you interested in your major?

Do I like my major? No! I love it! I really do love my major and in particular the subject matter and I really like the new friends I have made at this university/college/school. But I'm afraid I don't like the work. We are just so busy all the time. I'd prefer to be a party person but I have to buckle down and do the work. Even though I know it's a student's job to be busy and to work hard sometimes I would appreciate just a little bit of down time. I can remember being a high school student and thinking how life would be easy at university. What a mug I was. But I know that if I work hard then my future will be good and I will be able to enjoy my life more.

Why did you choose your major?

I chose to study Marketing because when I was a kid I can remember being fascinated by the adverts on TV. They drew me in and to be honest I was a bit hypnotised by them. I can remember always hassling my mum for brand-name clothes and shoes. I was a little devil in that way. Now I can understand the psychology behind the adverts and I can see how they entrance me. In the future I hope to work for a big advertising agency and hopefully one day I will see my adverts on the TV too.

What are the most interesting part of your major?

I have to say the most interesting part of my major is the photography option. I love taking photos and I have my camera with me always. In fact I always carry two, sometimes, three cameras. When I was a kid I was fascinated with my dad's camera. He gave it to me when he got a new one. I became a bit of a shutterbug. Now if I see something interesting then I can take the shots and maybe use them in my course work. So I can use my hobby to benefit my course work. In the future I am sure I will continue to take photographs, even if by then it's no longer part of my chosen career.

What are the advantages and disadvantages of your major?

If I were to tell you of all the good and bad things about my major we could be here all day. So I will keep it brief and just give you the highlights. The good things about my major apart from the subject matter are the friends I've made. When I was at high school I was scared I would have no friends when I moved. But now I have friends I know will last a lifetime. The bad things? Well there's too much. Sometime we work like dogs running here and there to different classes. I long for the summer holidays when I can lie back in the sun somewhere and just relax. But even that is a bit of a pipe dream because of the work we have to do.

Will you take up a job related to your major?

Will my major lead me to a job? Well that's a difficult question to answer completely. Obviously I am trying to go to a foreign university and who knows where that will lead me, which in itself is very exciting. When I was at high school I was pretty sure about what I wanted to do after my university studies. But now, so many doors seem to be opening and I have so many choices. Things are available that I didn't even know about back then. Nevertheless, I think my parents would like me to work back here in China and raise a family and do those traditional things. But you know China is changing and so are we—the young people. The world is becoming our oyster too.

What is the best time of a day for you to study?

The best time of a day for me to study is at night. I'm a night owl. I do all my best work in the early hours of the morning. I don't know why. When I was at high school you know I had to do my work when I was told to do it, even my homework. Now at university I have a free hand in organising my time. I think night-time is best for me. My dorm is as quiet as a grave and I can concentrate. There's no chitchat from my friends either to distract me. But I do look forward to the time when I can get a good night's sleep but until then I'll still burn the midnight oil.

▶ *Food and Cooking*

Who does the cooking at home? Why?

You know this might come as a surprise but my dad does most of the cooking at home. When I was a kid I can remember him doing the cooking and he has always done it. But when my grandma visits dad does give up and lets her do it. This makes us laugh because she totally reorganises his kitchen, which drives him as mad as a hatter. My dad is a good cook though and when I get home today I know there will be delicious food waiting for me. You know when I have a kid I will make sure that he learns how to cook so that he can cook for his family too.

What do you think of cooking programmes in China?

Cooking programmes in China are really popular on TV now. I can remember when I was a kid I hardly saw a cooking programme, but if there was one on I would sit and watch it. Now cooking programmes are all over the TV like a rash. I was even watching one this morning while I was having breakfast. I'll keep watching them because I can always learn something and one day, if I get around to it, I might cook one of those dishes.

When was the first time you cooked anything? What did you cook?

When I was a kid and was staying with my grandma during the summer, I cooked for the first time. The dish I cooked was tomato and egg which was my favourite food at the time; I ate it all the time. Now I think I am a pretty good cook. Although I am a bit of a lazy bones and tend to eat out a lot rather than cook at home. But when I have a kid I know that I will teach him or her to cook. It's an important skill for them to learn.

What food did you like to eat when you were a child?

My favourite food when I was a child was tomato and egg. I used to eat it all the time. My mum said she used to despair sometimes because all I would eat was tomato and egg. She said if I didn't get it I was a terror. Nowadays kids want to eat KFC and fast food like that. But I think our traditional food is best. It's more tasty and healthy too. When I have a kid I will teach him/her to cook and I hope they love tomato and egg as much as I still do.

Do you think it's good to take a child to restaurants?

Children can go to restaurants but in my opinion they should not go to restaurants like KFC and McDonald's. In my view these restaurants are unhealthy for children plus the kids do not learn any manners about eating. When I was a child I was never taken to restaurants such as these. We always went to traditional eateries to eat healthy food. Nowadays it's common to see children in restaurants. When I have a child I will always take them to different restaurants so they can learn about different food and how to have good manners.

Do you think it's important to cook at home? Why?

It's very important to cook at home for many reasons. I can remember in my parent's house we rarely went out for a meal. We ate at home and my mum or my grandma cooked. Now I tend to go out to eat more often but I do still cook at home. I am a bit of a lazybones sometimes and it's nice to pop out to the local eateries to grab a bite. When I have a kid I am sure that I will stay at home more and cook for my family. I can be a real homebody too.

What are the features of home-made food?

Everybody thinks that homemade food is the best. Well let me tell you that depends on the cook. If the cook is ham-fisted and a sloppy Joe then the food will be bad. I can remember going to one of my relatives during the Spring Festival to eat. When we ate, the food was almost inedible. On the other hand my grandma is the most incredible cook and like many women of her age, she can make a silk purse out of a sow's ear. With the minimum of ingredients she can make exquisite meals. I just hope that when I am her age I will be able to cook like her too.

What kind of food is popular in your country?

The most popular food in my country apart from rice would have to be dumplings. We all eat dumplings. When I was a kid we ate dumplings every day I think. Or so it seemed to me. I loved those dumplings made by my Grandma. Nowadays some Western food is becoming more popular. I even had KFC today. KFC is a very popular destination for Chinese people to snatch a bite to eat. But this kind of fast food is not so healthy. But I think in the future we will see more of Western influence in the food we eat and if we are not careful, we might lose a taste for our own traditional food.

Do different people in different places like different kinds of food?

China is a very big place with lots of different people eating different styles of food. I have relatives in Sichuan who like spicy foods. I can remember visiting them when I was a kid. When I ate I used to think my tongue was going to be burnt out of my mouth. In the southern part of the country the food is a little sweeter. I prefer to eat food that is not so spicy perhaps because I still remember those trips to Sichuan when I was a kid. But in my holidays I look forward to trying different cuisines and different tastes. If I can I will often search out those restaurants that claim to offer local home-cooked food just to taste the differences.

Who usually does the cooking in your family/at your home?

Usually my dad does the cooking in my family. Both my mum and dad are busy people but he just loves to cook. When I was a kid my grandma used to do most of the cooking but now she is a bit old. So my dad took over. I do love my dad's cooking though. He likes to make spicy food which I love. I often give him a hand because I want to learn to cook like him too. I hope that when I have kids we can cook together like my dad and me.

Did you learn to cook when you were younger/when you were a child?

I learnt to cook when I was a child at my home, usually my dad loves to cook. So I can remember right from being a kid I have given him a hand with the cooking. At first I was just his bottle washer, but gradually he gave me more and more things to do. Now I think I am a good cook and love to make special dishes for the family. I hope that when I have a kid we will cook together just like my dad and me.

In the future do you think you will be cooking more than you do now, or less?

I think I will be cooking more in the future. At the moment I'm a student and I live in a dorm. Having no cooking facilities, I always eat in the canteen or in a restaurant. In the future I hope to have a family so I can cook for my husband/wife and my child. When I have a family we will have to be careful with our money and not fritter it away by going to restaurants. Of course home cooking is not only cheaper but also much healthier for us all.

What kind of food do you think is healthy?

The kinds of food I think are healthy are fruit and vegetables. We all know you should have at least five of these every day. I can remember my mum getting frustrated when I was a kid and did not want to eat any vegetables. I only wanted to eat junk food. Now I see kids in KFC and McDonald's eating all that stuff and they are getting fat. When I have a kid I will make sure they eat healthy food and know what's good for them.

Do you think Chinese people's diet is healthy?

I do think that the Chinese people's diet is healthy. We love vegetables, fish and chicken and we never eat too much. I can remember the lovely healthy food my grandma used to make. But now I despair at seeing all the people in places like KFC eating all this fast food. Even the kids are getting fat now. We should stick to healthy diet or we will have the same obesity problems as Western countries.

Will you change your diet habit?

I think I would like to stick to my habit of eating Chinese food and not change. I think it is a healthy diet. I remember that I have been to a few Western style restaurants with some Western student friends. The food was OK I suppose, but I'm not really a fan. I don't like fast food like KFC either. I just love home-cooked food like my grandma makes. I hope in the future I can cook the traditional dishes just like her.

Do you like tasting new food?

Yes I do like tasting new food. But I have to say I would like to stick to my habit of eating Chinese food and not change. I think it is a healthy diet. I remember that I have been to a few Western style restaurants with some Western student friends. The food was OK I suppose but I'm not really a fan. I don't like fast food like KFC either. But you know I'll try it once just to see what it's like.

Do you like lunch or dinner?

Mm difficult question. I have to say I like both lunch and dinner but for different reasons. For lunch I usually eat with my mates and we can have a laugh and then of course we might go back to the dorm for a nap before class. I like dinner because when I am at home I am with my family and we can sit around, eating my grandma's appetising food and just chatting about this and that. So both lunch and dinner have their plus points.

▶ *Time Management*

How do you organise your time?

I'm a student so I have a very full timetable at school. Nearly every minute counts. In my social life I just use my smart phone diary like everyone else. It's a godsend really because I can set alarms which reminds me when I have a meeting or an appointment. I hate being late for things so my phone is so important as a timekeeper.

Do you think young people organise their time in the same way?

Of course young people organise their time in the same way. Most of us have smart phones or iPads now. I can remember what seems like yesterday when we had to use diaries and things like that. Now some people don't even wear watches because everything is on the phone. In the future my kids will have something even better, I'm sure.

Are you ever late for anything?

I am never late for anything except for one class which I am nearly always late for. I get hugely embarrassed tiptoeing into the class. It's a 7:45 class and I work late the night before. I set my alarm but I often snooze too much then it's too late. I have to leap out of bed and sprint to the class. I even miss breakfast and don't have time for a shower, so I'm a mess when I get there. In the future I am really going to try to clean up my act.

What excuses do you use when you are late?

The excuses I use when I am late have all been used up as I've been late so many times and my favorite excuse is I forgot to set my alarm, especially when I was late for school.

What excuses do people use when they are late?

The most popular excuses people use when they are late is to blame the traffic. It's easy to give this white lie and it trips off the tongue so easily. You can say: "Oh I was on the bus but you know the traffic was so bad, there must have been an accident or something." I try not to lie, but it's difficult not to when you are late and it's simply your fault for being a lazybones.

Do you like it when others are late?

I absolutely hate it when others are late. I'm always punctual and on time. Indeed I often arrive early when I have an appointment. I think it's rude when people leave you hanging about and I do admit sometimes I get impatient if they are really late. I remember once I was waiting for a date and that person was over 20 minutes late. So I just took off and left. He didn't get a second chance with me.

In your country do people forgive others when they are late?

I can't forgive people if they are late. But then I'm a very punctual person. I don't like hanging around waiting for someone. I do admit sometimes I get impatient if others are really late. I remember once I was waiting for a date and that person was over 20 minutes late. So I just took off and left. He didn't get a second chance with me. I don't really know what other people do.

If you had more time what would you do with the extra time?

If I had more time what would I do with it? Well I expect most people would give you a worthy answer like learning an instrument or taking up painting or writing that novel that's lodged in their heads. But personally, I think, if you have a busy life there's nothing wrong in just sitting back and smelling the roses for a while. I suppose that would get boring after a bit so in the future I would have to work out what to do with my time, but not just now.

▶ *Emails and Letters*

Do you write many letters or emails?

I write many letters but mainly in the form of emails. I can't remember the last time I actually wrote a letter and posted it. If I think about it, apart from some official forms and documents I haven't put pen to paper in years. I have friends all over the world so email is the most efficient and fastest way to keep in contact. I think if I had a boyfriend/girlfriend I might write him/her a letter with some romantic words or a poem in it as it seems to be more intimate. But I suppose you can do that in an email too.

What's the difference between emails and letters?

There are some obvious differences between emails and letters. Clearly letters are nothing more than snail mail, they are so slow. Whereas emails are as so quick and efficient. The downside of emails are people don't seem to attach much importance to them and they can just disappear and people can deny ever receiving your email. With the snail mail at least you can get the delivery recorded so important post doesn't go missing.

What kind(s) of letters/emails do you think is/are the hardest to write?

The hardest kinds of letters to write are those to a boy/girl that you have upset or you don't want to see anymore. The Dear John letters are tough to write. You want to end up your relationship but you want to try to let the person take it easy. So there is a lot of emotions on the page and you have to be careful that your tears don't smudge the ink. I remember that I did write one to a boy/girl who was keen on me once but I couldn't feel the same way. I hope that in the future I don't have to write any letter of this type.

How do you feel when you receive a letter or an email?

When I receive a letter or an email I experience different emotions. Receiving an email is often a non-event this is because my inbox is always being clogged by about a million spam mails. So after wading through that I am too worn out to feel anything about clicking on an email. But receiving a letter is special because you know that the person has put some effort into sending you the missive. Unless, of course, it's a bill, which nobody wants.

What kinds of emails/letters do you receive that make you feel happy?

The kinds of emails that make me happy are the long ones from my friends. I can remember letters from one of my friends who was in New Zealand on a placement for her course. The letters she sent to me really brightened up my day. I was missing my friend so much. But getting those letters kept our friendship close and I was happy to know that she was enjoying her time abroad. Now she's back we still write and keep in touch.

Do you think people will still write letters in the future?

Of course people will still write letters in the future. The only thing that will change is the medium we use to send letters. We might not be putting pen to paper like in the old days but we will still want to stay in contact with our loved ones and friends. I hope when I'm older I'll still be getting letters from my friends and family.

Do you keep letters?

I keep letters that are especially important to me. I have some old letters that are part of the history of my family, some old love letters that my granddad sent to my grandma. I hope that one day I will have some of my own love letters to add to my stash. Then perhaps one day my children will carry on the tradition of keeping these letters and occasionally reading them.

How do you get on the Internet?

At college I can connect to the Internet by the Wi-Fi system that the college provide for us. If I'm out and about I can dive into a coffee shop like Starbucks to connect with their Wi-Fi system. I also have a smart phone which can connect me to the net via 3G or Wi-Fi if it's available. So it's almost impossible not to be connected to the Internet in this day and age. I'm only young but I can still remember the old days when connecting to the Internet was really difficult and expensive. But now it's readily available and in most cases free.

Is the Internet popular in China?

The Internet is very popular in China. It impacts on nearly every aspect of our lives. For example now it's becoming so difficult to get a taxi because everyone has a taxi app on their smart phones so hailing a cab on the street is nearly impossible. And where would we be without all the ways we can communicate with everyone else. You know it's made the world a smaller and more open place and that's good for China.

How do people learn things on the Internet?

You can learn things on the Internet just by logging on. But some of the things you learn might not be correct. Even using a site like Wikipedia might lead you down the garden path with wrong information. And Google has become a verb, for example, "I'll just Google that." There are traditional learning materials online too so people can take classes or watch informative videos and documentaries on the Internet.

Do you write letters to your parents often?

I have to admit that I don't write letters to my parents. We all have mobile phones now so I ring them regularly and my mum is always calling me about this or that or with news updates about the family. I remember I sent my mum and dad a postcard when I was on holiday once and they were really pleased to get it. I'm kind of pleased that the card is still hanging in the kitchen in my parents home. You can't do that with an email.

▶ *Gifts*

What was your favourite gift?

My favourite gift of all time was my bike. Without a doubt I can still remember the day that I was given it. It was my tenth birthday and all my family were there. Then my dad wheeled my bright blue bike in. I was over the moon. I was so happy that I actually jumped for joy and ran around the room like a madman. I think a bike is the best present and I hope one day I'll buy one for my kid and get the same reaction.

Have you ever received a gift that you didn't like?

I did once receive a gift I didn't like. It was an aquarium. It's not clear quite why mum and dad thought I would like an aquarium. I'm not sure. I had been pestering them for a pet, but I wanted a dog or a kitty, not a fish. I was a bit underwhelmed. Of course I didn't do my best for these fish and eventually the poor things died and the aquarium was consigned to a cupboard where it never again saw the light of day.

When was the last time you received a gift?

The last time I received a gift was just last week actually. My friend had been to Korea for a short trip and she bought me back some sweets and snacks. I was over the moon to receive the treats she bought for me. When I go on my holiday in the summer I will be sure to bring her back a little something to delight her taste buds too.

Do you prefer receiving or giving a gift?

You know to be honest I'm a giver rather than a taker. I much prefer to give a gift than receiving a gift. It's not that I'm ungrateful but some of the gifts I have in the past have been so inappropriate or just downright useless I wonder if the person really knows me at all. I love giving a gift; in fact I love the thinking about it and even the actual shopping for it. It is a great pleasure of mine to while away some time gift shopping.

Do you think it's difficult to choose what gift to give people?

Choosing what gift to give people is half the pleasure of giving. I love the process of thinking about what I should get for someone. And then I adore the shopping, wandering around the shops, whiling away some hours, trying to find one perfect thing. And as for the wrapping, don't get me started. I think maybe I'm a bit strange but wrapping the gift is so much fun with the coloured paper, the string and little cards. Yes. I do love choosing and giving gifts to people. It's not difficult at all.

What were the gifts you sent to others recently?

Well the gift I sent most recently was some flowers on my mother's birthday. I am away in college so I couldn't get home for her birthday. So I used the website Taobao to buy some flowers that were delivered right to the door. She told me she was so happy that she was quite over the moon to get the flowers. She said it had made her day. So I was pleased that I had had the brainwave to go online to find the gift.

Do you like giving gifts to your friends?

Yes. I do like giving gifts to my friends. In fact we are constantly giving little gifts to each other. Giving a gift doesn't mean that you have to spend loads of money. It might just be a biscuit or a drink. It's basically just a token of our affections for each other. So sometimes we do it unthinkingly but we always do it with love.

▶ *Painting and Drawing*

Do you like painting/drawing? Why?

Yes. I do like painting and drawing. I can remember that I have been drawing since I was a little kid. In fact my parents still have some of my childhood paintings hanging on the wall. It's a bit of a source of embarrassment to be honest; I mean I'm all grown up now. More recently I have been trying to paint more seriously. I enjoy whiling away a few hours on an evening daubing away on a canvas.

Do you think children should learn drawing?

I don't think children need to learn drawing. I think they draw naturally. You only have to give a kid some crayons and paint and they will naturally start to draw things. It's good to encourage this creativity when they are naturally curious and artistic. I love looking at kid's drawings. It's like seeing the world through their eyes.

Why do primary schools have painting class?

Primary schools have painting class because these small kids are just so naturally drawn to drawing and painting. I think even if they didn't have a painting class the kids would be drawing over every inch of the walls. It's good to encourage this creativity in school when the kids are being naturally curious and artistic. I love looking at kids' drawings. It's like seeing the world through their eyes.

Why do people display artworks/paintings at their homes?

Many people display artworks and paintings at their homes. For many people a good painting will add a splash of colour to their lives. Some artworks might hold some significant meaning for the owner. Of course you can spend millions on some artworks if you are rich but a lot of artworks are more reasonably priced so people can buy it and enjoy it.

Have you ever bought any paintings?

I have never actually bought a real painting but I have bought posters of famous paintings to hang on my wall. One of my most favourite paintings is Van Gogh's *Starry Night*. I love that picture and can sit and look at it for hours. It's on my wall at home and it brings me a great deal of pleasure.

Do you think painting or drawing is important for adults?

Yes. I do think painting and drawing is important for adults. I know that painting and drawing are used as therapy for people who might have some problems with their moods or their lives. It can be a calming and relaxing hobby. It's great to be able to while away a few hours in an evening or a weekend daubing a canvas with some paint or sketching a nice view.

Do you still draw those pictures you did in your childhood?

No. I don't think that I still draw my childhood pictures. Those pictures were so naive. Now I don't really paint or draw much at all which is a shame. But if I did I am sure it would be more figurative or even more abstract. As adults we see the world in a different way from children do. We see its faults and its contradictions. It's not all about big yellow suns and big green trees.

▶ *Patience*

Is it important to be patient? Why?

I am probably the most impatient person in the world. I hate waiting for people to do things. So

I don't think it's important to be patient. They say good things come to those that wait. Well I don't believe that. If someone is late for a meeting with me then they are likely to find an empty space when they turn up because I will have turned tail and run. It's just so impolite.

Is it easy to be patient? Why?

Oh no, it's not easy to be patient. I am probably the most impatient person in the world. I hate waiting for people to do things. So I don't think it's easy to be patient. They say good things come to those that wait. Well I don't believe that. If someone is late for a meeting with me then they are likely to find an empty space when they turn up because I will have turned tail and run. It's just so impolite.

How can people be patient?

In my view people can only be patient if they bite their tongue, say nothing and believe that good things will come to those that wait. Well that's not me. I am probably the most impatient person in the world. I hate waiting for people to do things. If someone is late for a meeting with me then they are likely to find an empty space when they turn up because I will have turned tail and run. It's just so impolite.

What do you do when you're waiting for a bus or doing something else?

When I'm waiting for a bus I'm like a cat on a hot tin roof. I hate waiting. I am so impatient. I'll check my mobile phone like a million times, look up and down the road to see if the bus is coming, walk up and down like a solider on parade and do all manner of things to try and kill time. They say good things come to those that wait, but I just hate waiting.

Are people now less patient than people in the past? Why?

I think people are less patient than people in the past. We seem to live our lives at a fast pace and we need everything being done quickly now, from fast food to fast and speedy communications. So we try to jump on every bandwagon and grab whatever's going. But we really need to spend some time to smell the roses, to chill out and just let the world drift by a bit. But I suppose we just don't have the time.

▶ *TV Programmes*

Do you like watching TV?

I don't like watching TV, I love it! I might have what you call square eyes from watching so much TV. I can remember as a kid being mesmerised by it. And now I try to catch my fave programmes as often as I can. I'm really going to have to cut down in the future if I want to do well in my studies but you know TV is always there in the corner of the room, calling me.

How often do you watch TV?

I watch TV as often as I can. When I'm in my dorm, it's difficult to see any TV and of course as a student I'm very busy. But when I am back home with my parents, I get my square eyes again from watching too much TV. It doesn't help that my parents recently splashed out on a large flat screen TV. Now I'm really hooked.

What kinds of programmes do you like to watch?

The kinds of programmes I like to watch are really varied. I'll watch anything from Korean soaps, American reality shows to homegrown drama. Of course I also try to catch the news and some current affairs programmes because as a student I need to keep abreast of current issues.

Do you watch TV with your family or friends or by yourself?

I love watching TV with my family and friends. Its so much fun discussing what's going on, or who's doing what in a soap or just shouting at some of the idiots making fools of themselves in those reality shows. I'm OK watching TV alone too but when there's a gang of you sharing the fun it makes for a fun night.

Do you think you watched too much TV when you were a child?

I don't think I watched too much TV when I was little. I actually watched too little. I can remember that I always wanted to watch stuff but my mum and dad said no. Sometimes I was over the moon if I was allowed to watch something as a treat. In retrospect I think my parents did the right thing and I will probably do the same with my kids.

▶ *Trees/Forests*

Did you climb a tree when you were a child?

I climbed many trees when I was a child. My mates and me were always shinning up trees for one reason or another. We were fearless then. I suppose now I couldn't even climb to the lowest branch. I remember once going up a tree and finding a nest full of eggs. Well we took those eggs and I was so proud. But it was a false pride because my dad was really angry with me for taking those eggs and he made me see that it was totally the wrong thing to do.

Do you like to go to the forest for a vacation? Why?

Going to the forest for a trip or a vacation is always like finding a green oasis in your life. The trees are the lungs of the world's breathing life and are giving oxygen into the atmosphere so the air is always sweet and clean in the forest. In the heat of the summer, it's also a place to cool down and relax away from the heat and the hustle and bustle of the city. There's nothing better than pitching a tent for a few nights under the stars in the green woods.

Do people need to protect trees? Why?

Of course we do need to protect trees. Trees are the lungs of the world's breathing life and are giving oxygen into the atmosphere. I am appalled when I see the logging activity going on in China and the way the Amazon basin is being stripped bare. It's a crying shame and the authorities should pull out all the stops to protect our lovely trees.

Is it comfortable/nice to live in a place with lots of trees?

It's really comfortable to live in a place with lots of trees. The city where I live has lots of wide boulevards and avenues lined with beautiful trees. In the summer they offer cool shade from the burning sun overhead and in the autumn they drop their beautiful golden brown leaves over the pavement. It's such a relief just to get out of the sun sometimes and these trees act like huge sunshades. I could linger there for hours in the delicious coolness of their shade.

Have you ever planted a tree?

In fact I have planted a tree. When I was a kid my grandpa was a keen gardener and one day after I ate an apple he showed me how to take the seeds out. Then together we planted those seeds in a little pot and they sprouted and grew into little twigs. My grandpa always had green fingers. Then one day we planted those little twigs into the ground and now it's a wonderful apple tree that bears loads of juicy apples.

Do we need to plant trees? What are the effects of trees/forests?

Of course we need to plant trees. We can't just keep using this natural resource without replacing it. It would be shortsighted to think otherwise. Even in the short term we need trees for many different purposes—building, furniture even paper making. But we do need to develop sustainable forests that will allow us to use wood without resorting to stripping the rain forests and destroying valuable habitats.

▶ *Being Busy*

Have you been busy recently?

Yes. I have been busy recently. I'm still a student of course and it seems like I've been burning the midnight oil more and more recently as I try to keep up with my studies. I can't remember ever being so busy. I feel like I'm wearing my fingers to the bone with the amount of typing. I have to write papers for my courses. I could do with some down time.

When was the last time your were busy?

No. I haven't been busy recently. I don't know why sometimes at college we seem to be racing ahead at full speed and sometimes we have nothing to do. Maybe it's just the lull before the storm and soon we will be burning the midnight oil again. The last time I was really busy was just before the-mid term exams. They really put us through it and we were wearing our fingers to the bone, churning out paper after paper for our courses.

Do you like being busy?/Do you prefer to be busy or to be free?

I have to say I'm a busy bee so I like being busy. If I have time on my hands then I soon get bored. I have a low threshold of boredom so if I'm inactive I just have to find something to do. Sometimes I drive my dorm mates crackers especially when they are chilling out and watching TV or something. I just can't do that I have to do something. So I'll be cleaning or doing my work.

Was there a time when you felt stressed out/under pressure because of a busy schedule?

I have to say that as a university student I always feel stressed out because of my busy schedule. From the moment I wake up it feels like my feet never touch the ground. Sometimes I'm in bed and wondering where the day has gone. Sometimes I feel like I might blow my top or explode but I've been doing some yoga recently so I think I can now cope with the stress.

Have you experienced stress at work?

Experiencing stress at work seems to be part and parcel of my working life. I don't really experience much stress because the work is good and I can cope with it easily. But I have to say the boss is an idiot and he is the major cause of all the stress. He can't keep his nose out of our business. He thinks he knows better all the time so whatever you do is wrong. So that is the root cause of my stress at work.

How do you handle stress?

I handle stress with a mix of tai chi and yoga. My grandpa taught me the basics of tai chi years ago. He was a real master and an instructor in my hometown. Lately one of my colleagues encouraged me to go to yoga classes with her. I must say doing that has been a breath of fresh air in my life. Yoga and tai chi together has been a real stress buster for me and I hope to be doing it for many years to come.

Do you think you will be busy in the next few years?/Do you think you will be busier in the future than you are now?

In the next few years I will graduate and start to work so I will definitely be busy in the next few years. I know that to pass my exams I will have to burn the midnight oil to get the work done. So I will just have to buckle down and do it. And then after graduating I will be the newbie at work. So I will have to prove myself by working twice as hard as everyone else. But you know I am really looking forward to it.

▶*News*

Do you read the news?

Well I don't read the news in the traditional sense. I mean I don't read newspapers. What I do is catching up with the news via the news apps I have on my phone. I mean we are all geeks now, right? So I have apps for that. I have the BBC and CNN news apps on my iPhone. I have also been watching the English language news on CCTV to help me with my English.

How do you get news? Reading newspapers or in other ways?

Well I don't read the news in the traditional way. I mean I don't read newspapers, that seems so old-fashioned now. I do it in other more modern ways. What I do is catching up with the news via the news apps I have on my smart phone. I have also been watching the English language news on CCTV to help me with my English.

Who do you think prefers to read the news, young people or old people?

I have to say I think reading the news is for the old people. I don't think I have ever seen any of my friends reading a newspaper. It seems to be so uncool and the news is a bit boring. Young people like to read magazines about lifestyles and living. It's probably a bit shallow, but if I want to look at the real news I do have an app on my smart phone.

How do you make yourself keep up to date?

I can keep up to date really easily. I have an news app on my smart phone where I can check out what's happening. It also sends me bulletins if there are any breaking stories. If I need any news in depth I can always get up-to-the-minute news by surfing online. There's a hundred and one news channels I can look at so I can feel really connected to what's going on.

▶ *Shopping/Clothes/Fashion*

What types of clothes do you like best?

The kinds of clothes I like best are the simple uniform of jeans and a T-shirt. This is what I feel comfortable in for my day-to-day life. My mum thinks I'm a bit of a scruff but this is the common look for young people. I'm nothing special and I don't like to stand out in a crowd. So this is a simple anonymous look and I like it.

Who chose clothes for you when you were young?

Well I'm not sure who chose my clothes when I was young. I guess it was my mum. But judging by the old photos of me she either didn't have much choice or just had horrendous taste in clothes for her kid-me. When I look at those old photos I cringe a bit from embarrassment but I do keep my lips sealed because I know my mum and dad had it hard so they probably did their best for me so its not really a problem.

Can you give advice to your friend about choosing clothes?

I am actually hopeless giving friends advice about choosing clothes. Some of my friends have aspirations to be models or clotheshorses as I call them and they are always parading about in classy gowns while I slob about in jeans and T-shirts. I don't have the slightest interest in the latest fashion so when a shopping trip is on the horizon I try to make my excuses and disappear.

Do you like the clothes you wear?

Of course I like the clothes I wear. I mean I actually bought them using my own money so I should like them. I think you would probably be a bit deranged if you wore clothes you didn't like. I'm a casual sort of guy happy in jeans and T-shirts. But if I have to go somewhere formal I have clothes to fit that occasion too.

What is important for you when you buy clothes?

The most important thing for me when I buy clothes is price. I'm a student so I have scarce resources. This means I'm usually broke. I'm not into buying brand's for the brand's sake. If I see some branded clothes and it's a bargain I'll probably buy it. Otherwise run-of-the-mill clothing is good for me. But I must say I will check that the quality is OK. I still want my money well spent.

Where do you usually do your shopping? Where do you buy your clothes?

I usually do my shopping in shopping malls. I am a mall rat. I love hanging out in malls because there's so much to see and do. You can shop, browse the rails, grab a bite to eat or sit in a coffee shop and watch the world going by. You can usually get a good bargain in the malls as there are often sales and good discounts in the shops.

Do you enjoy shopping in big shopping malls/big shopping centres?

I do enjoy shopping in big shopping malls. I'm a mall rat. I love hanging out in malls because there's so much to see and do. My mates and I can shop till we drop. We can browse the rails, grab a bite to eat, share the juicy gossip or sit in a coffee shop and watch the world going by. You can get good bargains at the malls too as there are often sales and good discounts in the shops.

How often do you buy clothes? What styles of clothes do you like to buy?

I have to say I don't often buy clothes. The reason for this is first I'm a student so I'm broke half the time. Also I'm not really into fashion. I'm a sort of jeans and T-shirt person so the glossy mags and people on TV do not influence me. I do have some nice stuff though/even though I plead poverty I am a bit entranced by some brand names.

Why do some people not like shopping?

Why do some people not like shopping? Well you must be talking about my dad. My dad hates shopping. He becomes such a grump if he has to go out to the shops with my mum. If they go in the car, he sits in the car in the car park, fuming away until she gets back. It's also impossible to send him to do shopping as he always comes back with the wrong stuff. My mum even buys all his clothes for him. He doesn't seem to care either. But at the end of the day, dad is dad and we all love him.

What do you think about fashion trends?

I don't really care about fashion trends. I'm not much of a trendsetter myself. I'm more of a run-of-the-mill/jeans and T-shirt type of person. To be honest when I see some of the fashion shows on TV I tend to gasp in astonishment. Some are quite out of this world. You never really see that stuff on the streets so it's never been part of my world.

Have you ever bought clothes that you (now) don't like?

The clothes that I now don't like are mostly those I have bought on impulse or on the advice of friends. I have just totally ignored my inner voice which is screaming "no, no, no" and put my hand in my pocket and forked out for something that has probably never seen the light of day/stuck in the back of my wardrobe.

Do you think you will wear a different style of clothes when you are older?

Who knows if I will wear a different style of clothes when I get older? Maybe things will change but I think I'll always be a jeans and T-shirt kind of person. I mean, you do see older people out and about now wearing jeans and T-shirts, they are not all stuck in that sort of drab 1980's look. Some look really good and trendy.

What types of clothes are in fashion now?

I don't really know what types of clothes are in fashion now. I'm not a trendsetter so I don't follow fashion. Some of the things you see on TV blow my mind though because you never see them on the street. Most people seem to be wearing jeans and T-shirts. But you do get the occasional fashion conscious person wandering about and it always seems to look good on them.

Do you think fashion trends will be the same when you are old(er)?

Fashion is always changing so I doubt they will be the same when I am older. But anyway I'm not a trendsetter. I'm a jeans and T-shirt type of person and I think these types of clothes will always be with us. Strangely they have turned into a sort of uniform that everyone, young and old, wears so I think they will be timeless.

Are you very interested in fashion and clothes?

I'm not very interested in fashion trends and clothes. I mean I'm not much of a trendsetter myself. I'm more of a run-of-the-mill/jeans and T-shirt type of person. To be honest when I see some of the fashion shows on TV, I tend to gasp in astonishment. Some are quite out of this world. You never really see that stuff on the streets so it's never been part of my world.

Do you like to wear fashionable clothes? Do you wear designer clothes?

I'm not very interested in fashion trends and branded clothes. I mean I'm not much of a trendsetter myself. I'm more of a run-of-the-mill/jeans and T-shirt type of person. But I suppose I stick to what I like—Levis jeans, Nike trainers and so on. So I suppose I do wear designer clothes—the common ones not the real high-end stuff.

Do you have a lot of nice clothes?

I'm a student so I don't really have the money to have a wardrobe full of nice clothes. But I have got clothes for going to weddings and parties and things like that. I am lucky that my dad put his hand in his pocket a few times and bought me some nice clothes. I try to keep them nice so I can always look my best on these occasions.

Is there anything that you used to wear in the past that you don't wear now?

Yes. I have a few things that I used to wear in the past that I don't wear now. When I was a bit younger I got into the Goth scene a little bit. So I had a lot of black stuff. It was all a bit over the top but at the time I thought it was great. But actually I soon grew out of it and most of those clothes have either been chucked out or consigned to the bottom drawer of my wardrobe.

How often do you go shopping for clothes?

I must say I don't go shopping that often for clothes. I'm a student so I'm usually broke. When I go home my dad often takes me out shopping and puts his hand in his pocket to cover the bills. So I do have some nice stuff. I'm not a trendsetter, but I have some nice clothes that make me feel good when I'm out and about.

▶ *Politeness*

Is it important to be polite?

Of course its important to be polite, otherwise we'd all be at each other's throats. I have to say that though politeness seems to go out the window when it comes to getting on the bus or metro. It seems that every man is for himself as everyone bumps and barges to get on and get that one elusive empty seat. I admit that have to bite my tongue at times so as not to shout at these rude people.

How to be polite?

We all learn how to be polite at a young age, well I hope we do. I learnt my "please and thank you" at my mothers knee. She was strict with us about being polite, especially to our elders. And I still am. My mum also taught me my table manners. So I think that in these types of social situations it's important to be polite.

Is being polite different now from the past?

Yes, being polite now is different from the past. In China people used to bow to each other, as they still do in Japan. But now the handshake is the norm when you meet a new person or a friend. The European cheek kiss however does seem to be a step too far for some people. My mates and I often give each other a hug to say hello though.

▶ *Friends and Family*

Do you have any/many close friends?

I don't have so many close friends but those I have I cherish. As a student I know lots of people who are my friends too but not ones that I would trust with my inner most secrets. My close friends are the kind that I can ring in the middle of the night and pour our all my troubles. We are always there for each other whether it be a shoulder to cry on or someone with whom to share the good times.

What qualities make them good friends?

The qualities that my good friends have are that they are trustworthy and that they are always there for me in both the good times and the bad times. We've known each other since high school so we have a shared history and loads of shared secrets. I'd be lost without my mates.

Do you live with your family?

I'm a student so I don't live with my family. But I visit them as often as I can, when my studies permit. I was scared of leaving home at first but now that I've found my feet I love being so independent. I'm not so sure that my mum is over the moon about me being so far away but we all have to leave sometime, right?

Do your family and friends still live in your hometown?

Yes, all my family and most of my friends still live in my hometown. Of course some of my friends are students like me and we've been scattered like grains all across China for our studies. But during the holidays we all get back together in the hometown, visiting all the old haunts, having fun and catching up with all the hometown gossip.

Do you think family members should live together? (Why/Why Not?)

I'm not sure if family members should live together. In the past because money was tight then this probably was the norm, but now I think things have changed. The younger generation are more independent and free. I don't think I would want my mum and dad and relatives to live with me. I'd never get a word in edgewise and they would know all my business and I don't want that at all.

When do you spend time with your family? What do you do together?

I spend time with my family during all the big holidays like the Spring Festival. Like everybody else, I have to fight tooth and nail to get a train ticket home and usually by hook or by crook I get there. When I am at home I usually spend all my time eating and watching the TV. The

Spring Festival Gala is important for my family and it's a must-see show. All the relatives come around and they always bring appetising dishes with them so we have a blowout feast as well.

Do you often go out with your friends?

When I am with my university friends we go out as often as we can. We go shopping or to the cinema. Sometimes we might just hang out in Starbucks doing our homework surfing on their free Wi-Fi. I don't get to see my best friends in my hometown that much but when we do get together we will often go out for a blowout supper, maybe a hotpot, which is my favourite.

Is your family very important to you?

I would be a liar if I said my family was not important to me. In fact they are very very important to me; they are my whole life. I'd be lost without them. I miss them so much when I am at college. When I was first away I was so homesick. I thought that I would die. I ring my mum nearly every day just to say hi and chat about this and that, make sure every thing's OK.

Do you prefer to spend time with your family or your friends?

I'd say it's fifty fifty when it comes to spending time with my family or my friends. I love my mum and dad to bits but sometimes even they are a bit like hard work. So I need the time out with my friends, especially after a hard day's studying. We can go for coffee or a meal and just relax. With mum and dad I always feel like I have to be on my best behaviour so I just can't relax with them.

What do you do in your free time with your friends?

In my free time with my friends the world's our oyster. When we come out of class it's like a weight's been lifted and we can have some fun and relax after a hard day. So we might go to our favourite hotpot restaurant for a blowout meal. Or we might go to Starbucks to chat about this and that over coffee, surfing the free Wi-Fi on our smart phones. And of course we like to hang out at the mall, window-shopping is so much fun with my mates.

Are there any times when you prefer to be alone?

Yes, there are times when I prefer to be alone. I mean I like reading and that's a pretty solitary pastime. There's nothing better than snuggling up in my warm bed with a good book. I get annoyed when my phone rings or buzzes with people wanting to chat or sending me messages I don't want to read, so I usually switch it off if I remember. But I'm a pretty gregarious person when all is said and done so I like being with my mates as well.

▶ *Walking*

Do you like walking?

Yes I love walking. It's a good way to fit exercise into the daily grind. I get the bus to college. I often jump off a couple of stops before I need to just so I can walk there. I love to walk in the forests too, especially in the summer under the cool shade of the leaves keeping me cool and out of the burning sun. Walking in the countryside near where my mum lives is one of the things we do when I go home; we often go out for a stroll after lunch.

How often do you take a walk?

Well naturally I walk every day. It's a good way to fit exercise into the daily grind. I get the bus to college and I often jump off a couple of stops before I need to just so I can walk there. At the weekends I love to walk in the forests or I go walking in the countryside near where my mum lives. This is one of the things my family does when I go home; we all go out for a stroll after lunch.

Do you prefer to walk in the countryside or in the city?

Well naturally I prefer to walk in the countryside rather than in the city. This is because I'm a country girl/boy at heart so I love walking through the fields and forests near my hometown. The air in the city is just so polluted that sometimes I really don't want to set foot outside my front door. So there's no pleasure to be walking in the city, unlike in the countryside.

▶*Sunshine*

Do you like the sunshine? Why?

Who doesn't like the sunshine? On a sunny day you just have to look about you and everyone has a smile on his/her face. So the sunshine brings with it sunny moods. Plus everything is more colourful and much brighter. Everyone sheds their drab winter clothes and puts on their summer best. Even the plants start to poke their heads out above the soil to greet the sun. I love sunshiny days.

What do you like to do in the sunshine/on sunny days?

What I like to do on sunny days is having a picnic in the sunshine. My mates and I will grab some food and a blanket and head off to the park. Soon we will have found a place and laid out our feast. Then we can relax and sunbathe, dozing in the warm rays of the sun. It's great watching all the other people out and about enjoying the sunshine too. How we miss it during the grey days of winter.

What things do you think are hard to do in the sunshine? What do you dislike to do when it's sunny outside?

When it's sunny outside how I hate being in the classroom. I can look out of the window and see all the other students, not in class, lounging around, sunning themselves while I have to sit and listen to some boring lecture. So it's hard to go to school or even to work. I want to sit in the sun with friends over a cold drink, putting the world to rights and just chilling out.

Do you like going outside on weekends on sunny days?

I live for the weekends and if it's sunny so much the better because I love going out in the sun. If it's going to be sunny all weekend my mates and I might organise a picnic somewhere where we can have fun. Maybe the beach or down by the lake where we can splash about in the water if the sun gets too hot for us. We've been known to stay there all night just to watch the sun come up especially on the balmiest of nights.

Have you ever been to a place without sunshine?

The place I went to without any sunshine was a week on the coast. We had planned a great summer holiday. We had packed all the beach stuff, the swimsuits, the sun cream. We were cock-a-hoop that we were going on holiday. When we got there it was raining. It rained all week. The sun didn't shine once. We were all so miserable. It was the worst holiday in the world.

▶ Leisure Time

How much free time/time to relax do you have (per week)?

Well as I'm a student I don't have much free time. I suppose that technically my weekends are free. But I am often busy doing my coursework and my homework. I don't seem to have much time to relax. I tend to relax quite late at night, watching some TV or a movie. I hope that in the future, when I'm at work, I might have more free time to spare.

What do you do in your spare time/free time?

I am usually busy in my spare time. I can't just sit and stare into space or while away my time in front of the TV. So I'm usually off somewhere, meeting up with my mates, having a laugh. We might go for a blowout meal or linger over a coffee in Starbucks, surfing their free Wi-Fi. I guess sometimes I'll have some downtime. I do like reading but I usually do that when I'm free in the evening when there are not so many of my mates available.

In the evenings do you prefer to relax at home watching TV or go out with your friends?

Relaxing at home watching the TV is just one of my many options really. I can go out with my friends maybe for a blowout meal at our favourite hotpot place or if the mood takes me I might just stay at home curled up on the sofa with a good book or a movie on the TV. So it just depends on the circumstances really.

Do you have a lot of fun in the city?

The city is just the best place to have fun. There's so much on offer, I don't know where to start. When my mates and I go out we tend to start off with a meal, probably a hotpot because we all love hotpot. Then we might go to a bar or a club to try and catch some live music. Once we've been there we might be inspired to sing ourselves or trot to a KTV. It's hilarious that none of us can hold a tune but we love singing ourselves. Yes, the city is a great place.

Do you think it's important to (have time to) relax?

It is very important to have time to relax. If you get too stressed out then you might get ill. I know some guys who are just workaholics but what does it get you. These guys are overweight and so unhealthy from their stressful lifestyle. I think sometimes you need to be able to lie back and smell the roses. I really do make sure I relax in my spare time. It doesn't take much to relax or even too much time but it's worth it all the same.

Do men and women relax (=spend their free time) in the same way?

I think men and women relax in different ways. Some men might like to do sports or run to relax while some women might like to do crafts like knitting. But I guess it depends on the individual because I know some girls who love running just as much as the man does. I mean I love a hot bath as a way to relax and I know that many men and women do too. Soaking in a hot tub is my idea of bliss.

When do you spend time with your friends or your family?

I spend as much time as I can with my friends and family. I work hard as a student so as soon as I have some free time I'm off to have some fun. When I'm with my family we seem to do an awful lot of eating and laughing. I really look forward to have home cooked-food with my family. But I also love meeting my friends, lingering over a coffee, chatting about this and that.

What's more important to you? Your family or friends?

Well that's not difficult to say; obviously my family is the most important thing in my life. I don't know what I'd do without them. I mean sometimes they are so frustrating that I feel like tearing my hair out. But at the end of the day they are my family and I know that they would move heaven and earth for me. My friends are important to me too. But my family will always come first, after all blood is thicker than water.

▶ *Bicycles*

Do you ever ride a bicycle?

I ride a bicycle every day to school. But believe me, you do need to have a bit of a death wish to cycle in my city. The drivers there are maniacs and even though I always stick to the cycle path I'm always in fear of my life as I dodge the scooters, cars and even lorries bearing down on me. Even so I do love cycling and it keeps me fit and healthy.

How old were you when you learned to ride a bicycle?

The first time I learned to ride a bike was probably when I was about seven or eight. I remember that my parents bought me a bike for my birthday. Oh I was so over the moon that I literally jumped for joy. Then there was the thrill of sitting on that blue bike while my dad held me upright and encouraged me to pedal. I probably fell off more times than you can count but eventually I could ride it. I was so free that summer; you just couldn't keep me off my blue bike.

Are bicycles popular in China?

Bikes are very popular in China. Do you know that song "9 Million Bicycles in Beijing" by Katie Melua? Well I would guess that's a serious underestimation. Everywhere you go in China you will see a bike in one form or another being used for transport. They are a cheap and reliable form of transport. I'm just glad that the neighbourhood where I live is nice and flat so I can speed around on my mountain bike.

Would you say it's difficult to learn to ride a bicycle?

I would say it's not particularly difficult to learn to ride a bike. My dad helped me and I would say that within half an hour or so I was off with the wind in my hair zooming around like an old pro. I guess I fell off more times than I'd care to mention. But once you've mastered the thing, nothing can stop you.

What are the reasons why people ride bicycles?

There are many reasons why people ride bikes. I like to cycle so that's why I ride my bike. It keeps me healthy and I can get to school much quicker than taking the bus. Many people might be using a bike or something like a tricycle. It's easy for them to get in and out of traffic. The cost is low and it's much more reliable than say an electric bike.

What are the advantages (or benefits) of riding a bicycle?

There are many advantages to ride a bike. The first one is that if you regularly cycle somewhere then you are keeping fit and healthy. Secondly it's good for the planet. You are not adding to the pollution problem by belching out exhaust fumes. Thirdly it helps for cutting down on the congestion on our streets. There are just too many cars nowadays. And finally it's cheap and reliable. It's the transport for the common man. You can see them everywhere in China. I really enjoy riding my bike.

What kinds of people ride bicycles?

All kinds of people ride bikes. Young people, old people. People are cycling everywhere. People cycle for health, for their businesses or just to get somewhere. There are loads of people cycling in the city.

Do children also ride bicycles in your country?

Of course children ride bikes in my country. But in the city, it's quite dangerous for them to cycle even though we do have cycle paths. When I cycle in the city, I always do it with my heart in my mouth. I'm so scared. Also I believe that children under the age of fourteen are not allowed to cycle on the roads in the city. In the countryside, it is different. The roads are safer and young kids can enjoy the real freedom of cycling.

Why do children enjoy riding bicycles?

I think children enjoy riding bikes because of the freedom it gives them. It's a new skill but it always carries with it a hint of danger. I must have fallen off my bike a million times when I was a kid but I always got back into the saddle and zoomed off again at breakneck speed. The thrill of riding down rough tracks with your mates is not one that's soon forgotten.

Would you say bicycles are suitable for people of all ages? Can you think of any people who are not suited to riding a bicycle?

I think that biking is suitable for people of all ages, both young and old people. The young people love it because it gives them freedom and thrills like when you freewheel down a long hill enjoying the speed and the wind in your hair. It's good for old people too. It helps them be independent and is good exercise for their knees and joints. I don't think there are many people that are not suited to cycling.

Do you think bicycles are suitable for present society?

I think cycles are more than suitable for our present society, in fact I would say they are essential. Some of our major problems could be cleared up if more people cycled. For example the pollution caused by all the cars on the roads in our cities could be cut if cars were banned in the city and people had to use bikes. Also, another problem—the rising level of obesity would be solved. Cycling is good exercise and it would help people lose weight and be healthy.

What do you think are the advantages (and disadvantages) of bicycles compared to cars?

There are many advantages of bikes over cars. First and foremost is we could help to cut pollution if we all got out of our cars and biked to work. Secondly cycling is such good exercise. When the road is flat, it's not hard to cycle anywhere quite quickly. I guess one of the main disadvantages of cycling in the city are the mad drivers especially the taxi drivers who cut you up and never give you any space. I am often cycling with my heart in my mouth as cars, buses and even lorries use the cycle lane.

Would you say it's safe/suitable to ride a bicycle in the city (or in China)?

While I would say it is safe to ride a bicycle in the city I would still say it is risky. I am often cycling with my heart in my mouth as cars, buses and even lorries use the cycle lane. But usually the flow of traffic is quite slow and Chinese drivers are very cautious mainly because most of them don't want to scratch their car. I don't think cyclists concern them too much. However, saying that I do know a couple of people who have been knocked off their bikes. I'd have to say it's mainly e-bike riders who are the real menace though.

▶*Mobile Phones*

Do you have a mobile phone (= a cell phone)? What do you use it for? Is your mobile phone important for you in your daily life?

Of course I have a mobile phone, who doesn't nowadays? My mobile phone is totally important for my daily life. I use it all the time. It's a smart phone so I have downloaded loads of apps on to it. So I use it for messaging like with QQ or WeChat, I can use maps if I'm lost and my diary keeps me up-to-date with the things I have to do. I cannot imagine what I would do if I lost it.

When did you get your first mobile phone?

I really can't remember exactly when I got my first mobile phone; I think I was in middle school. It was a birthday present from my mum and dad and I know I was over the moon. All my mates had phones and I was feeling a bit left out. I loved that phone and I loved the funny games like snake. We were all addicted to snake at school. I think we drove some of our teachers mad because we were always looking at our phones trying to get a better score.

Is there anything you dislike about using mobile phones?

Now I'm a student. The thing I dislike most about mobile phones is often the people that use them. In my class there are a couple of kids who are always playing on their phones, even in class. This is so rude to the teacher and I know it drives her crazy when she is trying to teach us important things and these guys are paying no attention to her; they are just playing games or sending messages. So basically I think they are idiots.

Do you think you will continue using your mobile phone in the future?

Of course I will continue using my mobile phone in the future. It's an important part of my life and you know they are here to stay. We can't simply un-invent them. In fact I am totally looking forward to the new generation of phones. I mean what is going to happen in the future? What new developments will there be? I've already seen a phone that you can wear like a watch on your wrist. It's amazing.

Do people in your country like using mobile phones?

People in my country love using mobile phones. When you are on the bus or metro there's the constant jibber jabber of people chatting on their phones. Or people have their heads down staring at the screen, watching movies, reading or just playing games. So mobile phones have become an important and integral part of our daily lives, people just can't do with out them. It's a bit like an addiction.

How do you think mobile phones will develop or change in the future?

I think mobile phones will develop into something which interfaces with our bodies in a more personal way. I've seen some science fiction films where the director has tried to show this. In the film even the chips and things are inside your bodies so you don't really have to carry around a block of plastic like you do today. But that might just be fiction. But I know the developments are getting faster and faster. Just look at how the iPhone has changed.

▶ *Music*

Do you think it is necessary for children to learn a musical instrument?

I don't think that it is particularly necessary for children to learn a musical instrument. I think you have to first see if the child has an aptitude to learn. I can remember my parents wanted me to play piano, just like my grandma. But I'm actually tone-deaf; I just didn't have an ear for music. Those lessons I had were torture and I was so unhappy. But my parents soon noticed this and the lessons stopped.

What kinds of music do you like best?

I like all kinds of music but I have to say because I'm a student, I do like rock and pop the best. I really like some of the K-pop bands and a couple of J-pop bands. But mainly I listen to rock and some classic rock from the 80's and 90's. Classical music is OK I suppose and I don't listen to much of it, but it's good sometimes to have it on in the background when I'm studying.

Have you ever been to a live concert? When was the last time you attended a concert?

I have never been to a live concert. I am not really into going to classical music concerts. But as I am a student I have been to lots of live gigs. Most Saturday nights my mates and I will go downtown to catch some of the live bands playing in clubs around town. Maybe one day if someone special comes to town I will go to a live concert, who can tell?

Would you like to go to a concert in the future? If you have the chance, will you attend the concert?

I would love to go to a concert in the future and in fact I am planning on attending one soon. I am hoping that my favourite Western band will tour China soon and if they do I'll be first in the queue for tickets. If I get the tickets, and I know they will sell out fast, I'll be over the moon. I never in a million years thought I would get to see them and this opportunity will be just too good to be true.

Would you prefer to watch a concert on TV or attend a live concert?

Watching concerts on TV is great because it gives you the opportunity to see bands that might never get to China for one reason or another. So I'll often watch live concerts on TV or get the DVD of the concert to watch, but the great thing about life concerts has to be the atmosphere. After all this is a great event with lots of people all there to enjoy themselves, so the atmosphere is electric.

What is the most popular concert in China?

Well I have to say that the most popular concert in China may well be Beijing Opera. There is a whole TV channel dedicated to the Opera and people in their millions watch it. It is very traditional. I must say though it is not my cup of tea. I much prefer something more modern and-up-to date like Korean Pop. My favourite band at the moment is Big Bang.

What type of music did you like when you were a child? What about now?

You know, when I was a child the type of music I liked was the Beatles music. For some reason my Dad had an LP of their music. I forget its name now but I loved that record. I used to dance and dance until I dropped to that music. More recently I like a much more varied mix of music but the Beatles have always remained a favourite.

Do you have a lot of classmates who play musical instruments?

A lot of my classmates do play musical instruments. A lot of them are in the school band. I'm afraid I'm tone-deaf and cannot carry a tune on any instrument so I don't have to play in the band. I know some of my classmates are unhappy because their parents force them to play the instrument. But I am lucky; my parents let me off when they realised how reluctant I really was.

▶ *Birthdays*

Do you like birthdays?

Who doesn't like birthdays? I love birthdays. I love getting presents and eating cake and being with my family and friends. Having a birthday has always been a big event for me and we celebrate it religiously every year. Going to other people's birthdays is also great fun too. I like buying birthday presents for people and like I said birthday cake is always a big bonus.

Do people in China celebrate birthdays?

Of course people in China celebrate birthdays, in fact we like celebrating them so much that we have two birthdays, our Gregorian birthday and our Lunar birthday. You see we like to have our cake and eat it too. So it's great having two birthdays; it means I get to eat cake twice without having to feel so guilty about my heath.

Are any birthdays (reaching a certain age) especially important in your country?

The important birthdays in my country are when you get to twenty and fifty. When you are twenty you are then deemed legally to be an adult so you have to take responsibility for your own affairs. At fifty you are deemed to be getting on a bit. But nowadays fifty seems quite young as people are now living longer and longer because of better food and health care so maybe we will start celebrating sixty and seventy more.

How do Chinese people celebrate birthdays?

Well you know we Chinese people love to eat so it makes sense that we celebrate birthdays with a big blowout meal. We might have a much more intimate gathering at home with just our close relatives and appetising home-made food and then if it's a big birthday like a fiftieth we might go to a fancy restaurant and invite all our friends for an evening of food and entertainment.

Who do you like to celebrate your birthday with? With your friends or family?

I really like to celebrate my birthday with my family. It's important for me to be with my mum and dad on this occasion. They brought me into the world and I know that they struggled at times to bring me up when money was tight. So when I go home my mum will cook all my favourite dishes and I can sit in the bosom of my family and bask in their love. I do feel really blessed at these times.

Do all your friends know when your birthday is?

Of course all my friends know when my birthday is. It's no secret and of course on my birthday I want loads of presents so my friends need to know when it is. We all have a big cake too. I love my birthday with my friends, but if I can I will go home because it is very important for me to spend my birthday with my mum and dad who I love very much. So by hook or by crook I try to get home each year on my birthday.

Do people in China have birthday parties? (Why/Why not?)

Yes, of course people in China have birthday parties. You know in China we have two birthdays. We have our Gregorian birthday and our Lunar birthday so we like to have our cake and eat it too. But we usually only have a party on our main birthday and that is always fun with delicious food and cake. We generally invite all the relatives around to our house to enjoy the festivities and then we might end up by going to KTV to sing the night away.

Do you think it's important to give a (special) gift to someone on his or her birthday?

I think it's important to give someone a gift on his or her birthday. I love both giving and receiving gifts on birthdays. I must say that I do love thinking about what to buy for someone on his/her birthday and then wandering around the shops looking at the knick-knacks and trying to buy that perfect thing for my friend or relative.

Do children and adults celebrate birthdays in the same way?

I think that basically we all celebrate birthdays in the same way because we all love a party, right? And who doesn't love birthday cake? Birthdays give us as adults a chance to get in touch with the child we once were. So we might have a cake with candles that we still blow out to make a wish. And the table will be full of our favourite food cooked for us by our doting mum. So yes I think adults and children celebrate birthdays in the same way.

What do children do when they have a birthday party?

In my experience what children do when they have a birthday party is running around and making a lot of noise. They get so excited even if it isn't their own birthday. Of course there are nice snacks to eat and then the cake. When the cake comes everyone sings "happy birthday" and the birthday boy/girl then has to blow out the candles all at once and then make a wish. Probably all the uncles and aunties are there so the lucky kid will get some nice presents to open too.

▶ *Photographs*

Do you like taking photographs?

Yes, I love taking photos. I take them all the time. It's so handy now because most smart phones have good cameras in them and also the apps so you can edit them there and then. I also like posting my photos online to places like Instagram and Flickr. I am a bit of a shutterbug so apart from my phone I do have three or four other cameras.

How do you take photographs?

I usually take photographs on my phone. Phones now have fantastic cameras in them so they are great to use for snapping pictures on the move. I also have a Digital SLR camera for when I want to take some real good photos and I also have an old camera that uses actual films that I have to get developed. You can do some really interesting things with films that you cannot really do with a digital camera.

Do you like cameras?

I guess I do like cameras. I have about four cameras, not including my phone. I have a small digital camera I keep in my pocket and a larger format digital DSLR camera. I also have two older cameras which take films so I have to search online for the film cassettes and then I have to get the pictures developed. So I guess you can say I'm a bit of a shutterbug.

How do you organise/keep/save your photos?

I have literally thousands of photos. The vast majority of my images are kept safely on an external hard drive. There are also hundreds of photos on my computer. Those pictures I take using films and are developed I keep in albums to keep them safe. It's also good to get those albums out occasionally and I can show my friends and family some of the work I have been doing.

How do you think you will keep/save your photos in the future?

I think in terms of saving my photographs the future is already here. Once I kept my photos in an album, then with digital photos I kept them on my hard drive. Now my photos are stored in something called the cloud. I do not have the foggiest idea what that is except that my images are safely stored on a server somewhere in the world and I don't think they will ever be lost. What I think will change are the devices we use to look at those images.

Are there any photos on your wall at home?

The photos I have on my wall at home are the usual family photos. Pictures of my mum and dad and I have some really interesting black and white photos of my grandparents days. They are real revolutionary sort of photos from those old days. I sometimes think about getting some of my photos made into pictures, I guess I might get around to it one day.

Would you say photographs are a good way to preserve memories?

Of course photographs are a great way to preserve memories. Only recently my mum gave me a bunch of photos from when I was a child. There were so many things that I had already forgotten about so it was great to be able to refresh my memory and check out some of the things I got up to as a child. I'm going to put them all in an album so that I can show my kids and it's made me think about doing the same thing when I have a kid.

Do you think it's important to preserve memories?

Of course it's important to preserve memories and photographs are the perfect way to do that. I have some lovely photos of my grandparents taken when I was a kid. When my mum gave them to me I was over the moon, as I didn't have any memories of that time really. It was all a blur when I was a kid. Time passed so quickly and I had forgotten a lot of what I had done with them so it was great to get the photos. I put them in an album and I take it down and look at it regularly.

▶*Schools*

Did your parents choose a secondary school for you?

My parents had a huge say in what secondary school I went to. However I had the responsibility of passing the entrance exams to get in. I had to work really hard and had to burn the midnight oil to make sure I got a really good score. All that hard work did pay off in the end and I'm happy to say that I went to the best high school in the city.

Which school did you like the most? Will you send your children to that school?

I have to say that the school I liked the most was my high school. It's actually a private school and I really worked hard to get in. But you know hard work paid off. I was over the moon to get a place in that school. I don't know if I will send my children to that school. Once I am qualified I might be working in a different city rather than my hometown. But I do know I will try to get the best education for my child. Money will be no object.

How did you go to school every day?

Actually I didn't have to travel to school every day because I was a boarder and I lived on the campus in dorms with the rest of my classmates. When I was younger, in my primary school, I had to take the bus every day, but my mum always took me to school. I was too young to travel across the city on my own. Sometimes, if I was very lucky, my dad would drive me to school in his car. I would be over the moon sitting in the back watching the world go by on my way to school.

What was the first school you attended?

The first school I attended was a kindergarten near my mums workplace. Depending on her shift work either my mum or my grandma would take me to school, drop me off and then pick me up again in the afternoon. It was at the kindergarten that I first had a foreign teacher teach me English. It was from then that I started to love to learn English.

Where was it?

I know that my kindergarten was downtown close to where my mum worked but I don't know what the street was called as I was too little to know that. I do know that where it once stood is now a shopping mall. How times have changed. My mum told me this once when we were having coffee in the Starbucks in the mall. She said we were probably sitting right on top of what used to be my kindergarten. How strange is that?

▶ *Relatives*

How often do you pay a visit to your relatives?

Now I am a student. I don't often visit my relatives too much. I do get to see them on some of the big holidays but that's about it. Some of them are a bit irritating to be honest. They are always poking their nose into my business. Do I have a boyfriend/girlfriend is a huge topic of conversation when I'm in the room. Often they will just talk about me as if I'm not there. That's so irritating.

What do you usually do at your relatives'?

There is never really a lot to do when I'm at my relatives'. The older relatives just want to sit drinking and gossiping. Or the women will be in the kitchen cooking the meal for everyone. I sort of hang around mostly trying not to get in the way of anyone or get to be the focus of the gossip. Sometimes there are relatives who are of my own age so we might watch TV or a DVD. Going to my relatives' is never a big deal for me.

Do you prefer to visit your friends or relatives?

Most of my friends are students like me so they do not have their own homes, so at the moment I prefer to visit my relatives. Sometimes there's not too much fun to be had at my relatives' places. I might just be hanging around while the food is being cooked or I might get roped into doing something I just don't want to do. I think it's too rude just to sit there playing games on my phone or staring at the TV so I do try to get involved but sometimes I just don't want to be bothered.

Will you buy anything when you pay a visit?

It depends on who I am visiting to be honest. If I am visiting my favourite aunty or grandma I might take her some flowers or some chocolate. It will just be a small thing because I'm still a student so I am usually broke. They always protest that I shouldn't buy things for them but I can see by their smiles that they really appreciate it. And it makes me happy too.

▶ *Toys*

What toys did you like to play with when you were a child?

When I was a child my favourite toy was my bike. I just loved my bike and I was over the moon with joy when my parents gave me one for my birthday. I think that summer I was in the saddle every day. I was zooming here and there, visiting my friends, showing off my cycling skills. I think I must have fallen off about a million times. I still have the scars. But my blue bike was the best thing in the world for me.

Do you think you learned anything from playing with toys?

I think that you can learn a lot from playing with toys. Some toys teach you how to be imaginative and creative. Other toys teach you some skills. Also when you are playing with friends you have to learn about sharing and those hard lessons about winning and losing. I was always such a bad loser that I can remember running to my mum in floods of tears if I lost. But she always made me go back to try and try again. Those were good lessons for the future.

Did you (prefer to) play with those toys alone or with other children?

Playing with friends or other children was always important to me. Like everyone else I don't have any brothers or sisters so the local kids became like my brothers and sisters. When we were not in school we would all meet up like a big gang and play all those games kids would play. So in the evening we'd all be bruised and ragged with cut knees when our mums called in for supper. I remember those days like it was yesterday.

If you have children in the future, what will you give them?

I think the choice of toys for kids is important. I know that I will not want to buy guns if I have a boy. There are too many guns in the world even toy guns. And I will definitely not be buying dolls if I have a girl. I know this will probably be undermined by the grandparents and the relatives, but at least I can keep my conscience clear and make sure my kids have the right sorts of toys.

▶ *History*

Are you a student?

I'm currently a university student. I'm studying at XXX and my major is XXX. Obviously as I'm taking this test I want to continue my studies at a foreign university. So it would seem like I will be a student for many years to come yet.

Do you like history?/Do you think history is interesting?

Yes, I love history but I'm not a history buff if you know what I mean. I enjoy watching historical dramas and documentaries on TV but I don't think I would want to plough through some dry history book. I also enjoy visiting historical places and learning about the history of my country. So yes history is interesting but I couldn't study it seriously.

Do you think the Internet is helpful in learning history?

The Internet is a wonderful tool for learning about anything and in particular for learning about history. There are many websites that you can visit and even chat rooms where you can ask academics and professors questions about any historical subject you want to know about. So just at the click of a mouse you can find out about any historical subject you want. It's just amazing.

Do you think it is a good way to learn history online?

Learning anything online is fraught with danger. Many things are posted online about any given subject; it's hard to drown out the noise. What I mean is there is so much stuff that a lot of things there are just plain wrong or false. So you have to be really clear about how authoritative the source is before you use that information, say in an essay for school or university.

Do you think the resources on the Internet are reliable?

It's a well-known fact that not all the resources on the Internet are reliable. A lot of information sites like Wikipedia are open sources, this means just anyone can post anything they like on any subject. So many things are posted online now about any given subject; it's hard to drown out the noise. What I mean is there is so much stuff that a lot of things there are just plain wrong or false. So you have to be really clear about how authoritative the source is before you use that information, say in an essay for school or university.

How often do you watch programmes or films relating to history?

That's difficult to quantify. I guess I do watch a lot of films and programmes relating to history although some of them are fictional histories like *Game of Thrones*. I've also been watching a great series on the History Channel called *Vikings*. It's a fictional story but based upon real events and history. Some of the BBC programmes like *Downton Abbey* are really good too. They give me an insight into what life was like in the past.

▶ *Countryside*

Have you ever lived in the countryside for a long time?

I have always lived in the city so I have never lived in the countryside at all. Of course I have spent time in the countryside but I am a city girl/boy at heart. I like the bright lights and the hustle and bustle of the city. The countryside is just too slow and boring for me. You can't buy nice things in the countryside. I mean where would I get my daily fix of Starbucks coffee? No. I'm a city girl/boy through and through.

What are the advantages and disadvantages of living in the countryside?

One of the great advantages of living in the countryside is the fresh air. The city air is always so polluted and dirty. I get fed up having to wear a mask nearly every day. In the countryside the big disadvantage for me is that there is never anywhere to go shopping. I'm a shopaholic, I love shopping. In the countryside the nearest mall will be miles away. That's just not good at all.

Compare the availability of services such as education, health services and transportation in the city and in the countryside.

I think that the provision and availability of social services like health, education and transport in the city and countryside is like chalk and cheese. They are completely different. In the city it is really easy to get access to any of these services whereas in the countryside it's much more difficult. In the countryside people might have to travel a long way, even walk to the nearest school or hospital. That's why I love living in the city so much. I'm a real city boy/girl.

What are some of the differences between city people and country people?

There are many differences between city people and country people. In many ways they are like chalk and cheese, totally different. City people like the fast lifestyle of the city with its fast food, fast cars. Everything is just a few minutes away. We can get what we want and we can get it now. Whereas in the countryside the pace of life is slower. Maybe the farmers and country people are more attuned to the seasons than we are. Plus life is healthier, the food is better and the air is fresher. So there are many pros and cons about living in either place.

Which place is more beautiful than the countryside?

Although I think that the countryside in China is very beautiful, I do think that the seaside or the coast is a place to behold. I love being on the coast watching the sunset and the crashing waves.

The scenery is always changing as the weather changes its moods too. Being on the beach in a raging storm is actually my idea of bliss. It's just lovely watching Mother Nature at her rawest.

Which do you think is the more relaxing place to live, the city or the countryside?

Clearly the countryside is the more relaxing place to live. The pace of life is slower, the air is cleaner, but that's me a city boy/girl speaking. However, if you are a farmer and you live and work in the countryside, well I guess you would find life pretty hard work. The daily grind of planting and harvesting is hard work and probably not that relaxing. We city people think that the countryside is a rural bliss but people still have to work like dogs to make a living there.

▶ *Daily Routine*

What are you usually doing at this time?

I'm currently a student so this time in the morning I will be at class. Each of my classes at university is an hour long, but usually we have double periods so a class might be about 2 hours long. After class I might have a bit of time to grab a coffee or a bite to eat. But then before I know it, I'm rushing off to my next class.

Do you do the same thing(s) every day?

As a student my days are varied so I'm not doing the same things every day. Some days I might be in classes, studying all day. Other days might see me in the library, researching for a paper. We also have time when we can do sports or hobby clubs so I like to play badminton with my friends or use the university gym. So my life is busy. I don't get bored.

Tell me something about your daily routine.

My daily routine starts with me being up at the crack of dawn. My alarm wakes my up at about 6 am. Then I have to leap out of bed to shower and get dressed. Then I get to the school canteen to grab a bite of breakfast. I'm usually in my first class by about 7:45. Classes in the morning continue until about 11:30 when we stop for lunch. Around this time I'll try and get my head down for a little nap. Most afternoons are spent researching papers in the library and doing the writing. But also if I'm lucky and I think I can get away with it, I'll meet with my friends for coffee in the local Starbucks for a chat about this and that. In the evening I do homework and whatever housework I've got to do.

In a typical day, what do you do in the classroom?

If I am in the classroom that means I'm being a typical student. So if the teacher is good I'll be listening and taking notes. I'll be the image of the perfect student. But if the subject or the teacher is bad then I'll be snoozing at the back or playing games on my phone or, if we think we can get away with it, not be there at all. We'll head for the local coffee shop and spend our time chatting about this and that. Of course we would be in so much trouble if we got caught but luckily we have got away with it so far.

For you, what's the best time of the day for studying/working?

The best time for me to study is in the evening. I have to say I'm a bit of a night owl. So many an evening will see me burning the midnight oil. When I am stuck in my dorm, it's much quieter after my mates have gone to bed and are asleep then I can fully concentrate on my work. I try to catch up on my sleep during the midday nap time. So far it has worked out fine and I feel that this time is very productive for me.

Is your life now the same as it was before?

I have to say my life is completely different than it was before. After all in high school I was just a kid and I thought that university would be a breeze. But in reality I have been proven wrong. It's a tough life being a university student but the rewards are great. Plus I do have enough free time to enjoy life to the full. I have some great mates and we get up to all sorts of fun things. So I have to say life is even better than I thought it would be.

If you could make one change to your daily routine, what would it be?

The one change I would make to my daily routine is to add some exercise into my life. For most of the day, I sit down doing sedentary work like reading and writing. I've noticed that I'm getting fat around my belly. So I do need to work out and get fit again. But you know it's tough when I have so much to do to try and change that routine.

If you had more free time, what would you do?

If I had more free time I would do something useful like running or working out. I'm getting fat. I spend all my time being a bookworm in the library or burning the midnight oil writing papers for my professor. I really do need to get exercising so I don't feel so slothful.

How do you plan/organise your study time? Do you ever/do you often change these plans?

I tend to organise my study time around my university timetable. That makes the most sense because the days fly by so you have to keep up with what's going on in your timetable. So once I have the basic structure I can work out what I need to do and when. I think it's a pretty good system and I haven't really had to change these plans much. I occasionally have to tweak it here or there but in the main it works OK.

Can you think of any improvements to your daily routine?

I could probably think of a ton of improvements to my daily routine but the main one would be not to get up so early every day. I love my bed but the alarm clock rouses me from my beauty sleep at 6 am every morning, rain or shine. I am a bit of a night owl when it comes to studying. I often go to bed late at night, so the 6 am start always comes as a bit of a shock.

第3章

高分攻克

PART 2

- 现状和基本注意事项
- 评分要点详解
- 如何有效审题及寻找合适观点
- 如何快速展开话题（编码口语学）
- 如何利用好1分钟准备时间和记录关键词
- 官方高频题库及『编码口语学』高分范文

第1节 现状和基本注意事项

Describe a present you received when you were a child.

You should say:

what the present was

who gave it to you

how you used this present

explain how you felt when you got this present.

剑桥官方明确规定，在第二部分允许考生准备1分钟并记录相关要点，然后开始独白（独白的定义：用自己的个人经历去自然展开话题，说“小故事”给考官听，而不是传统意义上的演讲，演讲通常是比较正式的）。题目中的describe 准确的解读应该是“talk about”，独白时间为1～2分钟，中间考官无权打断（但是现在很多考官违反官方规定），当时间达到2分钟的时候，考官会说“Thank you”，然后你必须立刻停止。所以学会控制独白时间是非常重要的，在后面章节中会详细说明。目前，P2独白最佳时间长度为1分40秒左右。

P2开始时，考官会千篇一律发布同样指令，通常是：“Now I’m going to give you a topic and I’d like you to talk about this topic for one to two minutes. Before you speak, you’ll have one minute to think about what you’re going to say and you can make some notes if you wish on this piece of paper.”考官会同时给你一支铅笔和一张纸，然后问：“Do you understand?”你可以简单回复“Yes”或者“Sure”。接下来，考官会说“Here is your topic”，同时考官会采取这样的方式把题目读一遍“I’d like you to describe + topic”，并且把卡片给你。考官不会读出题目之外的其他信息。你收到卡片的时候，1分钟记时开始。

你不能要求考官更换卡片，因为剑桥官方认为这些都是非常普通的话题，适合每个考生，考生应该具备一定的想法。但是中国学生一般只关注学习，不太关注生活，知识面狭窄，而且习惯于“假大空”的思维，所以有些话题确实很难想出好的观点，即使想出观点也很难去展开（后面章节会详细介绍如何寻找合适的观点）。如果话题实在难以想出合适的观点，那就可以去编，毕竟雅思口语是语言考试，考官不在乎你说的是真是假。

在考官队伍中，有一些考官在提供话题卡的时候喜欢给考生意想不到的“挑战”，比如“体育”类型卡片给女生或“衣服”类型卡片给男生，目的是为了真正测试考生的词汇量。所以，在平时备考中，不要忽视任何一个话题。

不要在话题卡上写字，你可以将要点记在考官给你的那张要点纸（key point paper）上，考官不在乎你纸上写的是什么东西，中文甚至画图都可以，关键是要有效提醒自己该说什么（后面章节将提到如何有效书写关键词）。考官会在你讲完后收回要点纸。

如果对考题有疑问，需要在准备时间内提出，但仅限于对话题卡所表达的意图产生疑惑，如“Describe a family business”，你可以问：“Can I say something about the business run by my family or any other family business?”如果问了，考官会延长几秒准备时间，通常不会太多。不过最好不要提问，有些考官比较冷漠，甚至不予理睬，会影响到你的心情。这就要靠平时备考时请富有经验的雅思口语老师来帮你提前解惑答疑。

1分钟准备时间结束后，考官会说："Alright? Now remember, you have one to two minutes to talk about this topic and don't worry if I stop you—I'll tell you when the time's up. Could you start speaking now (please)?" 当你听到 "now" 的时候，必须立刻开始独白。在你独白的时候，你可以保留话题卡。独白结束后，考官会收回。

你在说的时候，考官无权打断或提问，即便他没有听清或听懂。在你独白的时候，考官有时会说 "Mm" "Oh" "OK" 等语气词表明自己在听你独白，不用去在意。在独白过程中，你不允许向考官提任何问题。

在你独白过程中，考官可能会时不时看自己的手表或教室内的时钟，不要太在意，这是考官在严格确保你的独白不超过2分钟。当你说到1分钟就停的时候，考官如果觉得已经了解到你的水平，独白就此结束。倘若考官觉得你没有充分发挥水平，他会用手势或简答的语言鼓励你多说。通常情况下，如果你说到1分15秒左右停止，考官就会说 "thank you" 。到2分钟的时候，考官会立刻阻止你说下去，同时会说 "thank you"，你应当立刻停止，即便有一句话没有说完也不行，如果只剩个别词就可以收尾，考官基本可以接受。

独白结束，剑桥官方规定考官可以继续问1~2个 "后续问题" (follow-up questions)，这些问题已经写在考官的问题书里，考官不允许即兴提问。这些问题不是用来测试你的语言水平，是为了显示考官对你所说的 "小故事" 感兴趣 (P2独白大部分内容应该是个人经历)。如果考官在你独白后直接跳到P3，你可能认为考官对你所说的完全不感兴趣，从而影响你的信心，在这一点上，剑桥官方还是非常人性化的！"后续问题" 基本上都是 "yes/no" 问题，考生在回答时不需要太长，但也不能简单到只有 "yes/no"，或 "Yes, I did" "No, I haven't"，最好要说得稍微长点，举例："Have you told this story to anyone else?" "Yes, I have. I told my father and he thought it was very funny." 考官也可能不问你后续问题，主要有3种可能：1.问题书上的问题不适合你的独白内容。2.你在个人经历中已经回答了这些后续问题。3.考官自己忽略了。

考官在开始P3时一般会说："You've just been speaking about + the topic of Part 2 + and now I'd like to ask you a few more general questions on the topic of + the topic in Part 2." P2中考官想获得更多你的具体信息，P3中话题一般比较笼统和抽象，后面章节中会详细介绍。

第2节 评分要点详解

在第二部分中，考官主要看重的是你的叙述能力，比如讲故事的能力。叙述能力中最关键的评分要点是：

你的流利度：你具备连续独白且保持自然速度的能力。

你的连贯性：你具备使独白易懂的能力，包含以下几个因素。

① 独白完整性

② 表达逻辑性

③ 每个小要求的展开信息之间的关联性（过渡词或句）

当然，考生要尽可能展示词汇能力和复杂语法结构，这是考官在P2部分非常看重的。

下面我们首先来学习平时如何训练流利度（主要是为了避免不自然的长时间停顿）。

对中国考生来说，保持独白的连续性是个非常大的挑战，如果独白中出现大量的不自然停顿，会大大影响最终的分数，所以这是考生第一步需要加强的！下面是短期改善的3条建议：

(1) 备战中勤加练习

① 考生需要找一个练习口语的小伙伴，每天坚持和对方用英文聊天，可以聊聊每天发生的事情，探讨一些感兴趣的话题（如都教授为什么在中国这么受欢迎），重点是一定要互相交换信息。记住，在给出信息的时候，不要忘了说出自己的感受。这个属于基本口语练习，可以让考生对口语没有陌生感，因为很多中国考生是很少开口说英文的。

② 和小伙伴在一起按照雅思口语模式练习P2话题，最好是之前没有准备过的话题，严格按照时间要求，记录关键词，努力去说1~2分钟。这可以培养你的"brainstorm"能力，对考试非常有利！

③ 朗读并理解多叔范文（本章第6节），但千万不要背。现在市面上也有很多范文素材，但内容基本上是客观描述，更像演讲，不是自然的独白！所以不建议去使用。

(2) 有足够的信息去说（本章第4节中会介绍）

(3) 训练自然长停顿能力

当你用中文独白的时候，也会出现一些长停顿，这些长停顿是非常自然的。但在雅思口语P2中，我们通常在长停顿的时候会冷场，这样做是非常不合适的。在独白的时候允许有长停顿，但是要保证让考官知道你在思考，这也是考官所谓的"speak your thoughts"中的一部分。除了内容表达上比较连续，长停顿的时候嘴里也要有话说（think aloud），这样整个独白听起来就比较顺畅。

Um, let me see. What else can I tell you?

Mm, what else is there?

What else can I tell you about old Nanjing Street? (if you are describing a street)

What have I forgotten to tell you?...Oh yes...

还有一种特殊情况是，考生在较短时间内完成了独白，但是发觉时间还远远达不到最佳标准（1分40秒），可以采用以下方式继续说下去，避免尴尬！

Oh, when I told you about...I forgot to say that...

As I mentioned before...

As I was saying...

I forgot to mention/I forgot to add/I forgot to tell you...

记住，考生要在平时训练中刻意练习这种长停顿方式，在实际考试中如果出现此类停顿，嘴里会习惯性地念念有词，但是脑子却在思考后面到底该说些什么。

其次，我们需要了解如何使P2独白更具连贯性。

总体来说，如果考生的P2独白更具完整性、逻辑性，就更容易让考官听懂。很多中国考生喜欢信口开河，说到哪儿是哪儿，完全不顾及题目的要求，也很难保证完整性。

① 要学会审题，不要偏题（本章第3节将会详细介绍）

② 要多训练标记语（discourse marker）的使用，比如：

as a matter of fact, as far as I know, as far as I can remember, luckily, surprisingly, accidentally, actually, as you probably know

③ 小要求展开信息之间要有过渡表达（承上启下），结尾要有总结

承上表达：

OK, so I've just given you some information on...

OK, so, I guess you understand/see/know...

启下表达：

Now let me turn to...（切忌读出小要求，要简单转换）

Now I'd like to talk about...

结尾总结：

So I think you already have a pretty good picture of...

So I hope by now you have a good idea of...

第3节　如何有效审题及寻找合适观点

考生在审题时要牢牢记住两点：

(1) 对题目中的形容词或副词要特别重视，在独白中要重点描述。

举例：Describe a historic building you visited.

你在独白中要用大量篇幅说明这个形容词“historic”，你可以介绍其他和题目相关的信息，但不能喧宾夺主。多叔在教学过程中发现，很多考生喜欢套用范文，把类似的素材直接拿过来，看似都在讲同一个事物，但是逻辑重点不同，考官一眼就会识破你在背诵或套用。

题目下面的小要求不能遗漏（有不少雅思口语教师说这些只是提示，这种理解是错误的），每个卡片上都明确标明“you should say”，其含义是“you should include these points but you can also include other suitable points”。从侧重点上来说，最后一条小要求是至关重要的，最好要用自己的切身经历来说明。另外，很多同学经常问这些小要求是否需要按顺序说，答案是否定的。除了第一个要求一开始就要点明，其他小要求可以打乱顺序。

(2) 合理寻找观点。

许多中国的考生觉得很多P2话题比较难，比如描述一部法律等，甚至一些普通的话题，如描述一个对中国重要的名人，考生都需要考虑很久，好不容易想出一个观点却无法继续说下去。

主要原因有两个：① 知识面太窄，不关心生活；② 习惯“假大空”的思维。

老外喜欢“真小实”，因此考生在寻找观点的时候千万不要“think too big”，要从接地气的观点入手，而且最好选择自己比较熟悉的，在讲的时候要实实在在告诉考官你的想法及理由。举个例子：描述一个你感兴趣的国家，首先是不要纠结什么叫感兴趣，其实感兴趣就是你觉得这个国家有什么东西吸引你，你觉得好玩，比如韩国，你就说那里有很多出色的流行音乐街头show，然后具体描述你是通过何种手段知道的，并且结合自己真实的感受和想法。再比如：描述一顿特殊的饭，考生绞尽脑汁思考什么叫特殊，其实非常简单，你要学会赋予意义然后解释充分就可以了，你完全可以说大学里的“散伙饭”（farewell dinner）。最后，我想说的是老外觉得考题都非常简单，只是我们和他们的思维方式不同而已！

好了，现在我们来学习寻找观点的捷径，多叔总结出8字法则：

“宁熟不新，宁词不熟。”

宁熟不新：有时候考生喜欢追求新奇的观点，想借此来给考官留下好的印象，但是需要注意的是，你在说的时候可能完全没有东西可以呈现，所以不要图一时口快。我们应该去寻找自己比较熟悉的观点，说到这儿，肯定有考生会说：“如果很多考生都说过这个观点，那我岂不是就没戏了。”这种理解是错误的，考官不在乎你说的观点是否陈旧，他只在乎你是否在说自己的经历。每个人的经历都是不同的，即便是同样的观点，内容也千差万别。

宁词不熟：我们面对话题时，可能会想到2~3个比较熟悉的观点，这个时候要注意了，要选择自己词汇量相对充足的观点。举个简单例子，当考题是“描述一个你去过的旅游景点”时，有的考生会同时想到两个景点，“九寨沟”和“南京夫子庙”，一般来说，后者可能会更好展开，考生储备的词汇也会多些，因为针对夫子庙考生可以说当地的工艺品店或者演出，但是九寨沟主要是自然美景，中国考生在这方面词汇稍微欠缺。

第4节　如何快速展开话题（编码口语学）

▶实验

在学习“编码口语学”之前，我们先来看一个有趣的实验：

我曾经让10个英语口语水平良好的考生面对10个不同的话题，按照雅思考试要求做独白性描述，然后录制他们的答案，最终形成文字数据，经过统计学分析，得出一个惊人的结论：他们语言中82.3%的潜意识是相同的，只不过根据题目的改变，呈现潜意识的语言相互有别。

1. 概念

这里面有3个概念。

概念1：描述

从主观视角呈现事物的状态，并通过切身体验表达自己的感受。

概念2：潜意识

在描述一件事物的时候，潜意识指的是在脑中形成的习惯性想法。

概念3：语言

语言是潜意识的外在呈现方式，其本身不具备“可移植性”。

2. 解读

在学习完这3个概念之后，我们来解读上面的实验。

雅思P2考题都是描述性话题，而描述是一种人类对事物的常规解读方式，所以，考生在思维层面上一定有一套习惯性潜意识去实现描述行为，然后根据被描述对象的不同而改变语言呈现方式。思维是语言的载体，思维不变，语言却可以变化万千。这样就解释了前面实验中出现的现象，10个考生因为面对10个不同话题，所以语言表达各有不同，但思维层面上却有很多相同的潜意识。下面就详细介绍这一整套潜意识。

目前雅思口语话题只分为四大类：人物、地点、物体（具体物体和抽象物体）、事件。

想把这些对象描述清楚，考生仅需要传递四组信息。

信息1：描述对象是什么

信息2：对象特征是什么，包括具体特征和抽象特征

信息3：相关经历是什么

信息4：影响体会是什么

这四组信息分别包含对应的潜意识，整体加起来就构成一整套潜意识。我们拿第一组信息举例子，“对象是什么”里面包含潜意识“对象名称、怎么知道的、过去什么情况”，这些都是我们在平时生活中描述“对象是什么”的时候，通常有的习惯性潜意识。考生可能会产生疑问：题目的小要求可以通过这些潜意识满足吗？答案是肯定的。因为题目本身就是描述，所以出题者列出的小要求自然包括在这些潜意识里。

举例说明：

Describe a famous person who is important to your country. **You should say:** **who this person is** **how you know about the person** **what sort of life they had before they became famous** **how this person became famous** **explain why this person is important to your country.**

这个话题中前三个小要求完全可以用第一组信息“对象是什么”来充分诠释：

The famous person that I would like to say something about is Mo Yan. Actually he is the writer of a famous novel called *Big Breasts and Wide Hips*. In my view I really think he is quite a talented novelist.（对象名称及相关信息）I do remember I found something about him on a domestic website called Sohu.（怎么知道的）I was surfing online just for fun and from a news report I knew that he used to be a poor farmer in a small village.（过去什么情况）

理解了上述基本原理之后，下面我们来系统学习P2思维拓展神器“**编码口语学**”。

我们把所有的话题都视作“A”，根据前面所学，将描述应该包含的四组信息进行编码，其中“对象特征”拆分为“具体特征”和“抽象特征”，故总计五组信息。

A1 **描述对象**	A11 对象名称
	A12 怎么知道的
	A13 过去什么情况
A2 **具体特征**	
A3 **抽象特征**	A31 特征是什么
	A32 举例说明
	A33 有什么效果/结果
A4 **相关经历（小故事）**	A40 过渡句
	A41 场景
	A42 当时的行为
	A43 突然的发现
	A44 细节描述
	A45 切身感受
A5 **影响体会**	

举例说明：

> **Describe a person who visited your home.**
>
> **You should say:**
>
> **who the person is**
>
> **when the person visited you**
>
> **what you and this person did together**
>
> **explain how you feel about this visit.**

* A1 描述对象

A11 对象名称

这个涉及如何合理开头，不少考生喜欢绕半天才讲到主题，如 “in my life, there are so many..., however, I would like to...” 考官喜欢开门见山，并最好同时转述 (paraphrase) topic!

编码结构： topic + your general view

举例：The person who visited my home that I would like to say something about is my dear friend. In my view I really think she is quite nice.

A12 怎么知道的

一般情况下，我们都习惯使用 “在什么情形下” 及 “大概什么时间” 来表述如何知道一件事物。

编码结构：situation + time

举例：I do remember that the first time she visited my home was when I was still a freshman.

A13 过去什么情况

我们在介绍一件事物的时候，总喜欢提及其过去，就如同导游一说到某地就喜欢来点历史背景，否则索然寡味。

一般由 “获知渠道” + “相关信息” 构成。

编码结构：access + information

举例：I heard from my mum that she had been selected for the Chinese squad in the Olympic games, so she's sporty too.

* A2 具体特征（只有人物、地方、具体物品含有这个编码）

人物

我们在介绍一个人的时候，喜欢提及年龄、体型及典型面部特征。

编码结构：he/she is + age + body shape + facial feature

举例：She is about 30 years old with a slim figure, and you can see a lovely dimple on her left cheek when she smiles.

地方

我们在介绍地方的时候，具体特征一般包括位置、周边有什么及距离多远。

编码结构：location + surrounding + distance

举例：It is situated in the northwest of my hometown. Not far away from it, you can find the central train station, only 5 minutes' walk.

具体物品

我们在介绍物品的时候，常常习惯谈到形状、材质及颜色。

编码结构：shape + material + color

举例：It has a shape of swift and is made of wood, which impressed me by its flame red outer skin at the first sight.

* A3 抽象特征

A31特征是什么

特征都是别人给出的评价，所以首先要说到相关人群，然后给出特征。

编码结构：related people + feature

举例：All her friends consider her to be really intelligent and have a really sharp mind.

A32 举例说明

这个就比较简单了，可以用各种举例的方式，如"for instance"，当然也可以不说。

举例：For instance, she has a very good understanding of maths but you know, it's all Greek to me.

A33 有什么效果/结果

和上面一样，可以简单明了地使用"therefore""as a result"来表达抽象特征带来的结果。

举例：Therefore, we have often sat together and she has shown me how to do some of the more difficult sums in my homework.

* A4 相关经历（小故事）

在解析A41场景的时候，需要在其前面加上A40（过渡句），原因很简单，A4是用来回答最后也是最重要的一条小要求，所以我们要先用A40来过渡并强调。

A40 过渡句：一般的表达方式为"Finally, I would like to..."或"Finally, I would say..."

举例：Finally, I would like to give you a little story about why I like this girl visiting me so much.

A41 场景

我们说故事时，通常喜欢用场景开头而不是简单的具体时间，比如"那是一个寒冷的冬日下午"就比较有故事带入感。

编码结构：weather + time

举例：It was on a freezing cold winter's afternoon.

A42 当时的行为

我们说完场景之后，就会习惯性地提到当时自己在干吗，这样的描述会很有画面感，同时可以更好地导出后续的故事。

编码结构：(at that time) I was doing... + place

举例：I was preparing for my final examination at home.

A43 突然的发现

因为最后一条要求是解释你的感受或表达原因，在说故事的时候提到“突然的发现”，就直接找到焦点，引出你的评论和感想。比如谈饭店的时候，你可以说突然发现这个饭店的“焦点”是服务特别好，从而自然谈及相关细节和最终的感受。

编码结构：At that moment + ...grabbed my attention

举例：At that moment there was a heavy knock on the door which grabbed my attention.

A44 细节描述

这一条属于考生自由发挥部分，考生可以直接添加自己的信息。

举例：To my surprise，standing there was my good friend with a big smile on her face. She had come here just to help me. With her guidance I finished my work very quickly. I feel very happy not only because I passed my examination but that I had such a good friend.

A45 切身感受

表达感受有两种常见方式，练好一种基本上就可以了。

编码结构：I + *adv* + *v*（+ ...）或者 I was *v*-ed(+ by...)

举例：So I really enjoy her visits because she is always a breath of fresh air in my life.

* A5 影响体会（机动部分，如果实际考试中时间差不多了，这条可以省略）

最后抒发一下你迄今对描述对象的印象或感受。

编码结构：Even so far, I still + *v* + ...,which/who brought me...

举例：Even so far, I still remember that visit from her, which brought me a good memory.

注意：

① 不是每个话题都要涵盖所有编码，根据实际需要，有些可以省略。

② 编码根据题目需要，部分可以打乱顺序，这样表达起来更加灵活，同时更好满足题目要求。

③ 如果话题是关于未来的，如“你想去的一个旅游景点”，只需要改变编码中部分时态即可。

第5节　如何利用好1分钟准备时间和记录关键词

如何利用好1分钟准备时间？首先，拿到题目之后10秒内要想出到底该说什么，并决定怎么开头，不少考生在时间过去大半的时候还在纠结到底该说些什么，或者准备开始说的时候突然卡壳，不知道该怎么说出第一句话，从而造成不必要的紧张，甚至对后面考试的信心产生极大损害。

考生只要记下编码口语结构中的关键词来提醒自己，尤其是动词(包括时态，因为考生很容易在动词时态上犯错)，同时用斜线“/”将记录下的关键词隔开，这样既方便又清晰。

第6节　官方高频题库及“编码口语学”高分范文

People

> **Describe a person who visited your home.**
>
> **You should say:**
>
> **who the person is**
>
> **when the person visited you**
>
> **what you and this person did together**
>
> **explain how you feel about this visit.**

**Answer:*

The person who visited my home that I would like to say something about is my dear friend. In my view I really think she is quite nice. Thinking back I do remember that the first time she visited my home was when I was still a freshman. I heard from my mum that she had been selected for the Chinese squad in the Olympic games, so she's sporty too.

All her friends consider her to be really intelligent and have a really sharp mind, for instance, she has a very good understanding of maths but you know, it's all Greek to me. We have often sat together and she has shown me how to do some of the more difficult sums in my homework.

Finally I would like to give you a little story about why I like this girl visiting me so much. It was on a freezing cold winter's afternoon and I was preparing for my final examination. It was a hard slog. At that moment there was a heavy knock on the door which grabbed my attention. To my surprise, standing there was my good friend with a big smile on her face. She had come here just to help me. With her guidance I finished my work very quickly. I feel very happy not only because I passed my examination but that I had such a good friend. So I really enjoy her visits because she is always a breath of fresh air in my life.

**Idioms:*

think back: to remember something

Example: Melissa and Jay both fell silent, thinking back to the dreadful time when Jack had almost died.

it's all Greek to me (informal): something that you say when you do not understand something that is written or said

Usage note: This phrase comes from Shakespeare's play, *Julius Caesar*.

Example: I've tried reading the manual but it's all Greek to me.

slog (informal): to work very hard or to use a lot of effort to do something

Example: You've got this wonderful man who slogs his guts out for you, and all you do is criticizing him!

grabbed my attention: to draw or attract someone's attention

Example: The scary movie grabbed my attention.

a breath of fresh air: someone or something that is new and different and makes everything seem more exciting

Example: Angela's like a breath of fresh air when she comes to stay.

Describe someone you had a good time with or someone you enjoy spending time with.

You should say:

who the person is

how you knew this person

what you did together

why you would like to spend time with this person.

**Answer:*

The person I would like to say something about is my dear friend Mr. Dou. In my view I really think he is quite nice. Thinking back I remember that the first time he visited my home was when I was still a freshman. I heard from my mum that he has a reputation as a famous math teacher.

All his friends consider him to be really intelligent and have a really sharp mind, for instance, he has a very good understanding of maths but you know, it's all Greek to me. We have often sat together and he has shown me how to do some of the more difficult sums in my homework.

Finally I would like to give you a little story about why I like spending time with this man so much. It was on a freezing cold winter's afternoon and I was preparing for my final examination. It was a hard slog. At that moment there was a heavy knock on the door which grabbed my attention. To my surprise, standing there was my good friend with a big smile on his face. He had come here just to help me. With his guidance I finished my work very quickly. I feel very happy not only because I passed my examination but that I had such a good friend. So I really enjoy his visits and spending time with him, because he is always a breath of fresh air in my life.

Describe a famous person who is important to your country.

You should say:

who this person is

how you know about the person

what sort of life he had before he became famous

how this person became famous

explain why this person is important to your country.

Answer:

The famous person that I would like to say something about is Mo Yan. Actually he is the writer of a famous novel called *Big Breasts and Wide Hips*. In my view I really think he is quite a talented novelist. I do remember I found something about him on a domestic website called Sohu. I was surfing online just for fun and from a news report I found that he used to be a poor farmer in a small village.

For all of his die-hard fans, he is considered to be really hardworking. He never stops writing; he is a born scribbler. He finally got the chance to win the Nobel Prize in Literature, which seemed to be incredible for Chinese writers of the past decades.

Finally I would say that his contribution to the status of Chinese literature in the world today is immense. Maybe a little story can help you to understand. It was on a cold winter's afternoon, at that time I was watching a talk show online. Suddenly the experience of a guest of honour grabbed my attention. The focus was on the first Chinese writer to shock the world with his novels. His works depicted the true picture of Chinese society in the 1960s and soon I was completely amazed by his importance to China. Without him we would have no opportunities to know so much about our past. Now you can see why I admire him so much! He is a great writer who has brought much honour to China.

Idioms:

surf online: to browse around in the contents of the Internet

Example: I spend an hour a day or more surfing online.

die-hard: to end with difficulty

Example: It is a nightmare for die-hard smokers who now can only smoke in the open.

guest of honour: a guest who gets special attention from everyone; the person for whom a party, celebration, or ceremony is given

Example: Bob is the guest of honour, and many people will make speeches about him.

Describe a time when someone helped you.

You should say:

who the person is

where and when the person helped

how the person helped you

explain how you felt after the person did this.

Answer:

The person who helped me that I would like to say something about is my mum's friend who teaches maths at the local university. I do remember that the last time she visited my home was when I was still a freshman. I heard from my mum that she had also been selected for the Chinese squad in the Olympic games, so she's sporty too.

I would like to give you a little story about how this teacher helped me so much. It was on a freezing cold winter's afternoon and I was preparing for my final examination. It was a hard slog. To my shame I'm quite hopeless when it comes to maths. All her friends consider her to be really intelligent and have a really sharp mind. She also has a very good understanding of maths but you know, it's all Greek to me. At that moment there was a heavy knock on the door. To my surprise, standing there was my mum's good friend with a big smile on her face. She had come here just to help me. With her guidance I finished my work very quickly.

I feel very happy not only because I passed my mathematics examination but that I had such a good teacher. So I really enjoy her visits because she is always a breath of fresh air in my life. She is always very patient with me as she goes through all the difficult sums and equations and shows me the ropes. We have often sat together and she has shown me how to do some of the really difficult sums in my homework. She is such a helpful person and so modest too.

Describe an intelligent person.

You should say:

who this person is

when and where you first met him/her

what kind of person he or she is

explain why you think this person is intelligent.

**Answer:*

The person who I think is really intelligent is my mum's friend who teaches maths at the local university. In my view I really think she is quite nice as well as being brainy. I do remember that the first time she visited my home was when I was still a freshman. I heard from my mum that she had also been selected for the Chinese squad in the Olympic games, so she's sporty too.

All her friends consider her to be really intelligent and have a really sharp mind. She also has a very good understanding of maths but you know, it's all Greek to me. But she is very patient with me as she goes through all the difficult sums and equations and shows me the ropes. We have often sat together and she has shown me how to do some of the really difficult sums in my homework.

Finally I would like to give you a little story about why I think this teacher is so intelligent. It was on a freezing cold winter's afternoon and I was preparing for my final examination. It was a hard slog. At that moment there was a heavy knock on the door. To my surprise, standing there was my mum's good friend with a big smile on her face. She had come here just to help me. With her guidance I finished my work very quickly. So you know this shows that not only is she an intelligent academic but that she also has emotional intelligence. She cared enough to come and help me. She is always a breath of fresh air in my life.

**Idiom:*

show somebody the ropes: to explain to someone how to do a job or activity

Example: The new secretary started working today so I spent most of the morning showing her the ropes.

Describe a person you enjoy talking with.

You should say:

how often you talk with this person

when you usually talk with him or her

what topics you usually talk about

explain why you enjoy talking to him or her.

**Answer:*

The person who I enjoy talking with is one of my lecturers at university, Mr. Dou. In my view I really think he is quite nice. I do remember that the first time I met him was when I was still a freshman at university. But now he often drops by at lunch for a chat with the students when he can. He has something of a reputation as a famous writer in China.

All his friends consider him to be really intelligent and to be as sharp as a tack. He also has a very good understanding of English romantic poetry but you know, it's all Greek to me. We have often sat together and chatted about this and that in the canteen over coffee or lunch. He has shown me how to write articles for my college newspaper and some romantic poems which he loves.

Finally, I would say some of his ideas are very interesting and creative. Maybe my personal experience can help you to understand. It was on a cold winter's afternoon. At that time I was attending his lecture in the multi-media classroom of my school. His ideas about campus love grabbed my attention. He said: "Campus love should be considered as a compulsory course for students!" I discovered that he had figured out many benefits of campus love that I had never heard before. I was totally amazed by these ideas. When I first met him I felt that talking with him would be a great pleasure and our talks together since have proved just that.

**Idioms:*

drop by: to visit briefly

Example: About 100 guests dropped by to celebrate the publication of his book.

as sharp as a tack: very intelligent

Example: He may be old in years, but he's still as sharp as a tack and knows what he's talking about.

this and that: one thing and another

Example: You can see a lot of activities in the park; people are riding bikes, playing ball, doing this and that.

Describe an occasion you met a friend who you hadn't seen for a long time.

You should say:

who the person was

when you met the person

how you keep in contact

explain how you feel about this person.

**Answer:*

The friend I met who I hadn't seen for such a long time was my friend Kim. She used to be my classmate in primary school. About 2 years ago, I was waiting for the city bus when quite unexpectedly I bumped into her. What a surprise we both had. I must say fate was on our side that day.

Let me tell you more about it. It was on a cold winter's afternoon and I was waiting to catch the bus in front of my university. It was freezing cold and everyone was bundled up but I noticed a familiar face standing next to me. Surprise surprise, it was my primary school classmate. I couldn't believe my eyes. We have not seen each other for nearly ten years. Luckily we were waiting for the same bus so we sat and chatted about this and that. I actually missed my stop because we spent so much time catching up with each other.

I promised her that I would organize a dinner for our reunion. Now we keep in touch by using our mobile phones or sometimes by Skype. As for how I feel about her, I am really pleased that we have got together again and even more pleased that she has gained some success as a novelist. She is especially good at romantic stories. Now when we are together having coffee or over lunch, we often talk about how to be more romantic.

**Idioms:*

bump into someone: to chance on someone; to meet someone by chance(not normally with physical contact)

Example: Guess who I bumped into downtown today.

bundle (oneself) up (against something): to wrap oneself up in protective clothing or bedding as protection against the cold

Example: Please bundle yourself up against the frigid wind.

Example: Bundle up before you go outside.

couldn't believe your eyes: if you say that you couldn't believe your eyes when you saw something, you mean that you were very surprised by it

Example: I could hardly believe my eyes. They'd made so many changes; it looked like a completely different house.

keep in touch: to maintain communications with someone; to maintain up-to-date knowledge about someone or something

Example: After my neighbour moved, we still keep in touch.

Describe an interesting wild animal from your country.

You should say:

where you learned about this animal

what it looked like

where you saw it

explain why you like this interesting animal.

**Answer:*

The wild animal I would like to say something about is the wild elephant. The first time I saw it was when I was having a trip to XX. I heard from the local residents that wild elephants used to be the best friends of their ancestors living cheek by jowl. They had worked and lived together, so both man and beast would have an intimate understanding of each other and they would work together as a team.

The first time I saw a wild elephant, I was a bit taken aback. It was so huge and looked so strong. It was a real beast of burden. Let me give you an example. The wild elephant has a very long and strong trunk compared with other elephants. It's so strong that it can even carry people on it.

Finally, I would say this wild animal means a lot to local people. Maybe my experience can help you to understand. It was on a cold winter's afternoon. I was talking with a local man and he told me about a wild elephant which grabbed my attention. I discovered that 10 years ago an elephant had saved a child's life by defeating a group of wolves. I was totally amazed by the greatness of wild elephants. Since then the elephant has been my favourite kind of wild animal.

**Idioms:*

cheek by jowl: side by side; close together

Example: The two families lived cheek by jowl in one house.

taken aback: confused or surprised by something unexpected

Example: Company executives have been taken aback by the criticism.

Example: I asked him directly if he was looking for someone with my skills, and I think he was kind of taken aback.

a beast of burden (literary): a large animal, which is used for pulling vehicles or carrying heavy loads

Example: Huskies are traditionally used in the Arctic as beasts of burden.

Describe a situation when you helped someone.

You should say:

what the situation was

who the person was

how you helped him/her

explain how you felt after helping him/her.

**Answer:*

I would like to describe a situation when I helped someone. Actually the person was my best friend at high school and we have been inseparable since we first met. We had been applying to universities and were waiting with bated breath for the letters. Then on this fateful day she got her university entrance scores and unfortunately she had failed by the skin of her teeth. She had wanted to enter this particular university for a very long time and suddenly her bubble had burst.

Finally I would like to give you a little story about how I helped my friend in her time of need. It was on a freezing cold winter's afternoon when I went to her place and took her out for a walk. Walking along the river I said to her: "I know you are in a very bad mood now but this is life. Sometimes life is hard but you need to fight back until you get what you want." I must have struck a chord with her because one week later she made the decision to try again next year. Finally I'm pleased to say she succeeded in getting her place. I was over the moon for her not only because of her success but that she also took my advice.

**Idioms:*

with bated breath: while holding one's breath

Example: We stood there with bated breath while the man hung on the side of the bridge.

Example: They listened with bated breath for the announcement about the winner.

by the skin of one's teeth: just; barely; by an amount equal to the thickness of the (imaginary) skin on one's teeth

Example: I got through calculus class by the skin of my teeth.

Example: I got to the airport a few minutes late and missed the plane by the skin of my teeth.

burst someone's bubble: to destroy someone's illusion or delusion; to destroy someone's fantasy

Example: I hate to burst your bubble, but Columbus did not discover Canada.

Example: Even if you think I am being foolish, please don't burst my bubble.

strike a chord: if something strikes a chord with someone, they are interested in it and like it because it is connected with their own lives or opinions

Example: Clearly the book has struck a chord, as we can see from the hundreds of letters we have received from readers.

Example: Her ideas on social reform will strike a chord with poor people everywhere.

be over the moon (informal): to be extremely pleased about something

Example: Marie got the job. She's over the moon.

Place

Describe a street where you like to go shopping.

You should say:

where it is

what you buy there

how often you go there

and explain why you like to go to this street for shopping.

**Answer:*

The street where I like to go shopping is Gold Street located in the northwest part of Nanjing. In my view I really think it is quite famous for the variety of shops and the warm-hearted people living there.The place is really buzzing along with people going here and there. The first time I paid a visit to this street was when I was on a trip to Nanjing. From my friends I heard that there were a lot of the world's top brands, so being a shopaholic, I just had to see by myself.

For the young girls who are really into shopping, like me, it is considered to be a great place for grabbing bargains. You can find whatever you want from diamonds to dumplings. Now, I go there almost once a week.

Finally I would like to give you a little story about why I like this place and why this street is extremely good for shopping. It was on a warm spring afternoon, I was wandering around the streets. At that moment a lovely pair of shoes caught my eye. I decided on the spur of the moment to buy them. But very unfortunately I found my purse had been stolen. Then the shop owner, a lady with a sweet smile, walked towards me and grabbed my attention. She calmed me down and called 110 for the police. She even gave me some cash so I could get back to school. So you can understand why I like this place now.

**Idioms:*

buzz along: to move along fast

Example: The cars were buzzing along at a great rate.

Example: The traffic is sure buzzing along.

here and there: at this place and that; from place to place

Example: We find rare books in used-book stores here and there.

Example: She didn't make a systematic search. She just looked here and there.

grab someone or something away (from someone or something): to snatch someone or something away from someone or something

Example: Harry's aunt grabbed the dirty candy away from him before he got it in his mouth.

Example: I grabbed away the meat from the dog.

catch somebody's eye: to attract someone's attention

Example: Out of all the beautiful things in the garden, the fountain was what really caught my eye.

on the spur of the moment: suddenly; spontaneously

Example: We decided to go on the spur of the moment.

Example: I had to leave town on the spur of the moment.

Describe a park or garden you visited and liked.

You should say:

where it was

what it looked like

what people did there

explain how you felt about this park.

**Answer:*

The park that I know best and I have visited a lot is the old Nanjing Park. The park means a lot to me. It's in the northwest part of Nanjing—the capital city of Jiangsu province. It is quite famous locally for its beauty, in fact it's the city's jewel in the crown. The first time I paid a visit to this park was when I was on a trip to Nanjing. I had heard from a local tourist guide that the park used to be considered one of the top ten parks in China.

For everyone that visits this park the old Nanjing Park is considered to be extremely peaceful. It's like entering an oasis of calm. Large dense green trees surround it and it's like entering a hidden forest. Let me give you an example: when you enter this park you feel like you are in the countryside, not the middle of a bustling busy city. People often go there to relax, doing things such as tai chi, walking or even dating, walking hand in hand with their lovers.

Finally, I would say that this park truly deserves a visit. Maybe my personal experience will help you to understand more. It was on a cold winter's afternoon. I was wandering around the park when a small pond grabbed my attention. I discovered that the pond was as clear as crystal so that you can see the fishes swimming in the water. I had never seen this kind of pond before. I was totally amazed by the beauty of the pond and of the whole park. Now you can understand my feelings about this park.

**Idioms:*

the jewel in the crown (+ of): the best or most valuable thing in a group of things

Example: The island of Tresco, with its beautiful tropical gardens, is the jewel in the crown of the Scilly Isles.

bustle around: to move about very busily

Example: The people were bustling around, trying to get things ready for the picnic.

Example: I wish you would stop bustling around.

clear as crystal: very clear; transparent

Example: The stream was as clear as crystal.

Example: She cleaned the windowpane until it was clear as crystal.

Describe a restaurant you like to go to/that impresses you.

You should say:

where this restaurant is

what type of food this restaurant has

why you go to this restaurant

explain why you like this restaurant.

**Answer:*

The restaurant that I like to go to is an old Nanjing restaurant. The restaurant is called "Old Nanjing". This restaurant is close to my heart. It's in the northwest part of Nanjing, the capital city of Jiangsu province. It is quite famous locally for its fabulous food and great service. The first time I paid a visit to this restaurant was when I was on a trip to Nanjing. I had heard from a local tourist guide that it used to be considered one of the top restaurants in China.

For foodies who love this restaurant, including me, the old Nanjing restaurant is very well known for a type of food called Huai Yang flavour. This is so delicious. I go to this restaurant just to experience these flavours on my tongue. The food is just out of this world.

Finally, I would say the service in this restaurant is pretty good. Maybe my personal experience will help you to understand. It was on a cold winter's afternoon. I was looking for some food to share with friends and we were all really peckish; we really needed a bite to eat. In the restaurant a lovely lady grabbed my attention when she came to help me order the food. She told us the background of each food and recommended choice dishes. So I was totally amazed by the great service in this restaurant. Now you can see how much I like it and why.

**Idioms:*

close/dear to somebody's heart: if something is dear to someone's heart, it is very important to them

Example: Animal rights is an issue very close to my heart.

out of this world: wonderful and exciting

Example: This pie is out of this world.

Example: My boyfriend is just out of this world.

bite (to eat): to get something to eat

Example: I need a few minutes to grab a bite to eat.

Example: Bob often tries to get a bite between meetings.

Describe a historic building you have visited.

You should say:

where it was

what people do there

why you went there

explain how you felt about this building.

**Answer:*

The historic building I have visited is the old Nanjing library. This building means a lot to me. It's in the northwest part of Nanjing, the capital city of Jiangsu province. It looks like an ancient castle built around 100 years ago. It is quite famous for its old book resources and the academic atmosphere inside. The first time I paid a visit to this library was when I was on a trip to Nanjing. I had heard from a local tourist guide that in recent memory this old library was one of the top ten oldest libraries in China.

For readers who love this library, including me, it is extremely well known locally for the facilities inside. Let me give you an example. When you enter the library, you can see the old wooden chairs and wide dusty bookshelves; this makes reading a mysterious adventure. You can wonder at who has sat on these chairs before you—famous authors, professors or just us bookworms.

Finally, I would say this historic building carries all the memories of Nanjing city. Maybe my personal experience can help you to understand. It was on a cold winter's afternoon and I was wandering about in this library, looking for a book. A wall full of photos grabbed my attention and I noticed that these images were taken lots of years ago. These old black-and-white snapshots reflected the scenes of the old days of Nanjing. I am amazed at the significance of this library for the people in the city. Now I guess you can see my feelings about this old library.

**Idioms:*

in recent memory: the period of time in which things are still remembered and discussed

Example: Never in recent memory has there been this much snow!

Example: I haven't been this happy in recent memory!

wonder at someone or something: to be amazed at or in awe of someone or something stilted

Example: We all wondered at Lee and the way he kept his spirits up.

Example: The people wondered at the bright light that lit up the sky.

wander about/wander around: to stroll or amble around without any purpose evident; to roam around

Example: We just wandered about downtown all morning, looking at the shop windows.

Example: It's fun to wander around in a strange town.

Describe a place (not in your country) you like to visit.

You should say:

how and why you would go there

how you know about this place

what the scenery is like in this place

who you would go with

and explain why you want to visit it.

**Answer:*

The place that I would like to describe is Jizhou Island, a tourist attraction in South Korea. It is quite an interesting and appealing destination for young people like myself. It would be great to go there by air to spend the spring festival, enjoying all the attractions. I do remember I found out about this island from a website called Sohu when I was just surfing the Net. Then I did a Baidu search to find out more and I knew that it used to be one of the top ten island destinations a few years back.

For travellers like me who love Jizhou Island, it has an extremely good reputation for its beauty and other attractions. For instance the blue blue sky, the long, soft beaches and of course the warm sea for swimming. In my dreams I would go to this paradise with my new lover. It's a heaven on earth in my view.

Finally, I would also say that Jizhou Island is a good place for foodies. Maybe a little story will help you to understand. It was on a hot summer afternoon and I was looking at sites on the Internet about Jizhou when a picture grabbed my attention. It showed a yummy South Korean dish being served to several holidaymakers crowded around a table. Every one of them was enjoying their food; you could see the delight in their smiles. I discovered that a lot of travellers went to Jizhou just for a taste of that special dish. I was totally amazed by the thought of this food and I fell in love with this place. I know that one day I will enjoy a bite to eat there. Now I suppose you can see why I want to go there so much.

**Idioms:*

surf the Net: to browse around in the contents of the Internet

Example: I spend an hour a day or more surfing the Net.

dream about someone or something/dream of someone or something: to have mental pictures about someone or something, especially in one's sleep

Example: I dreamed about you all night last night.

Example: I dreamed of a huge chocolate cake.

paradise (on earth): a place on earth that is as lovely as paradise

Example: The retirement home was simply a paradise on earth.

Example: The beach where we went for our vacation was a paradise.

heaven on earth: something extremely good

Example: Brian's parties are heaven on earth—the food is marvellous and the company is terrific.

fall in love (with something): to become enamoured of something

Example: I simply fell in love with the dress. I had to have it.

Example: I fell in love with the red car and bought it at once.

Describe a place you visited to learn another culture.

You should say:

where you went

what you learned

how you learned it

explain how you felt about this culture.

**Answer:*

The place where I visited to learn another culture is a small town located in the central part of Anhui province. Its name is "she" in Chinese. It is very well known for its unique local culture which is called temple fair there. As far as I can remember, I paid a visit to that town around 7 years ago when I was on my winter vacation. When I was there I learned that this culture has lasted for nearly 1,000 years.

For travellers who are interested in the temple fair, learning this culture is considered to be very easy and enjoyable. A typical example I want to tell you about is that by simply being in the crowd at temple fair, you can experience the charm of that festival. You can be doing things like eating local snacks, buying some souvenirs or just hanging out, watching interesting street performances. These things always make me very excited.

Finally I would say this Anhui culture definitely deserves attention. Maybe my personal experience will help you to understand. It was on a cold winter's afternoon and I was shopping with my mum at the temple fair when we noticed a small show not far way. This show grabbed our attention and getting close to it, we discovered that a lovely local girl was displaying her embroidery skills. She was able to make wonderful work within 10 minutes. She had such nimble fingers that she made a beautiful landscape of this town just with needle and thread in next to no time. All the things amazed me, especially the skills of the local people. So I guess you now know how I feel about the town and its culture.

**Idioms:*

as far as/(in) so far as: to the degree that

Example: As far as I know, he isn't coming to the party.

Example: The city once went so far as to threaten to shut off the building's water supply.

pay (someone or something) a visit/pay a visit to someone or something: to visit someone or something

Example: Bill paid a visit to his aunt in Seattle.

Example: Please pay a visit to our house whenever you are in town.

hang out (some place): to spend time aimlessly; to waste time

Example: Bill: "What are you doing this afternoon?" Tom: "Oh, I'll just hang out."

Example: Kids hang out too much these days.

in next to no time (informal)/in no time (at all) (informal): if something happens or is done in no time, it happens or is done extremely quickly

Example: It's only another mile or so. We'll be there in next to no time.

Example: He had the food ready in no time.

Describe a seaside place you like to visit.

You should say:

where it is

how you know it

what you do there

who you go there with

explain why you like to visit it.

**Answer:*

I would like to describe Qingdao, which is a beautiful coastal city located in the eastern part of China, I really think it is so impressive for its great seaside beauty as well as lots of small wooden houses. I do remember I found out about this city from a website called Sohu when I was just surfing the Net. Then I did a Baidu search to find out more and I knew that it used to be one of the top ten tourist attractions a few years back.

For travellers like me who love this city, it has an extremely good reputation for its beauty and other attractions. For instance the blue blue sky, the long, soft beaches and of course the warm sea for swimming. In my dreams I would go to this paradise with my new lover. It's a heaven on earth in my view.

But this time it was these houses that attracted me to visit again. Maybe a little story will help you to understand. It was a warm summer afternoon and I was walking towards the seaside and I was feeling very excited as I was on holiday. Then along the beach there were several wooden houses that grabbed my attention. They were all built in an old style and were a bit battered and weather-beaten but in my eyes beautiful all the same. In the same location you can also find lots of seafood restaurants serving delicious locally caught fish which I love. I was totally attracted by that kind of house. I still dream of having one of these houses so I can live in this special seaside town. Maybe if I am lucky one day I will live there—my fingers are crossed.

**Idioms:*

batter (someone or something up): to damage or harm someone or something

Example: Who battered up this desk?

cross your fingers/keep your fingers crossed: (often an order) to hope that things will happen in the way you want them to

Usage note: People often cross their middle finger over their first finger as a sign that they are hoping for luck.

Example: We're crossing our fingers and hoping that the weather stays fine.

Example: Keep your fingers crossed, everyone. Jane's only got to answer one more question.

Describe the ideal house that you would like to live in.

You should say:

where it would be

what type of house it would be

who you would like to live with

and explain why you would like to live in that kind of house.

**Answer:*

The ideal house that I would like to live in is a small wooden house near the sea. I really think it would be fantastic to live inside. I saw this kind of house when I was having a trip in Qingdao, a beautiful coastal city. I have to say it's my dream house.

For people like me who love this kind of house, it is considered to be extremely suitable for having a romantic and artistic type of life. When you open your windows, you can see the ocean and smell the fresh sea breezes and the light that comes of the sea is so clear and fantastic. Or you can choose to simply walk along the beach hand in hand with your boyfriend or girlfriend, shoes off, paddling in the warm shallow water.

Finally, I would say that this house is a paradise for living. Maybe a little story will help you to understand. It was a warm spring afternoon and I was walking towards the seaside and I was feeling very excited as I was on holiday. Then along the beach there were several wooden houses that grabbed my attention. They were all built in an old style and were a bit battered and weather-beaten but in my eyes beautiful all the same. In the same location you can also find lots of seafood restaurants serving delicious locally caught fish. It's foodie heaven. I was totally attracted by that kind of house and the lifestyle. I still dream of having one even after so many years. Maybe if I am lucky one day I will live there—my fingers are crossed.

**Idioms:*

dream house/dream home: an idealized home perfectly fitting the needs and desires of its inhabitant(s)

Example: This is our dream house.

hand in hand: holding hands

Example: They walked down the street hand in hand.

Example: Bob and Mary sat there quietly, hand in hand.

Objects (Concrete)

Describe something special that you saved money to buy.

You should say:

what it was

how long it took you to save money to buy it

why you wanted to buy this thing

explain how you felt when you bought it.

**Answer:*

The special thing that I saved up money to buy is the limited edition of a famous novel called *Future Love*, written by a Chinese writer Mo Yan. I made up my mind to buy it when I finished reading the first chapter of it in a local shop. Actually it was very expensive; it cost me nearly 2,000 RMB. I saved all of my money for 2 months in order to get it and it broke my bank.

For the readers who love this book, it is considered to be very valuable, not in monetary terms but in its cultural value. What I want to tell you is that it was the first book that reflected the true history of China in 1960s. Therefore, as a student who is very interested in history I really wanted to get it and by hook or by crook I did.

Finally, I would say this book really gave me a surprise. Maybe my personal experience can help you to understand. It was on a cold winter's afternoon. I was wandering around in a local bookshop as I just mentioned because I'm a bit of a bookworm. Then a book in the corner grabbed my attention. I noticed that it was the book that I had been longing for for a long time. I could not find it anywhere else before. I was completely amazed by this discovery. I'm sure you can guess my feelings when I bought it. I was over the moon about it and very happy.

**Idioms:*

save (up) (for something): to accumulate money in order to buy something

Example: I can't buy a car because I am saving up for college.

Example: I don't have the money now, but I am saving up.

make up your mind/make your mind up: to decide something, esp. what to do

Example: She's made up her mind to take dancing lessons.

Example: Once you've made your mind up, there's no turning back.

break the bank: to use up all one's money (alludes to casino gambling, in the rare event when a gambler wins more money than the house has on hand)

Example: It will hardly break the bank if we go out to dinner just once.

Example: Buying a new dress at a discount price won't break the bank.

by hook or (by) crook: by any means, legal or illegal.

Example: I'll get the job done by hook or by crook.

Example: I must have that house. I intend to get it by hook or crook.

long for someone or something: to desire or pine for someone or something

Example: She is longing for her old friends.

Example: Walter longed for his hometown in the mountains.

over the moon: extremely pleased and happy.

Example: When he sent me flowers and a note, I was over the moon.

Describe something that you enjoyed reading.

You should say:

what it was

how much does it cost

what it is about

explain why you like it.

**Answer:*

Something that I have enjoyed reading recently is a magazine called *Cuisine Life*. I really think it is very useful for me, as I love cooking. I bought it from a local bookshop when I had a trip to Nanjing and it only cost me 20 yuan. I knew that it was one of the top ten popular magazines in China.

For the lovers of this type of magazine, it is thought to be really excellent in introducing the cuisines of different places across China. As a foodie, I now read it quite often. I love trying the dishes out on my long-suffering friends.

Finally, I would say this magazine has given me a lot of pleasure. Maybe my personal experience can help you to understand. It was on a cold winter's afternoon. I was reading this magazine in a Starbucks in downtown Nanjing, just whiling away an afternoon. In the magazine a local dish called salty duck grabbed my attention. Then I noticed that the magazine even showed the detailed address of where to buy it. In a flash I had jumped on a bus and went to buy some. I was over the moon because without it I wouldn't know about this great food in Nanjing. Now you can see why I like this magazine.

**Idioms:*

while away something: to spend time in a relaxed way

Example: Commuters while away the time when they are stuck in traffic by listening to their favourite radio station.

in a flash: quickly; immediately

Example: I'll be there in a flash.

Example: Suddenly my wallet was gone. It happened in a flash.

Describe a time you forgot/lost something.

You should say:

what you forgot

when and where you forgot it

what are you doing at that time

explain how you felt after you forgot it.

**Answer:*

I would like to tell you about when I forgot something. I'm going to tell you about a photograph album that I lost. I bought it when I was on a shopping trip to Nanjing. My mum had given me a lot of old photos and I needed something to store these precious memories.

It was a couple of years ago on a cold winter's afternoon. I was walking around with my dad in a local shopping mall, just wandering about really with some time on our hands. There were so many things to see on each floor. But then a photo album in a corner grabbed my attention. I just thought that it was incredibly perfect in design; it even had a silk cover. I was impressed by the flame red words written on the cover saying "good memory". I knew this was just the thing for the family snaps so I bought it without any hesitation. Later we went to Starbucks for coffee and a bite to eat. But when we got on the train to go back home I suddenly found it was not with me. I must have left it there. I was so irritated by my own carelessness and how stupid I was.

When my family heard this, they said "what a pity", but even now they still tease me about my poor memory. Now when I forget something, they say: "Where's your album?"

Idioms:

time on your hands: a period when you have nothing you must do

Example: These kids have too much time on their hands, and they get into trouble.

Example: For the traveller with time on his hands, try a boat ride on the river that surrounds the city.

just the thing/the very thing: exactly what is needed

Example: A week's rest would be just the thing for her.

Describe a present you received when you were a child.

You should say:

what the present was

who gave it to you

how you used this present

explain how you felt when you got this present.

Answer:

The present I received when I was a child was a great kite in the shape of swift. It still sticks in my mind. Whenever I see a similar kite flying, it always takes me back. I remember that I got this gift from my dad when I was a little kid around 5 years old. I played with it almost every day in the spring. Even when there wasn't a breath of air, I would take it out, hoping for wind.

For me, this kite was sort of hard to play with well. Let me give you an example. At first, I was too clumsy to operate it. It would not fly very smoothly or very high. But even this poor performance could satisfy me. I had never flown a kite before and it was so exciting.

Finally, I would say that this gift meant a lot to me. Maybe my little story can help you to understand. It was on a warm spring afternoon. I was celebrating my fifth birthday with my whole family. We were all very excited about having a party. Then my dad conjured up a big box. It just grabbed my attention. After I opened it I discovered that it was my favourite toy, a kite. I was over the moon with joy. I could not help running and jumping in the house like a lunatic. This was the gift I had been longing for for a long time. I had seen all the other kids with them and I was green with envy. Now I guess you can understand my feeling after I got my big kite.

Idioms:

sticks in the/your mind: if something sticks in the mind, you remember it easily, often because it was exciting or strange

Example: Of all the things that we did in Crete, that boat trip really sticks in my mind.

Example: She had one of those faces that sticks in the mind.

take sb. back: if something takes you back, it makes you remember a period or an event

Example: That piece of music really took me back (to my schooldays).

conjure someone or something up: to make someone or something appear, seemingly by the use of magic

Example: The magician conjured seven white doves up.

Example: Then an old wizard conjured up a horse.

long for someone or something: to desire or pine for someone or something

Example: She is longing for her old friends.

Example: Walter longed for his hometown in the mountains.

green with envy: appearing jealous; appearing envious

Example: My new car made my neighbour green with envy.

Example: Bill was green with envy that I won first place.

Describe an old thing in your house.

You should say:

what it is

how (or when) your family got this thing

how long your family has kept it

explain why it is important to your family.

**Answer:*

The old thing in my house that I would like to say something about is an old TV set. Its brand name is "panda". I heard that it used to be the most popular kind in 1980s but now of course it seems as old as the hills. As far as I can remember, my dad bought it back when I was a kid of around 6 years old. Now it has been kept in my house for 20 odd years.

For my whole family this TV set is considered to be very significant. Back then watching TV was the only way to entertain ourselves. So we all cherish that TV, even now my mum even keeps it polished and gleaming with loads of elbow grease.

Finally, I would say this TV set means a lot to my family. Maybe a little story can help you to understand. I remember many years ago it was on a cold winter's afternoon. My whole family were preparing for the upcoming Spring Festival. Then my dad carried a big box in. This grabbed my attention, so I ran to open it. When I discovered that it was a TV set I jumped for joy. Soon the whole family were completely cheered up. We had a great Spring Festival because we could watch the Spring Gala for the first time. So I guess you can see the importance of this TV to my family.

**Idioms:*

old as the hills: very old; ancient

Example: That's not a new joke; it's as old as the hills!

Example: Our family custom of eating black-eyed peas on New Year's Day is old as the hills.

elbow grease: hard scrubbing

Example: Tom: "What did you use to get your car so shiny?" Mary: "Just regular wax and some elbow grease."

Example: Joe put a lot of elbow grease into cleaning the kitchen.

jump for joy: to be very happy about something good that has happened

Example: Tina jumped for joy when she found out she'd be in the team.

Describe an item of clothing that you wear on formal occasions.

You should say:

what this clothing looks like

where you bought it

on what occasions you wear it

explain why you wear it on that occasion.

**Answer:*

The item of clothing that I wear on formal occasions is a swallow-tailed coat. I guess you might know what it looks like. I really think it is quite the thing for someone like me. Thinking back, I bought it when I was having a trip to Nanjing around 3 years ago and I was a bit flush with money.

For young people who are into fashion and style like me, it's considered to be the best choice for some special occasions like wedding parities. Therefore, when my friends celebrate their big days I often wear this swallow-tailed coat. This coat helps me to show my deep respect to my friends but also lets me show off a bit too. I don't think it will ever go out of fashion either.

Finally, I would say that wearing that coat makes me look smarter and well dressed on these occasions. I guess I'm a bit of a dandy at heart. Maybe a little story can help you to understand. It was on a warm spring afternoon and I was attending the wedding party of my classmate Jerry and I was proposing a toast to my friends around me. Then I noticed people gazing at me. This grabbed my attention but I discovered that they seemed to be less interested in me, but more interested in my nice coat. I was completely amazed by the attraction of this kind of coat and how it can make you popular, especially with the girls/boys.

**Idioms:*

think back (to something): to remember back to something in the past

Example: Now, try and think back to the night of January 16.

Example: My mind is preoccupied with other things. I can't think back.

go out of fashion: to become unfashionable; to become obsolete

Example: I hope this kind of thing never goes out of fashion.

propose a toast: to make a toast before a celebratory drink

Example: I'd like to propose a toast in honour of your birthday.

Example: At the wedding reception, the bride's father proposed a toast to the new couple.

Describe a work of art you have seen.

You should say:

when you saw this work of art

where you saw it

what it looked like

explain your feelings about this work when you saw it.

**Answer:*

The work of art that I have seen is a huge wooden sculpture which quite took my breath away. Although it's big I really thought it was also quite delicate. The first time I saw it was when I was having a trip in an old street in Nanjing. I heard from my dad that it used to be considered a landmark in the city.

For people who have seen this wooden sculpture, it is considered to be an example of really excellent craftwork. It's shaped like a fish, therefore if you stand a little far away from it, it looks like a real fish swimming in the air.

Finally, I would say that it really stunned me at my first sight. Maybe a little story can help you to understand. It was on a warm spring afternoon. I was wandering about with my dad along the street. Then a huge fish appeared in front of me. It totally grabbed my attention and I was speechless for a second. Then I discovered that it was around 15 meters high and completely made of wood. You could even see the fish scales on the body. I was totally amazed by the high artistic standards of it. Now I suppose you can understand my feelings about this work when I saw it.

**Idioms:*

take your breath away: if something takes your breath away, you feel surprise and admiration because it is very beautiful, good, or exciting

Example: The beauty of the Taj Mahal took my breath away.

I'm speechless: I am so surprised that I cannot think of anything to say

Example: Mary: "Fred and I eloped last week." Sally: "I'm speechless."

Example: Tom: "The mayor just died!" Jane: "What? I'm speechless!"

Describe something (except computer or phone) that you can't live without.

You should say:

what the thing is

where and when you bought it

how often you use it

explain why you can't live without it.

**Answer:*

The thing that I can't live without is my digital camera. I really think it is indispensable for my life. I'm a bit of a shutterbug and I love taking snaps. I bought it on a trip to Nanjing about 3 years ago so it's getting on a bit now, but I still love it.

For the people who love taking photos, having a digital camera always comes in handy. Let me give you an example: Whenever you see a beautiful scene you can simply take it out of your pocket to take a picture. So I use it almost every day.

Finally, I would say it is very important for my life. Maybe my personal experience can help you to understand. It was on a cold winter's afternoon. I was wandering around in a forest park. Then a small pond grabbed my attention. I discovered that it was so clear as crystal that you can see the fishes swimming in the water. I had never seen this kind of pond before so I took a picture of it. Thanks to my digital camera, I can share the beauty of this pond with friends. Without it I would lose a lot of good memories. That's why I cannot live without my digital camera and I would even say it's like my third eye.

**Idioms:*

getting on (in years): becoming old

Example: She's getting on in years, but she's healthy.

come in handy: (for something) to be useful

Example: I think that this gadget will come in handy in the kitchen.

Describe a photo that you like.

You should say:

when it was taken

who took it

what was in it

explain why you like it.

**Answer:*

The photo that I like very much is a photo about a famous dish, "braised meat with persevered vegetables". I'm a bit of a shutterbug and am snapping pics all the time. I took it in a small restaurant when I was having a trip to Nanjing. I really think it is quite funny. I heard from my best friend Alex that this photo is considered to be my best work by my friends but I think they are pulling my leg.

But for the fans of this image in my Instagram account, the food in it is considered to be really attractive. After seeing this snap online, lots of people have been to that small restaurant in Nanjing just so they could have a bite to eat. Maybe I should ask for a discount next time I go there.

Finally, I would say that I am so proud of this photo. Maybe a little story can help you to understand. It was on a cold winter's afternoon. I was having a dinner in that small restaurant I had mentioned before. Then this wonderful dish grabbed my attention. I quickly took out my camera and took a picture of it. I discovered that the picture turned out to be so clear and showed all the good points of this food. Even when looking at it, it made my mouth water and luckily it tasted as good as it looked. I am totally amazed by the effect this photo had online. That's why this is my favourite photo.

**Idioms:*

pull someone's leg: to kid, fool, or trick someone

Example: You don't mean that. You're just pulling my leg.

Example: Don't believe him. He's just pulling your leg.

make someone's mouth water: to make someone hungry (for something); to cause saliva to flow in someone's mouth

Example: That beautiful salad makes my mouth water.

Example: Talking about food makes my mouth water.

Objects (Abstract)

Describe a film that you disliked.

You should say:

what it was

where you watched this film

why you chose to watch this film

explain why you disliked this film.

**Answer:*

Personally, a film I disliked was a bad film called "Over the Map". I really think it is very poor in both its style as well as the acting skill. As far as I can remember, I watched this film in a large theatre when I had a trip to Nanjing about 2 years ago. I heard later from a news report that it was considered one of the worst films in that year.

On the basis of the movie trailer, this film was thought to be extremely attractive, a must-see movie. People were talking about it at school and it was meant to be the new blockbuster of the year. So I chose to watch this film without any hesitation but made a fool of myself.

Finally, I would say this film really wasted my money. Maybe my personal experience can help you to understand. It was on a cold winter's afternoon and I was watching this movie together with my dad in the nice warm cinema. Then a ridiculous image grabbed my attention. I noticed that there was a plane flying in the air on the screen and you know that the film is set in 1649! I was completely shocked by the poor quality of this film. It wasted both my time and money. It was just money down the drain. That's why I disliked this film so much.

**Idioms:*

make a fool (out) of someone/make a monkey (out) of someone: to make someone look foolish

Example: John made a monkey out of himself while trying to make a fool out of Jim.

Example: John made a fool out of himself at the party.

Example: Are you trying to make a monkey out of me?

(throw/pour) money down the drain: to waste money; to throw money away

Example: What a waste! Buying that old car is just pouring money down the drain.

Example: Don't buy any more of that low-quality merchandise. That's just throwing money down the drain.

Describe a time when you are busy.

You should say:

when the time is

what you do at this time

how you arrange your time

explain how you feel during this busy time.

**Answer:*

The time when I am at my busiest is the end of last term at college. I really think it is very torturous time. I actually have a lot of trouble when I am preparing for the final exam. It is difficult memorizing a lot of academic terms.

By the way, for all the Chinese students like me, the final exam is considered to be the hardest as it covers a lot of ground. Therefore, I need to make a timetable to revise the different courses. I need to organize my life.

Finally, I would say something that happened which was quite time-consuming. Maybe my little story can help you to understand. It was on a cold winter's afternoon of last term. I was preparing for my English exam in my dormitory. Then suddenly an email grabbed my attention. I discovered that Professor Duo had given us a new assignment to do. We had to read 5 English novels within 10 days and write a report for him. I almost lost it. I was totally shocked by this terrible news. It was like he was kicking us when we were down. I was just like busy bee during this time so I guess you can see how I felt during that horrible fortnight.

**Idioms:*

cover a lot of ground: to deal with much information and many facts

Example: The history lecture covered a lot of ground today.

almost lose it: to nearly lose one's temper, composure, or control, as out of anger

Example: I was so mad, I almost lost it.

Example: When he saw the dent in his fender, he almost lost it.

kick somebody when he/she is down: to do something bad to someone when you know they already have a lot of problems

Example: His wife left him last month and I don't want to kick a man when he's down, but we simply don't have any more work for him.

be as busy as a bee (old-fashioned)/be a busy bee (old-fashioned): to be very busy or very active

Example: She's as busy as a bee, always going to meetings and organizing parties.

Describe an unforgettable advertisement (that you saw or heard or liked).

You should say:

where you saw or heard it

what kind of advertisement it was

what the contents of the advertisement were

and explain how you felt when you saw or heard this advertisement.

**Answer:*

The unforgettable advertisement that I would like to tell you about is a famous one called "NBJ". I really think it is very creative. As far as I can remember, I watched this advert on a video website named Youku when I was surfing the Net. My friend told me that it was chosen as one of the best advertisements in China last year.

This advert is considered to be a successful commercial. For example, the product "NBJ" became a household name just because it shows the exaggerated excitement of people when they get it. So these words were on everyone's lips. In fact it got to become a bit of a bore.

Finally, I would say this advertisement left deep impression on me. Maybe my personal experience can help you to understand. It was on a cold winter's afternoon. I was watching this advertisement online as I mentioned before. I heard the slogan being repeated several times which grabbed my attention. It said "we only want NBJ in the Spring Festival". This became a bit of an earworm so that after watching it, you still remembered the name and found yourself mindlessly repeating it to yourself. I was totally amazed by the effect of this advert. Yes, it was really an unforgettable advert.

**Idioms:*

a household name/a household word: well known by everyone; commonly and widely known

Example: I want my invention to become a household word.

Example: Perry Hodder has become a household name.

leave an impression (on someone)/leave someone with an impression: to provide a lasting memory for someone after one has left (akin to "make an impression on someone")

Example: Her performance was less than stunning. She didn't leave a very good impression on us.

Describe something you enjoy doing with an old person in your family.

You should say:

who the person is

what you enjoy doing with the person

where and when you do it with the person

explain why you enjoy doing it with the old person.

**Answer:*

The thing I enjoy doing with an old person is playing chess with my grandpa. I really think it is very funny and meaningful for both of us. I started to like playing chess at home when I was still a young whippersnapper of about 8 years old.

For my whole family, playing chess with my grandpa is considered to be a good way to learn from him. Typically he often plays chess with a lot of strategy. But I tend to play it impulsively, therefore I make lots of stupid mistakes. I'm a bit hotheaded in these games. Grandpa comes around my house most weekends and now I look forward to our chess games.

Finally, I would say playing chess with my grandpa is quite beneficial. I remember once I was wandering around in my community when I saw several old men sitting in a circle which grabbed my attention. Getting close to them, I discovered that my grandpa was playing chess with his old friends. Unlike me, he always thought for a long while before moving one chess piece. He is a bit of a master. I was totally amazed by his carefulness and cleverness. Since then I have found that playing chess with my grandpa brings me great enjoyment.

**Idioms:*

a hothead: a person who gets angry easily; hot tempered

Example: Phil, don't be such a hothead. Try to control your anger.

look forward to something: to anticipate something with pleasure

Example: I'm really looking forward to your visit next week.

Example: We all look forward to your new book on gardening.

Describe a course you learned at school, university or evening class.

You should say:

what the course was

what you did at school, university or evening class

who taught the course

explain what you learned from the course.

Answer:

The course that comes to mind is a training course for learning French. I really think it was very useful for me. I studied the language together with my roommate in the training centre of my university when I was still a freshman.

We all thought that the teacher is absolutely excellent. She was an enthusiastic teacher for whom nothing could faze her. A typical example I want to tell you about is that she often taught us with great patience and she had spent 5 years in France, so she was a bit of a Francophile.

The last point? Maybe my personal experience can make you understand. Thinking back, it was a warm spring afternoon and I was having a trip in Qingdao when a foreign couple asking the way caught my attention. I discovered that they came from France and nobody could understand them. I walked towards them and communicated in what I think was standard and fluent French. Even so they understood me and I showed them the right way to go. I was so proud of myself and over the moon that they understood me. Without that French course and my great teacher, I would not be able to speak so well and I couldn't have helped that couple.

Idioms:

come to mind: (for a thought or idea) to enter into one's consciousness or be remembered

Example: Do I know a good barber? No one comes to mind right now.

Example: Another idea comes to mind. Why not check in the phone book?

bring something to someone's attention: to make someone aware of something; to mention or show something to someone

Example: I would like to bring this problem to your attention.

Example: If there is something I should know about, please bring it to my attention.

Describe a subject that you want to give information to others.

You should say:

what the subject is

when people ask you information about the subject

what you would say

explain how you feel after people ask you information about the subject.

**Answer:*

The subject that I want to give information to others about is Chinese culture. I really think it is full of interesting things. And of course China is a hotbed of traditions and traditional activities. When I was selected as a teaching assistant, I received a lot of questions about this subject. I was over the moon because I knew that Chinese literature was the most popular subject in my university and I could give really good answers.

For teaching assistants, introducing this subject is an easy and interesting job. Once you start to tell people about culture, they can get the gist of what you are doing and they are off doing their own work. So very soon they are able to benefit from what they can get from this subject.

Finally, I would say I was as pleased as Punch when people asked me for information. Maybe my personal experience can help you to understand. It was on a cold winter's afternoon. I was checking emails when one email grabbed my attention. It contained lots of detailed questions. I could feel the curiosity and interest from the student who had sent this email. After I had answered all of the questions, I felt a strong sense of achievement. I knew I had done a good job. I was very satisfied with what I had done for that student.

**Idioms:*

hotbed of something: a nest of something; a gathering place of something

Example: This office is a hotbed of lazy people.

Example: My class is a hotbed of nerds.

pleased as Punch: delighted; very pleased (this refers to Punch from the "Punch and Judy" shows)

Example: Child: "Do you think Grandma will like the picture I'm making for her?" Father: "I think she'll be as pleased as Punch."

Example: Fred was pleased as Punch to discover that Ellen was making lemon pie, his favourite, for dessert.

Describe a type of sport you like to do.

You should say:

what it is

when and where you play it

how you play it

what equipment and clothes are needed for this sport

explain what benefits you get from playing this sport.

**Answer:*

The sporting activity I like to do is playing tennis. I really think it is very exciting and healthy for my body. I usually play it on the school tennis court when I finish my class. I'm not that sporty but I love bashing the ball about on a sunny day.

My friends take playing tennis very seriously. Let me give you an example. As a beginner, you need to move a lot and use the right moves otherwise you might get hurt. So we have to do warming up exercises before we play. Then they demand that we wear the proper stuff. So I put on my tennis kit, grab my racquet and probably tempting fate I take a first aid box with me when I play.

Finally I would say this sport offers a lot for both viewers and players. Maybe a little story can help you to understand. It was on a cold winter's afternoon. I was watching the Australia Open when, a girl named Li Na grabbed my attention. I discovered that she was passionate about the game. Apart from this she had a wonderful figure. I was so attracted by this sport that after seeing Li Na I play tennis very regularly that helps me to work up a sweat, release some stress and as a bonus exercises my body too.

**Idioms:*

bash someone or something around: to treat someone or something roughly (physically or figuratively); to beat on or abuse someone or something (physically or otherwise)

Example: Stop bashing me around, and let's talk.

Example: The robber acted as though he was about to bash around his victims.

tempt fate:

1. to do something which involves a risk and may cause something unpleasant to happen

Example: I always feel it's tempting fate to leave the house without an umbrella.

2. to cause bad luck for yourself by talking too confidently about a situation

Example: It's probably tempting fate to say so, but I haven't had a cold all year.

work up a sweat: to put a lot of effort into something

Example: The volunteers are working up a sweat to make sure everything is ready on time.

Describe a subject you disliked in high school.

You should say:

what the subject was

how the teacher taught

how long you studied

why you disliked it.

**Answer:*

The subject I disliked the most in high school was the singing class. I studied this subject for almost one year—it felt like an eternity. I clearly remember I began to be tired of this subject before I'd even finished the first class. This was because, honestly, I cannot carry a tune.

Also the way our singing teacher was teaching this subject was really boring. In fact it was mind-numbing. A typical example is that the teacher kept asking us to sing again and again without developing any useful skills. This is typical of Chinese teaching methods—repetition, repetition. This was so annoying that I spent most of the classes muttering under my breath bad things about my teacher.

For the last point, maybe my personal experience can show you the problem. If I think back, it was on a warm spring morning. I was taking that first class. The first song in the textbook was named "My Future Is Not a Dream"; this grabbed my attention, as it was a song I knew and loved. So we waited impatiently for the teacher to teach us how to sing it. Surprisingly I discovered that the teacher just wanted us to simply follow him like sheep. We kept doing this for nearly 10 minutes so soon I was totally irritated. So now you can see why the singing class was so dislikable!

**Idioms:*

carry a tune: to be able to sing accurately

Example: For such a complicated song, they should at least find someone who can carry a tune.

mutter something about someone or something: to say something softly and indistinctly about someone or something

Example: I heard him mutter something about being late.

Example: Sharon is muttering something about Dave. What does she mean?

under one's breath: spoken so softly that almost no one can hear it

Example: John was muttering something under his breath, and I don't think it was very pleasant.

Example: I'm glad he said it under his breath. If he had said it out loud, it would have caused an argument.

(be) like sheep (disapproving): if a group of people are (like) sheep, they all behave in the same way or all behave as they are told, and cannot or will not act independently

Example: They all followed him like sheep.

Describe a family business you know.

You should say:

what this business is

how you know it

what kind of people their customers are

explain why this business is so successful.

**Answer:*

The family business I know is the small flower shop owned by my uncle. In my view I think it is a very successful business. He started to run it with his partners when I was still a little kid in primary school. I heard from my dad that his flower shop used to be the most popular in the whole city. You could say my uncle was enjoying the sweet smell of success.

For people who know this shop, it's considered to be really well known for selling fresh flowers. Therefore most of customers are young boys and girls who often buy flowers for their lovers. How wonderful to be able to act like Cupid with his arrows, helping love to flower.

The last point is a personal experience which can let you understand. If I think back to a cold winter morning, I was walking by his shop and I noticed a crowd of people there which grabbed my attention. They were all waiting in a line beside the gate. I discovered that my uncle was helping a young girl choose her favourite colour and the most appropriate flowers very carefully and was asking her the reason why she was going to send these flowers. He was being the perfect gentleman. I was totally amazed by his considerate service as well as all his prospective customers. This is why this small business is so well known and successful.

**Idioms:*

in view of something: in consideration of something; because of something

Example: In view of the high cost of gasoline, I sold my car.

Example: I won't invite John to the meeting in view of his attitude.

the sweet smell of success (informal): the pleasant feeling of being successful

Example: He enjoyed the sweet smell of success.

Describe the season you like.

You should say:

what season it is

what the weather is like

what you usually do

why you enjoy this season.

Answer:

Personally the season I love so much is the summer. I really think this season is full of fun and games. I remember enjoying this weather even when I was still a little kid in primary school around 7 years old.

For students, whether at senior high or college, summertime is thought to be so exciting. A typical example I want to share with you is that almost every day is sunny and we can have a long vacation which always lasts two months. During this holiday, I often enjoy lots of interesting activities such as fishing and swimming. I love these lazy days of summer.

The last point I want to make can be explained by my personal experience. It was a hot summer afternoon. I was still doing my homework at home which made me feel very bored and irritated; my head was buzzing. I was hoping that the summer time could pass as quickly as possible. But then a loud voice grabbed my attention. It was someone saying, "Double duo, please get out and come swimming with me." I discovered it was my classmate and best friend Peter. Quick as a flash I ran out and we had a lot of fun in the local swimming pool. Soon I was totally addicted to summertime because I could do such great outdoor activities and have so much fun with my mates.

Idioms:

fun and games: playing around; doing worthless things

Example: All right, Bill, the fun and games are over. It's time to get down to work.

Example: This isn't a serious course. It's nothing but fun and games.

buzz with something: (for a place) to be busy or filled with something

Example: The room buzzed with excitement.

Example: The office had better be buzzing with moneymaking activity when I get there.

quick as a flash: very quickly

Example: I'll finish this work quick as a flash.

Describe something you did to help you learn another language.

You should say:

what you did

where and when you did it

who you did it with

and explain why it was helpful.

Answer:

What I did to help me learn another language is a training course for learning French. I really think it was very useful for me. I studied the language together with my roommate in the training centre of my university when I was still a freshman. We studied week in and week out religiously. I don't think I missed a class. I enjoyed it so much.

We all thought that the teacher was absolutely excellent. She was an enthusiastic teacher for whom nothing could faze her. A typical example I want to tell you about is that she often taught us with great patience and she had spent 5 years in France, so she was a bit of a Francophile.

The last point? Maybe my personal experience can make you understand. Thinking back it was a warm spring afternoon and I was having a trip in Qingdao when a foreign couple asking the way caught my attention. I discovered that they came from France and nobody could understand them. I walked towards them and communicated in what I think was standard and fluent French. Even so they understood me and I showed them the right way to go. I was so proud of myself and over the moon that they understood me. So thanks to that French course and my great teacher, I was able to speak so well and I could help that couple.

**Idiom:*

week in, week out: every week, week after week.

Example: We have the same old food, week in, week out.

Example: I've done the same thing—week in, week out—for three years. I'm tired of this job.

Describe a group you like to take part in.

You should say:

what the group is

what you will do in this group

who you did with

explain why you want to take part in.

**Answer:*

The group I like to take part in is my school choir. I started to notice this group when I was at a loose end. Now I really think it is very interesting and helpful to me. I started to have this passion for singing when I was a first year student in my university. I heard from my classmates that my school choir used to be the hottest one in the whole city.

The teacher of this choir is thought to be really brilliant. A typical example I want to tell you about is that he often uses interesting methods to teach us how to sing. For example, he even imitated the voices of different singers in order to help us carry the tune. I have to say that I don't have the voice of an angel, but he was able to coax a tune out of my mouth using these methods.

For my last point, maybe my personal experience can help to explain. Thinking back, it was a cold winter's afternoon. I was watching the school performance at the end of the first term. Then a powerful song named "My Future Is Not a Dream" grabbed my attention. I discovered that the group of girls that were singing very passionately on the stage were my classmates. I was green with envy. Why hadn't I known about this choir? At the end of the song, all the audience suddenly stood up to show their respect and clapped, shouting "encore, encore". I was totally amazed by the vocal skill of this choir and that's why it's a group I like to take part in.

**Idiom:*

be at a loose end: to have nothing to do

Example: If you find yourself at a loose end over the weekend, you could always clean out the garden shed.

Example: Sarah was at a loose end in a strange city when she first met Bob.

Describe a job you would like to do in the future/a future plan/an important decision.

You should say:

what the job would be

what you would do in that job

how you can get the job

explain why you would like to do that job.

**Answer:*

The job I would like to do in the future would be a TV presenter. I have great interest in this job. I really think it is quite funny that I had the brainwave of being a TV presenter when I was watching a programme named "Day Day Up".

People tend to think that this type of job is really challenging. A typical example I can tell you about is that I would have to learn how to speak standard Putonghua, and communicate well with the audience. I will have to be able to speak as clear as a bell.

My last point? Maybe my own experience can give you some insight. If I think back to a cold winter's night. I was looking for something interesting on the Internet and I was just surfing around looking at this and that. Then that programme I just mentioned grabbed my attention. I discovered that in this programme, a presenter called Wang Han was hosting a talk show before a live audience. His words were full of jokes and interesting cyber language. I was totally amazed by it and since then my dream is to be an excellent presenter like him. So this would be the job I would like to pursue in the future.

**Idiom:*

(as) clear as a bell: very clear, as with the sound of a bell

Example: I fixed the radio, so now all the stations come in clear as a bell.

Example: Through the wall, I could hear the neighbours talking, just as clear as a bell.

Describe a radio programme that you like to watch.

You should say:

what type of programme is it

when you watch it

what the contents of programme are

explain why you like this programme.

**Answer:*

The radio programme that I like to listen to is called "Cuisine Time". I accidentally caught this show in a hotel room when I was having a trip to Nanjing. I found from surfing the Net that it is one of the top ten cooking shows in China.

To those of us who love this radio show, it is extremely well-known for the information and knowledge about food. If you are a foodie like me, it's a must listen show. A typical example I want to share with you is that once it introduced a wonderful dish called "braised meat with preserved vegetable". The listeners to this show are always those people who treat eating as an important part of their lives. You can count me in amongst that number, as I live to eat.

As for the last point, my personal experience can provide an example. Thinking back to that cold winter's afternoon in the hotel room, I was staying alone and listening to radio. After I had tuned in to my favourite station a charming voice grabbed my attention. I discovered that this programme was so amusing. The presenter used humour and fun as a way to recommend a lot of speciality dishes across China. As a foodie myself I was totally amazed by the content of this show. So "Cuisine Time" is my favourite programme.

**Idiom:*

count me in: include me in your activity or plan

Example: You can count me in—I haven't been to a ballgame in years!

Describe an important message you received by phone, email or text.

You should say:

what the message was

who it was from

what you did after you got this message

and explain why this message is very important.

**Answer:*

An important message I received must be the short message by phone that made me feel so excited. I really think this message is quite incredible because it told me that I was invited to attend a great lecture delivered by my idol Ma Yun. I was over the moon that I had a place. I clearly remember that when I got the message from my head teacher, I just jumped for joy.

All my classmates thought that this chance was extremely precious. A typical example I want to share with you is that they all asked me to record the whole lecture, so I quickly had to dig in my pocket and buy a voice recorder to record the talk.

Finally my personal experience can provide some insight. It was a cold winter's afternoon and I was watching my favourite TV programme at home. To be honest I was feeling a little bit bored and at a loose end and was channel hopping a bit. On one station an energetic voice grabbed my attention. I discovered that a short guy on a large stage was giving a speech to almost 50 thousand people. It was my idol Ma Yun who used a lot of vivid and interesting examples to show his ideas. I was totally amazed by his passion and wisdom. In the meantime, I told myself I would try my best to listen to his live speech. After receiving that message, I did get to see my idol, so now you can see why that message was so important to me.

**Idiom:*

dig into your pocket: to use your own money to pay for something

Example: Parents of young children have to dig deep into their pockets at Christmas-time.

Events

Describe a picnic or meal that you ate outdoors.

You should say:

where you had this meal

who was with you

what you ate and drank

explain why you ate outdoors.

**Answer:*

The best meal that I ever ate outdoors must be a picnic that I had beside the sea. I really think it is quite unforgettable. I had this experience when I was having a trip to Xiamen, a coastal city. It was a blisteringly hot day but the sky was blue, the sea was cold and the food was really yummy.

Everybody at that picnic thought it was an extremely funny and enjoyable day, a red-letter day in fact. We drank a lot of beer, danced together, sang songs, swam and just basked in the sun. What is more, we got the chance to taste a wonderful local dish called "braised meat with preserved vegetable" which was so tasty.

Finally maybe my own experience can provide some insight to explain why it was so great. Thinking back to a cold winter's afternoon, I was looking for some interesting TV programmes at home and feeling a little bit bored and at a loose end. I was channel hopping when a programme about outdoor picnics grabbed my attention. I discovered that it was such a great way to release pressure and stress because you could get close to nature and do something crazy. I was totally attracted by this type of activity, so I contacted my friends and we had that great picnic outdoors by the sea. It's a great memory.

**Idioms:*

a red-letter day: a day that is very important or very special

Example: The day our daughter was born was a real red-letter day for us.

at loose ends: restless and unsettled; unemployed

Example: Just before school starts, all the children are at loose ends.

Example: Jane has been at loose ends ever since she lost her job.

Describe a recent change in your life.

You should say:

what the change was

when and where this change happened

what caused this change

what the result of this change was

and explain how you felt about this change when it happened.

**Answer:*

A recent change in my life that has meant a great deal to me is that I have become interested in playing tennis. Thinking back I remember that I began to love it about a couple of weeks ago but before that tennis was a strange thing for me. I've never been sports mad or a sporty person but yes this was life changing.

The main reason for this change in my life can be explained by my personal experience. It was a cold winter's afternoon. I was tuning the TV and looking for a programme I liked. I was just flicking through the channels, trying to kill time when a tennis match on CCTV5 grabbed my attention. The atmosphere there was really hot. I discovered that the girl who played so well was from China. Her name was Li Na and she was around 30 years old with a slender figure. She completely displayed the beauty of tennis. After that match I learned that she had won the Australia Open.

I was totally enthused with a passion for the sport and decided that I needed to change my slothful life for something more energetic. For me this change is fairly useful. I can share with you that I gradually fell in love with outdoor activities and have become pretty energetic every day. This is so beneficial for my work, especially when I work overtime because I can blast away the stresses and strains of my job on the tennis court.

Idioms:

a great deal: a large amount of something

Example: Keeping the house really meant a great deal to me.

kill time: to use something up, especially time

Example: I killed time reading a novel.

Example: The employees were not encouraged to kill time.

Describe an occasion when you moved into a new house or school.

You should say:

where you moved

when you moved

why you moved

and explain whether or not you like to move there.

Answer:

The occasion that I moved into a new house was when my family moved into a new flat in the downtown area that I liked so much. It is located in the northwest of the city and thinking back, we did it when I was still a primary school student.

For the whole family the environment of this new house is so satisfying. There are many kinds of shopping malls around the new house as well as the biggest park in the city. It is centrally located which comes in handy. The transport links are good which makes living there a piece of cake.

As for the last point, maybe my personal experience can provide some insight. It was a warm spring afternoon. My father and I were doing some exercises in the city park I just mentioned. We were really enjoying the surroundings here when a new building under construction just next to the park grabbed my attention. I was so amazed by the location of such a wonderful building. I told my father: "If we had enough money I would like to own a flat here". I was surprised then when my dad told me he had a secret but annoyingly he wouldn't tell me. I pestered him all day until just before bed he told me that he had bought one of those flats. I was so over the moon. I jumped for joy for about 5 minutes. When we finally moved in, it was just perfect and I've been happy there ever since.

Idioms:

come in handy: (for something) to be useful

Example: I think that this gadget will come in handy in the kitchen.

piece of cake: something easy to do; No problem

Example: When you know what you're doing, it's a piece of cake.

Example: Glad to help. It was a piece of cake.

Example: Rescuing frightened cats is my specialty. Piece of cake!

Describe a competition you would like to take part in.

You should say:

what the competition is

what cost you would have to pay to take part in this competition

how you would practice for it

explain why you would like to take part in it.

**Answer:*

The competition I would like to take part in would be the chess competition in my school. I have a great interest in chess and I really think it is a great chance to show my talent. Thinking back, I found out about the school annual competition from the campus newspaper when I was still a freshman. I heard from one of my classmates Jack that this used to be the hottest competition when compared with other competitions. A good bonus is the participants do not have to dig in their pockets to pay for it as it's free.

For the excellent players like me, preparation is extremely important. So I have to become a chess geek for weeks before a competition. For example, I would need to invest some time in practice of almost 3 hours each day to make myself perfect. Then I have to spend time being a bookworm and reading chess strategy books. It is also useful to find a good training teacher.

The last point will give you an insight into my personal experience. I remember it was a warm spring afternoon. I was having some fun with my roommates on the playground. Then a piece of news from the school broadcasting station grabbed my attention. In the broadcast, they released the spectacular news that a local businessman who was also interested in chess put up a 1,000 RMB prize for the champion. I was totally amazed by this exciting news as I knew that if practiced very hard that money was as good as mine.

**Idiom:*

invest someone's time in something: to put one's time, effort, or energy into a project

Example: Mary invests her time in charity work.

Example: I invested five weeks of my time building this model ship.

第4章

深度演绎

PART 3

- 现状及基本注意事项
- 高频学术表达及话题类型解析
- 最新题目类型总结、高分结构及标准答案

第1节　现状及基本注意事项

▶ 现状

在P2部分，考官问完1～2个follow-up 问题之后，P3就开始了。P3问题通常会非常宽泛和抽象，属于你和考官之间的讨论。部分题目是来自考官手中的“问题书”，和P2有联系，也有问题是考官针对你的P2独白随机提出的，更多的是深入讨论，即考官对你的回答中的观点进行“刨根问底”式的发问。P3难度自然要高出P1、P2很多。我们通常称这一部分为“加分项”，考生如果想获得7分或以上，就必须得好好重视P3的练习。通常，P3最佳回答长度为25秒，部分答案可以长达30秒。

(1) 考核目的

① 高级语言运用能力（高端词汇、高端语法、强连贯性）

② 深入挖掘观点能力（考官会测试你的口语极限：up limit）

(2) 总体特征

① 关于人和生活

② 有些话题和雅思大作文题目相似

③ 答案没有对错

(3) 问题类型

① Giving Information

② Stating Your Opinion

③ Evaluating

④ Comparing Two Things

⑤ Describing Changes from the Past to the Present

⑥ Speculating/Guessing

⑦ Suggesting

⑧ Describing Attributes/Qualities

▶ 讨论式

P3是你和考官之间对某几个话题的讨论，因此要尽量多说。有一点需要记住，P3和P1显著不同，不仅要回答问题，更要通过各种手段展开话题，说些与话题相关的信息。因此尽量不要回答很短的信息，尤其不能只说一句“I have no idea”之后就不说了。考官在此部分考核的是你语言的极限，不在乎你观点的对错，关键看你到底能说到什么深度，这样才可以给你合理加分！

下面就什么叫“讨论式”回答来举一个例子。

当谈到中国房价时，考官可能会问：“What's the government doing to help low-income people buy their own home?”或“Is the government doing anything to help low-income people buy their own home?"（这两个题目其实是一样的）

在实际考试中，如果你偶尔说“I have no idea”，然后继续表达自己的观点，是不会扣分的。下面的三种回答都是“讨论式”答案：

① "I have no idea but, if I were the government, I'd build many small, cheap apartments on the edge of the city where the land is cheap and I'd sell them to the low-income people at a low price, possibly even below the cost of construction because, after all, the government doesn't need to worry about making a profit."

点评：该考生提供了一个解决问题的方式，尽管没有直接回答问题，但这个回答符合我们讨论时的状态。

② "I have no idea but you know, I do agree it's a serious problem right now. For example, in Beijing, the average new apartment costs 2 million RMB, but the average Beijing resident only earns about 8,000 RMB per month."

点评：The candidate added information to confirm that a problem exists even though that was not the original question. In a discussion situation, this is suitable.

该考生进一步通过举例来说明这个问题非常严重，在讨论的语言环境中，这个回答是没有问题的。

③ "I have no idea but, you know, I do think the government has a responsibility to do something because, after all, China's government is a socialist government and the purpose of a socialist government is to look after the interests of the low-income people more than the interests of the high-income people."

点评：该考生继续说明这的确是政府的责任，符合双方在进行讨论时的语言风格，这个回答是没有问题的。

如果你能说出一条政府正在做的事情，再加上上述语言，考官将会对你的表现非常满意。

▶ 练习

这是关于提高“讨论感”的专项练习：

在平时训练中，考生可以和口语小伙伴自由讨论。激活讨论模式的方式很简单，大家根据下列热点话题尝试使用“well, the way I feel about..is”，然后提出鲜明的个人观点和对方展开讨论，这样很容易使你找到P3的“深度讨论状态”。

Divorce	Beggars	Homosexuality
Pollution	Television violence	Fast food restaurants
Smoking	Tourism	Crime

第2节　高频学术表达及话题类型解析

考生不仅在给出答案的时候要使用学术表达，在表示疑问或请求解释时也要和P1有所不同，毕竟P3对语言的要求更高，下面来系统学习一下。

▶ 请求解释和自我梳理

1. 请求解释

I didn't quite follow what you were saying about...

I'm afraid I'm not really very clear about what you mean by...

I'm sorry, could you explain what you mean by...?

2. 自我梳理

Let me put it another way...

Sorry, let me explain...

Well, what I am trying to say is that...

▶ 请求举例和自我细化

1. 请求举例

Can you show me an example of that?

Can you be more specific?

2. 自我细化

One example of what I was just saying is...

Just to illustrate my point, I would like to give you an example...

▶ 讨论变化

1. 学术表达

These days...has/have become...

...are getting more and more...

2. 经常讨论的话题

Divorce	Health	Crime
Lifestyle	Economy	Population
Role of woman	Transport	Social competition
Communication	Technology	

▶ 表达观点、喜好或偏好

1. 表达观点

My view is that...

It seems to me that...

The way I see it...

2. 表达喜好或偏好

I'm fond of...

I'm not much for/I don't go for...

...appeals to me more/I'm more attracted to...

▶ 表达解决方式

1. 学术表达

To solve this problem, I think we should...

I think this problem could be solved by...

2. 经常讨论的话题

Traffic jam

World poverty

Air pollution

Food safety

▶ 表达比较

这个是雅思口语P3的重点话题类型，下面我们要详细解读一下。

1. 比较对象通常有以下5种

(1) Males/females (boys and girls; men and women)

(2) Old/young ("old" can mean your parents' age and older; "young" means about 15 to 30 years old)

(3) Urban/rural (city and country)

(4) Children/adults ("children" are from about 3 to 12 years of age; "adults" are over 18 years old)

(5) Today/before ("before" usually means 20 to 50 years previously)

注意：有些问题通过"Yes/No" questions, "Prefer" questions or "Opinion" questions 来要求考生作比较，考生首先给出问题的"直接答案"："Yes" or "No", or what you prefer, or what your opinion is，然后给出细节，其中或多或少都要提到比较。

举例：Has the style of furniture in Chinese people's homes changed in recent years?

Yes, it has, people now buy more luxurious and more fashionable furniture than they did 30 years ago.

2. 形容词比较级的构成

中国考生经常不能正确使用形容词比较级，需要引起重视。

(1) 常规性形容词比较级

Types	Example Adjectives	Comparative Adjectives
Type 1: 一个音节	Big	"A is bigger than B."
Type 2: 两个音节以及ending with "y"	Busy	"People are much busier today than they used to be."
Type 3: 其他的 (not Type 1 or Type 2)	Expensive	"It's more expensive to study English overseas than in China."

特例：Quiet 的比较级应该为quieter。

以下15个形容词既可以用于Type 2，也可以用于Type 3。

common	handsome	narrow
polite	simple	cruel
likely	obscure	remote
stupid	gentle	mature
pleasant	shallow	subtle

(2) 非常规性形容词比较级

Adjectives	Comparative Adjectives
Good	Better than
Bad	Worse than
Little (uncountable)	Less than
Few (countable)	Fewer than
Much (uncountable)	More than
Many (countable)	More than

3. 如何进行比较

在口语表达中主要有三种比较方式。

Type 1: A Positive Statement Using a Comparative Adjective

A is bigger than B

Type 2: A Negative Statement using "not as + adjective"

B is not as big as A

Type 3: A Contrasting Statement

A is big but B is small

注意：当回答比较型问题时，尝试使用不同的比较方式会让考官觉得你具备“丰富句型”使用能力，这是口语高分的重要评分点。

▶ 谈论未来

1. 学术表达

There will (certainly etc.) be...

We will see...

I'm sure/confident/convinced/positive...

I imagine/expect/predict/foresee...

2. 经常讨论的话题

Transportation	Housing	The way people spend their free time
Work	Entertainment	Shopping
Clothes	The way people get their news	Communication
The environment	Society	Families
Medicine	People's eating habits	

▶ 谈论人群特质

1. 学术表达

I think...and...may be the words to describe it...

...are badly needed for that...

2. 思考以下职业（P3高频话题）需要哪些特质

Doctor

Bus driver

Waiter or waitress

Teacher

Lawyer

Accountant

Engineer

Journalist

第3节 最新题目类型总结、高分结构及标准答案

<table>
<tr><td>话题类别</td><td>对比类</td><td>题目类型</td><td>What are the differences between____.
How are ____ different from ____?</td></tr>
<tr><td>典型举例</td><td>• What are the differences between eating in the restaurants and at home?
• How are big cities different from those of twenty years ago?
• How are big cities different from small towns?
• How are the holidays different from those of twenty years ago?</td><td>高分结构</td><td>1. Firstly, ____. Secondly ____.
2. I'm not sure about ____ since I don't have much experience due to ____. However I am aware of some differences, for example ____.
3. I have to say there are lots of differences. Firstly, ____. Secondly, ____.
4. I think ____ are much more different today than they were ____ years ago. Firstly, ____. Secondly, ____.</td></tr>
<tr><td>标准答案</td><td colspan="3">1. Firstly, I would have to say that the difference between eating at home or in a restaurant is that home cooking is about food being made with love for the family, by a member of the family, be it mum, grandma or dad. Secondly, restaurants are often disappointing, perhaps the food is not good or the ambiance of the place doesn't appeal and you are always left with a big bill which can leave a sour taste in your mouth.
2. I'm not sure about how big cities are different from those of twenty years ago since I don't have much experience due to my age. However I am aware of some differences, for example, there must be many more cars on the road than there were twenty years ago. Of course the city center has boomed with those big brand shops and of course the shopping malls where you can buy things that perhaps didn't even exist in China twenty years ago.
3. I have to say there are lots of differences between big cities and small towns. Firstly, I would say that small towns are much more personal than big cities. In my small hometown I often bump into friends and acquaintances. But in a big city like Nanjing I can go for days without seeing any of my friends on the street. We have to make appointments just to go for coffee. Secondly, The range of shops are so different. In big cities you can buy almost everything from around the world, from fast cars, expensive jewellery to foreign food and snacks. Whereas, in my small hometown it's very difficult to buy these luxury goods and foreign foods. In the small towns the people are much more friendly too.
4. I think holidays are much more different today than they were twenty years ago. Firstly, I would say that they are much more glamorous affairs than they were twenty years ago. Nowadays we are much more likely to jet off to another part of the world, maybe Europe or America. We might think of a beach holiday in Thailand. But twenty years ago, many people didn't even have passports and were not allowed to travel. Secondly I think in the past, holidays were spent at home or at local resorts. But I would say that sometimes, these old fashioned type of family holidays might be better than wandering around some expensive resort halfway around the world, hoping that you will have a memorable experience and spending lots of money.</td></tr>
</table>

<table>
<tr><td>话题类别</td><td>选择类</td><td>题目类型</td><td>Do you prefer ____?
Which do you like better?</td></tr>
<tr><td>典型举例</td><td>• Do you prefer travelling abroad or in your own country?
• Which do you like better, living in a city or small town?</td><td>高分结构</td><td>1. If I were asked my preference for ____ or ____, I shall pick ____. For ____. But ____ has a ____ quality that attracts me as well. If it were not for ____, I probably would go for ____ instead.
2. ____ doesn't fit me unfortunately. ____ is ____ which is almost all I care about in the matter of ____.
3. Can I not choose any of the two? Well, if I must, I would go for ____. It doesn't make much of a difference to me but ____ looks/sounds prettier.</td></tr>
<tr><td>标准答案</td><td colspan="3">1. If I were asked my preference for travelling abroad or at home I would pick travelling abroad. For many people this is a new experience because for many years we could not travel abroad. But foreign travel has an exciting quality that attracts me. If it were not for the costs of foreign travel, I probably would go for an around-the-world trip instead of just short holidays.
2. City life doesn't fit me well unfortunately. My small hometown is the place which is almost all I care about in the matter of having a good life. City life is expensive and stressful. So when I can I have to escape back to my small town. I can meet my friends and stay with my family. Those few days away in my town allow me to recharge my batteries so I can face, once again, the rigors of city life.
3. Can I not choose any of the two? Well, if I must, I would go for small town living. It doesn't really make much of a difference to me but my hometown and the surrounding countryside looks much prettier than the crowded city streets where I work. It's also much quieter there which means when I visit, I can relax and catch up on some quality sleep without the noise of the city keeping me awake.</td></tr>
</table>

<table>
<tr><td>话题类别</td><td>列举类</td><td>题目类型</td><td>What does ____ do to ____?
What are ____?</td></tr>
<tr><td>典型举例</td><td>• What measures does your government take to protect wild animals?
• What's the main food in China?</td><td>高分结构</td><td>1. There are several different ____ about ____. Obviously ____ is the one that comes first, since ____. Secondly, ____ should also be taken into account for ____.
2. ____ are ____, ____, ____ and ____. The reasons are as follows. ____.
3. There are just too many ____ to be mentioned in this case. However ____ should be named because ____.</td></tr>
</table>

标准答案	1. There are several different government policies about animal protection in China. Obviously the protection of the Panda is the one that comes first, and has been in place since the 1950's. Secondly, the Snow Leopard has been protected since the 1970's. Of course the red panda is another endangered species in China which should also be taken into account for government protection. 2. The staple foods of China are rice, noodles, soybeans and vegetables, herbs and seasonings. The reasons are as follows. China for many years has been an agrarian society, so farmers grow the bulk of the food. It is only relatively recently that China has adopted the processes of industrialized food production. But still, the range of food and the range of flavours and tastes from across the provinces is remarkable. 3. There are just too many cuisines from the provinces to be mentioned in this case. However the cuisines that are most influential in China are those from Jiangsu, Shandong and of course Cantonese. Szechuan cuisine should be named too because of the bold flavours and its famous spiciness.

话题类别	态度类	题目类型	Do you think ____?
典型举例	• Do you think it is important for children to do some housework? • Do you think Internet can change our life? • Do Chinese people like to travel nowadays?	高分结构	1. Yes, I do. I believe that ____, after all ____ is making ____ much easier than it did before. Also ____ are becoming to realize that ____. 2. No, not really. I'm not buying the idea that ____. I understand that ____, ____ is expected to be taken more seriously at the moment. But to be honest, there are more important things to consider. So I just don't bother thinking about it. 3. I'm not sure. It depends on what you mean. Yes I know that ____, but when ____ is taken into account, I am afraid that ____.
标准答案	1. Yes, I do. I believe that children should do some housework. After all technology is making housework much easier than it did before. We have vacuum machines and dishwashers which help to save us time and which children can easily use. Also parents are becoming to realize that doing some housework is very important for children to be more independent. 2. No, not really. I'm not buying the idea that the Internet is life-changing. I understand that technology is a useful tool but we need to balance our real lives with the impact of virtual reality. In the 21st century technology is expected to be taken more seriously, but to be honest there are more important things to consider. So I just don't bother thinking about it too much, I just use the Internet as a useful tool to help my life, not change it. 3. I'm not sure. It depends on what you mean. Yes I know that during the Spring Break and the New Year everyone in China travels to see their family. But when foreign travel is taken into account, I am afraid that not so many Chinese people travel. I guess as time flies and foreign travel becomes within reach of people's pockets then, maybe more people will travel. Nowadays on some occasions I do enjoy foreign holidays. But seriously speaking, I don't see how farmers from the west of the country would be able to afford it.		

<table>
<tr><td>话题类别</td><td>态度类</td><td>题目类型</td><td>How do you think ____?
What's your opinion of ____?</td></tr>
<tr><td>典型举例</td><td>• What's your opinion of happiness?
• What's your idea of a perfect holiday?</td><td>高分结构</td><td>1. ____ is sometimes difficult to define, but ____. For instance, once I ____.
2. I can't define what ____ is as ____. But I can share my experience and opinion about it. It was ____ ago when I ____. I feel like that was supposed to be how ____ looks like.
3. ____, this is what ____ is about. Take me for example, when I was ____.</td></tr>
<tr><td>标准答案</td><td colspan="3">1. Happiness is sometimes difficult to define. I think it is important that we are happy. Life is sometimes difficult but if we can find happiness in our lives, maybe through love or even our work then we can say life is worth living. For instance, once I felt unhappy and frustrated. Things were not going right with my life. I was unfulfilled in my personal and work life. But then I found a wonderful person and now I must say I am happier than I have ever been.
2. I can't define what a perfect holiday is as everybody might have different opinions. But I can share my experience and opinions about it. It was a while ago when I was working hard and I needed a break. Luckily someone showed me where I could buy cheap tickets to Thailand, so I had a package tour to a beachside hotel. It was just like paradise. It was so beautiful with the blue sky and the blue sea. I feel like that was supposed to be how a perfect holiday looks like.
3. Having the perfect holiday—this is what happiness is about. Take me for example, when I was so exhausted from work, I was desperately in need of a holiday. I was unhappy and drained. So on the spur of the moment, I booked a beach holiday in Thailand. I have to say that this is the best thing I have ever done. It was the perfect holiday and even now, in my mind's eye, I can remember how beautiful the place was and how rested I felt afterwards.</td></tr>
</table>

<table>
<tr><td>话题类别</td><td>解释类</td><td>题目类型</td><td>Why?</td></tr>
<tr><td>典型举例</td><td>• Why is it important for us to give gifts to others?
• Why do people in China traditionally want to have a son?</td><td>高分结构</td><td>1. It's important to ____. Because it's ____. And apart from that ____ is another reason for it. And maybe the fact that ____ can also explain it.
2. The reasons of it are threefold. First of all ____. Second of all, ____. Finally, ____.
3. I don't know about it for sure. But if I have to illustrate, I would have to say that ____ would be a major reason. ____ ought to be reasons as well although they don't seem to be persuasive. But they are what this is about.</td></tr>
</table>

标准答案	1. It's important for us to give gifts to others because it's part of having a generous soul. And apart from that feeling happy is another reason for it. There is a saying, "it is much better to give than to receive" which shows the importance of giving. And maybe the fact that we also say "it's the thought that counts" can also explain it. Because it's not about the value of the gift, it's because we have thought about the person we want to give the gift. 2. The reasons offered are threefold. First of all it's an old cultural idea, a relic of the past from a time when male children were more valued than female children. This, of course, is outmoded now. Secondly people think that if they have a son, then in their old age there will be someone who will look after them financially. But of course in Modern China women can work too, so money and security is not so much of an issue. Finally, the one baby policy of modern times had a significant impact. So for the reasons noted earlier, parents felt that if they had a baby it must be a boy. Of course this has now created some social problems in China where the gender balance is now skewed towards boys. 3. I don't know about it for sure. But if I have to illustrate, I would have to say that nowadays the one baby policy would be a major reason. Financial and social aspects ought to be reasons as well although they don't seem to be so persuasive in this day and age. But they are what this is about.

话题类别	建议类	题目类型	What should be done?
典型举例	• What should we pay attention to in travel? • What is the best way to bargain?	高分结构	1. First of all, ____. Secondly____. Then ____. 2. I'm not sure about ____ since I am not an expert on this matter. However I am aware of a few of ____. It has something to do with ____. 3. I have to say there are lots of ____. Firstly, ____. Secondly, ____.
标准答案	1. First of all when we travel we should pay attention to our own personal safety. The big wide world can be a dangerous place, so we have to put that risk into perspective. Secondly when we travel we should get to know the people and places that we visit. We should not just live in the protected bubble of the hotel, never venturing further than the swimming pool. Then of course the most important things of all, when you leave, check your pockets for your passport, tickets and money. That's all you ever need, even if all your luggage is lost, those three things are the most important. 2. I'm not sure about bargaining since I am not an expert on this matter. I get a little embarrassed when I go shopping and I am expected to bargain. We all love a bargain, of course, but I just cannot bring myself to haggle with shopkeepers. I know I should and I know sometimes I pay too much for things. However, I am aware of a few of the skills of bargaining. It has something to do with starting to bid low and then trying to meet the shopkeeper somewhere in the middle. I know also you need to do it all with a smile on your face and to enjoy the experience.		

	3. I have to say there are lots of things we need to pay attention to when travelling. Firstly we need to make sure we know what time our trains or planes leave and we need to get to the station or airport on time. Secondly don't forget the tickets and passports. This is most important as it can ruin even the best laid plans for travel. Thirdly, I would say pay attention to where you are going. Enjoy the scenery and get to know the people and places. These will be your memories in the future.

话题类别	最高级类	题目类型	Most
典型举例	• What is the most important thing in your life? • What is most interesting in learning English? • What is the most important factor in choosing a job?	高分结构	1. The most important thing is ____. For me it seems to be the ____ because ____. Otherwise I would not ____. 2. The most interesting thing about ____ is ____. ____ should not just be about ____. It is more ____than that due to ____. 3. I don't see how ____ or what it can be but if I were to pick one that matters the most, it might be ____ since ____.
标准答案	1. The most important thing in my life is my family of course. For me it seems to be the be-all and end-all of my world because I could not live without them. Otherwise I would not be able to live. I depend on them so much. My Mum and Dad love me and I love them. I miss them when I am away from them and I try to keep in contact with them every day. Family is so important to me. I try to get home as often as I can and of course I always go there for the New Year and the Spring Break. 2. The most interesting thing about learning English is learning about the culture of the West. Learning English should not just be about grammar, spelling and pronunciation. It's more exciting than that due to learning about the foreign culture. I also consider reading and watching foreign books and films as useful. There is a veto on reading and watching in my own language too because I need to practice, practice and practice as my teacher instructs me. So yes, learning about the culture is the most interesting thing about learning English. 3. I don't see how I can pick the most important factor or what it can be, but if I were to pick one that matters the most, it might be the money since we work for money, not for fun, right? Secondly, I think I have to pick something that I would enjoy. I know I couldn't be an accountant for example, because I don't like maths and I don't want to work in McDonalds either. So an important factor is picking something that you like to do.		

话题类别	关系类	题目类型	Relationship
典型举例	• What is the relationship between happiness and money? • What is the relationship between your boss and you?	高分结构	1. Well first of all, there is great difference between these two. But they keep affecting each other in many ways. For instance, ____. Therefore they are closely bonded in some way. 2. The relationship between the two is quite ____. ____ controls ____ and ____ affects ____ in other ways.

<table>
<tr><td>标准答案</td><td>1. Well first of all, there is a great difference between these two. But they keep affecting each other in many ways. For instance, there is a saying that “Money can’t buy you love”—I think that’s correct. If someone only wants you for your money, you will never be happy. But money can make you happy in other ways. You can buy nice things, have good holidays, you can even be generous and give money to charity. This can make you happy. Therefore they are closely bonded in some way.
2. The relationship between us two is quite dynamic. My boss is a control freak so he always controls his workers in a strong and officious manner. But it’s different between me and the others. While his shouting affects some of the workers in other ways, with me he is a bit different. I don’t know why. I mean I don’t let him get to me either. At the end of the day it’s just a job and I know that I’ll soon move on to something better with maybe a better boss.</td></tr>
</table>

<table>
<tr><td>话题类别</td><td>衡量类</td><td>题目类型</td><td>Advantage/Disadvantage</td></tr>
<tr><td>典型举例</td><td>• What are the advantages and disadvantages of watching TV programs?
• What are the advantages and disadvantages of going on a package tour?</td><td>高分结构</td><td>1. Speaking off the top of my head, ____. However, ____.
2. The good thing about ____ is ____. However a bad thing might be that ____.
3. A few things about the advantages first. ____. Then we take a look at the disadvantages. ____.</td></tr>
<tr><td>标准答案</td><td colspan="3">1. Speaking off the top of my head, one of the main advantages of watching the TV is being able to relax in the evening. However, I must say that some of the programmes I watch are rubbish and I often think to myself that I should be doing something more useful instead. So that’s a disadvantage. I waste so much time sitting on the sofa and watching stupid people in stupid shows. But you know, there is something quite addictive about it.
2. The good thing about going on a package tour is that everything, for instance, the flight, the hotel, is organized for you by the travel company. At the hotel, the food is organized and of course all the fun activities are organized for you too. However a bad thing might be that you never leave the hotel and you just sit by the pool. So you live in a little bubble of security and never venture outside of the gate to sample the foreign people and places. That, of course, is simply a waste of a trip to a foreign country.
3. A few things about the advantages. Firstly everything on a package tour is taken care of for you. The flights are booked. The hotel is organised and even day trips are provided so you can see more of the country you are visiting. So you can feel safe and secure, confident in the knowledge that everything will go smoothly on your package tour. Then we take a look at the disadvantages. One disadvantage is that the package tour takes all the adventure out of travelling. Some of us enjoy planning our own itineraries down to the tiniest detail. Another disadvantage is that you usually have to travel in a group of people. These are people that you don’t know and you might have to spend two weeks with them. What if you don’t like them? So yes, there are advantages and disadvantages to the package tour.</td></tr>
</table>

话题类别	时间类	题目类型	When
典型举例	• When do most Chinese start to learn English? • When will people use professional photographers to take a photo for them? • When do you normally shop for clothes?	高分结构	1. Normally, ____. But sometimes it varies due to ____. 2. It depends on ____. I guess in most cases ____, but if ___. 3. ____ always ____ when ____. But it's not guaranteed that ____. If anything comes up we just need to make a second arrangement.
标准答案	1. Normally, I guess, most Chinese people start to learn English at school. Of course with television and new technology some kids might even have some English before they go to school to learn it. But sometimes it varies due to family background and the age of the person. Some families who work as farmers or factory workers might not have seen the value of learning English when they were young, but I expect that now all of their children have some English lessons at school. 2. It depends on the circumstances really. I guess that in most cases the first time people use a professional photographer is when they get married. Photography is so easy nowadays. We all have smart phones with cameras and digital cameras so it is easy to have lots of pictures. But if we want something special or if we want to remember a special occasion, it is better to have a professional to take the photos. 3. I always shop for clothes when there are sales on. But it's not guaranteed that I will find something that I like. If anything comes up when I need new or special clothes, I just need to make a special trip to the shops to get what I want. I don't mind that but I do love to find a bargain. That's why I love to shop for clothes during the sales.		

话题类别	阐述类	题目类型	What
典型举例	• What is success? • What is your idea of a perfect holiday? • Can you describe your personal target and personal achievement? • What are the characters of schools in China?	高分结构	1. ____ is not something that is guaranteed. I hope you understand what I am saying because this is one explanation that, I believe, makes sense. 2. ____ is like ____. They are similar for the fact that they ____. And if you catch the metaphor, you will be aware of it. 3. ____ means that ____. In my perspective, the notion of ____ has so many levels. First of all, it refers to ____. Then, it has something to do with ____. I hope these do explain it.
标准答案	1. Success is not something that is guaranteed. I hope you understand what I am saying because this is one explanation that, I believe, makes sense. We all want to be successful but we all have different ideas about what success means for us. It might mean making lots of money. It might mean becoming a big boss or a successful movie or pop star. Other people's notion of success might be different, for instance, the farmer who wants his		

<table>
<tr><td></td><td>crop to grow, the mother who is raising a child alone, the climber who wants to climb Everest or just the girl who wants to lose 10 kilograms. So mainly success is getting what you want.
2. Having a perfect holiday is like a dream to me. Like a rollercoaster ride I want my holiday to thrill me. They are similar for the fact that they have ups and downs, thrill and spills. And if you catch the metaphor, you will be aware that I don't just like to spend my holiday lying on a beach.
3. To set a personal target means that there has to be some achievements. In my perspective, the notion of achievement has so many levels. First of all, it refers to succeeding in what you are attempting to do. Then, it has something to do with completing the steps one by one as you move towards your target. Generally you will need some ambition to get to your target. But once you have achieved your personal target, you can spend some time reflecting on your past achievements. I hope this does explain it.
4. The schools in China have many different characters. In my perspective, education has so many levels. First of all, it refers to the main focus of the school. Maybe it is a high school or a middle school. Some schools might be foreign language schools where they teach English or even international school where foreign kids go to study there. Then, it has something to do with money and status because some schools are private schools where parents have to pay lots of money for their kids' education whereas other schools are public schools. I hope these do explain it.</td></tr>
</table>

<table>
<tr><td>话题类别</td><td>状态类</td><td>题目类型</td><td>Situation</td></tr>
<tr><td>典型举例</td><td>• What is the situation in the rural areas in China?
• What is the situation of computers equipped in your university?</td><td>高分结构</td><td>1. Not good in fact. ____ are affected by ____. It leads to ____. ____ announced new plans to ____. However it's not a good picture at the moment.
2. ____ pretty good. ____ has affected ____. It is simply beyond our expectation.
3. Not sure about it. What I do know is that ____ and it could lead to a chaos. But on the other hand, ____. But it's hard to say.</td></tr>
<tr><td>标准答案</td><td colspan="3">1. Not good in fact. At the moment many rural areas are affected by a lack of basic needs. Mostly this involves the lack of running water and poor transport system. It leads to restricted development in these areas. In 2013 the government announced new plans to help out these areas in terms of their development, raising farmers' income and encouraging new business development, so things might change in the end. However, it's not a good picture at the moment.
2. The situation in regard of computers at my university is pretty good. Nothing much changes though. The economics of running a big school means that the accountants have terrible influence on the purchasing of new equipment and new technology. I thought that a university would have top-of-the-range and modern IT equipment but when I first saw what I was expected to use, well, it was simply beyond my expectations.</td></tr>
</table>

	3. I'm not sure about it. What I do know is that if the government does not address the underdevelopment in the West, it could lead to chaos. But on the other hand, we need our peasants. We cannot encourage everyone to come to the east to work in factories. Who would grow crops then? So developing the western China economy may protect the peasants from being poor and deserting their traditional roles. But it's hard to say.

话题类别	途径类	题目类型	How
典型举例	• How do people do fitness in China? • How should parents divide their family responsibilities?	高分结构	1. Most of ____ choose to ____. While some others ____. People barely ____ but we can't be sure if it is the same elsewhere. 2. Different means can be provided. What I know about is that ____. Some say we can ____. Some say ____. 3. The best way of doing so is to ____. But if that doesn't work out well, we can always choose to ____. Other methods are easily accessible as well, like ____.
标准答案	1. Most of old people that I see choose to do exercise outside. Maybe they go walking while many go dancing every night and some others might use a gym to exercise regularly. People barely jog or run on the road like we see in the west. However, this might just be in Nanjing so we can't be sure if it is the same elsewhere. 2. When parents divide family responsibilities, different means can be provided. What I know is that when grandparents are involved in bringing up a child, then that child might well get spoiled. Some say we can ruin a kid by leaving him or her just with the grandparents. Some say that it's the mother's responsibility to bring up her own children. But then that would deny the child time with his or her grandma and grandpa who do have the time to care. Aunties and uncles would do the job too. 3. The best way of doing so is to share the responsibilities out amongst those people with the available time. But if that doesn't work out well, we can always choose to prioritize our own responsibilities, but that might mean some financial hardship if say mum cannot work. Other methods are easily accessible as well, like paying for an *ayi* or a nanny for example.		

话题类别	评估类	题目类型	Importance
典型举例	• How important is patriotism in international games? • Is interest important in a person's career? • Is it necessary to make plans ahead?	高分结构	1. Personally, I don't think ____ plays a huge part in ____. As a matter of fact I don't even see how it comes to be a great concern. There are lots of alternatives to be picked in this matter. 2. Sure ____ is important. ____ couldn't run without a proper ____. These are the only things needed. 3. Let me put it this way. Provided you ____, then ____. I'm sure ____ because ____.

标准答案	1. Personally, I don't think patriotism plays a huge part in international games. As a matter of fact, I don't even see how it comes to be a great concern unless of course that patriotism turns into blind nationalism. However, this only seems to be a problem for football whereas in terms of other sports there are lots of alternatives to be picked in this matter where nationalism doesn't raise its ugly head. 2. Sure interest is important in terms of one's career. One needs to be interested in their job otherwise you couldn't run without a proper incentive. Money cannot be the be-all and end-all of why we go to work. We need to have interest and career fulfillment; these are the only things needed. 3. Let me put it this way. If you do not plan ahead you are likely to trip yourself up and come a cropper. Provided you at least do some minimal planning, then you should at least reach your target or achieve your aims. I'm sure good planning was not seen in any failed activity because as we know, if you do not plan well, no good could come of it.

话题类别	预测类	题目类型	In the future
典型举例	• Do you think we will have more ways to relax in the future? • What will future houses look like?	高分结构	1. I do believe that ____. ____ is on the track to play a much more important role than it does now, for example ____. Of course it might not change straight away. But we shall see it coming. 2. I am not really sure ____. As long as ____ stays firm, there wouldn't be any further steps for ____ to take. 3. It is hard to tel about ____. If ____ were to make a difference, then I imagine ____.
标准答案	1. I do believe that in the future there will be different ways to relax. Technology is on track to play a much more important role than it does now in how we relax, for example we might have a chance to let our mind travel. Of course it might not change straight away but these things move forward in leaps and bounds. The virtual world is not quite here yet but I am quite sure we shall see it coming. 2. I'm not really sure what a future house will look like. As long as the housing market stays firm in China, I am sure the house of the future will develop. New technology of course will help tremendously and there wouldn't be any further steps for developers to take. But it's up to the foresight of the new architects to make the house of the future a reality. 3. It's hard to tell how we will relax in the future. If new technology were to make a difference, then I imagine computers will be helping us relax rather than making us depend on drugs and alcohol. There might be some worries about hooking oneself up to a computer program but I'm sure all the wrinkles should be dealt with long before that. Therefore it's really up to the designers and future-thinkers to come up with these new ways to help us relax.		

图书在版编目（CIP）数据

舌尖上的雅思 / 钱多多编著. —北京：中国人民大学出版社，2015.2
ISBN 978-7-300-20529-8

Ⅰ.①舌… Ⅱ.①钱… Ⅲ.①IELTS-口语-自学参考资料 Ⅳ.①H319.9

中国版本图书馆CIP数据核字（2015）第000440号

舌尖上的雅思

钱多多 编著

Shejian Shang De Yasi

出版发行	中国人民大学出版社		
社　　址	北京中关村大街31号	**邮政编码**	100080
电　　话	010-62511242（总编室）		010-62511770（质管部）
	010-82501766（邮购部）		010-62514148（门市部）
	010-62515195（发行公司）		010-62515275（盗版举报）
网　　址	http://www.crup.com.cn		
	http://www.1kao.com.cn（中国1考网）		
经　　销	新华书店		
印　　刷	北京宏伟双华印刷有限公司		
规　　格	185mm×260mm　16开本	**版　　次**	2015年2月第1版
印　　张	15.00	**印　　次**	2015年2月第1次印刷
字　　数	334 000	**定　　价**	45.00元（附赠光盘一张）